Childhood
Studies

KT-406-977

Martial Rose Library
Tel: 01962 827306

26 JAN 2009	14 DEC 2012	
18.3.09		
16 NOV 2009		
25 JAN 2010		
3 MAR 2010		
18 NOV 2010		
13 DEC 2010		
17 DEC 2010		
- 9 NOV 2011		
- 9 DEC 2011		
26 JAN 2012		

To be returned on or before the day marked above, subject to recall.

WITHDRAWN FROM
THE LIBRARY
UNIVERSITY OF
WINCHESTER

KA 0304941 8

Childhood *Studies*

An Introduction

EDITED BY
DOMINIC WYSE

UNIVERSITY OF WINCHESTER
LIBRARY

© 2004 by Blackwell Publishing Ltd
except for editorial material and organization © 2004 by Dominic Wyse

BLACKWELL PUBLISHING
350 Main Street, Malden, MA 02148-5020, USA
9600 Garsington Road, Oxford OX4 2DQ, UK
550 Swanston Street, Carlton, Victoria 3053, Australia

The right of Dominic Wyse to be identified as the Author of the Editorial Material in this Work has been asserted in accordance with the UK Copyright, Designs, and Patents Act 1988.

All rights reserved. No part of this publication may be reproduced, stored in a retrieval system, or transmitted, in any form or by any means, electronic, mechanical, photocopying, recording or otherwise, except as permitted by the UK Copyright, Designs, and Patents Act 1988, without the prior permission of the publisher.

UNIVERSITY OF WINCHESTER
03049418 305.23 WYS

First published 2004 by Blackwell Publishing Ltd

2 2005

Library of Congress Cataloging-in-Publication Data

Childhood studies / edited by Dominic Wyse.
p. cm.
Includes bibliographical references and index.
ISBN 0-631-23396-2 (alk. paper) – ISBN 0-631-23397-0 (pbk.: alk. paper)
1. Children–Study and teaching. 2. Children–Social conditions.
3. Child psychology. 4. Children–Services for. I. Wyse, Dominic, 1964–
HQ767.85.C482 2003
305.23'071–dc21
2003007536

ISBN-13: 978-0-631-23396-1 (alk. paper) – ISBN-13: 978-0-631-23397-8 (pbk.: alk. paper)

A catalogue record for this title is available from the British Library.

Set in Rotis 10/12½ pt
by Graphicraft Ltd, Hong Kong
Printed and bound in the United Kingdom
by TJ International, Padstow, Cornwall

The publisher's policy is to use permanent paper from mills that operate a sustainable forestry policy, and which has been manufactured from pulp processed using acid-free and elementary chlorine-free practices. Furthermore, the publisher ensures that the text paper and cover board used have met acceptable environmental accreditation standards.

For further information on
Blackwell Publishing, visit our website:
www.blackwellpublishing.com

Contents

Plates

Tables

Notes on Contributors

Jane Baker began her career within early years and primary education as a nursery nurse. She then worked for five years at a refuge and six years at a drop-in centre for women and children who had experienced violence. Having trained as a counsellor she became involved in providing training for volunteers and professionals throughout a range of services, which led to an increased interest in the rights of children to voluntary and statutory services. Jane has worked within the field of special needs as a school governor and in a number of parent support agencies. She is currently a lecturer in Health, Childhood and Social Studies at Hugh Baird College of Further Education.

Robert Banton is a Senior Lecturer in Child Health and Programme Leader for the BA Childhood Studies at Liverpool John Moores University. He began his career as a paediatric nurse before moving to the field of community child health as a health visitor. His recent research is in the area of professional involvement of health visitors with families whose children are on the child protection register. He is co-author (with Tilly Jones) of *Keeping Kids from Harm*. He is involved with other contributors to this book in a British Council research and teaching project examining child protection and children's rights in Jordan.

Angela Brennan trained and worked as a paediatric nurse, working in both acute and community settings before entering nurse education. She then undertook a law degree and qualified as a barrister in 1995. Her areas of teaching, research and consultancy focus on children's rights from a national and international perspective, as well as child law and child protection. She has worked in these areas in the UK as well as in Tanzania, India, Russia, Jordan and Colombia, where she has worked extensively with government and NGOs in the setting up of training and policy initiatives on children's rights and child protection. She is currently the Director of the School of Midwifery and Child Studies at Liverpool John Moores University.

John Clarke works as Faculty Learning, Teaching and Assessment Development Manager at Liverpool John Moores University and teaches on the BA and MA

Childhood Studies programmes. As a sociologist and an educationalist he has worked in schools, further education, and adult and higher education since 1975. He is interested in the links between childhood, education and the broader society, particularly from a historical point of view, as well as the ways in which the professions of teaching have developed and are seen today. He has worked in a range of teaching and staff development roles. For ten years he was an 'A' Level Sociology Chief Examiner and has developed courses and programmes for learners at many different levels. He has established and run courses for teachers in post-16 education as well as in universities. He has been involved in a range of evaluation projects, examination board scrutinies and university subject reviews. His main current research interest is in how higher education teachers view their own professionalism.

John Harrison is Senior Lecturer and Associate Programme Leader for BA Childhood Studies at Liverpool John Moores University. He gained his master's degree from the University of Liverpool in 1998. He has worked in a range of healthcare settings, from paediatrics to the military, including as a mental health nurse. His recent research has been in child mental health, an area in which he has presented at a number of conferences. He is currently completing his PhD on the perceptions of care staff toward children who self-harm.

Russell Jones is a Senior Lecturer in Childhood Studies and English at Manchester Metropolitan University. After seven years of manual work in heavy industry he completed a degree in English and moved into Education. He has worked with children in a wide range of settings, from nursery/reception to young offenders, and now has particular interests in literacy issues and in the rights of the child. After completing his PhD he wrote the book *Teaching Racism*, which was Book of the Week in the *Times Educational Supplement*. Since then he has contributed to several publications, including *Teaching English Language and Literacy* (with Dominic Wyse). He is currently working on literacy mentoring and on creative approaches to modern primary education. His book *Creativity in the Primary Curriculum* (with Dominic Wyse) will be published later this year.

Nicola Leather is a Principal Lecturer and Head of the Centre for Childhood and Child Health in the School of Midwifery and Child Studies at Liverpool John Moores University. She began her career as a paediatric nurse in the area of neurosurgery and ENT. She undertook a psychology degree and certificate in education, and moved into Child Nurse Education, taking a master's degree in psychology. Her research interests include child development, adolescence and psychology, with an emphasis on the young person as an individual. She is currently undertaking her doctoral studies in young people's quality of life and risk-taking behaviour.

Nicholas Medforth is Principal Lecturer and Head of Cross School Development in the School of Midwifery and Child Studies at Liverpool John Moores University, where he has been involved in the development and leadership of Childhood Studies programmes since the mid-1990s. His previous work as a nurse was as a specialist in children's nursing. His academic development has focused on psychology and its application to the study of childhood. He is currently involved in collaborative projects with children's organizations, including Childline Northwest. He is also a youth worker and is involved with other contributors to this book in a British Council research and teaching project examining child protection and children's rights in Jordan.

Ali Mekki is the Service Manager for Child Protection and Review for Liverpool City Council. Previously he held a range of posts, including social worker, team manager and childcare consultant. He has contributed to child programmes at Liverpool John Moores University and Liverpool University. He is currently completing an MBA. His research examines young people's engagement with formal processes, including democratic involvement, and the impact of strategic policies.

Nell Napier is Programme Leader for the Childhood Studies Degree at Manchester Metropolitan University. She has been a childcare worker in the voluntary sector (working with children with disabilities), a nurse and a primary school teacher. Her research has included comparison of nurse and teacher education, perceptions of practitioners in early excellence centres, and she is currently engaged in research on the recruitment of under-represented groups on childhood courses.

Áine Sharkey is an experienced early years practitioner who has taught in a wide range of nursery, infant and primary schools in the UK and overseas. Her most recent experience in the UK has been at university, where she taught on a variety of Childhood Studies and Early Years courses at Liverpool John Moores University. She has a particular interest in children's language development and is committed to working in partnership with parents. In 2003 she returned to Ireland to work with families and schools in a project designed to break the cycle of disadvantage.

Dominic Wyse teaches on the Childhood Studies programme and Education programmes at Liverpool John Moores University, where he is a Reader in Primary Education. He published the first qualitative research to analyse children's participation rights in English schools. The book *Children: A Multi-Professional Perspective* (edited with Angela Hawtin) was the first to adopt a multi-professional writing process to support its interdisciplinary focus on childhood. His recent articles have provided a critique of government policy on the teaching of English at primary schools. His most recent book is *Becoming a Primary Teacher* and his recent work on children's rights will appear in *An Introduction to Contemporary Issues in Education* (edited by Keith Crawford). He is currently managing a research project on creativity in schools.

Foreword

The context in which this book has been written is one of rapid change and development for children, families and the communities in which they live.

One of the most significant changes has been the degree to which the many government departments, sectors and professions responsible for the care and education of children have come together and are represented in decisions affecting young lives. The three Cs – Communication, Collaboration and Coordination – were highlighted well over a decade ago in the government report *Starting with Quality* (1990) as being essential to securing 'a continuing expansion of high quality services to meet children's and their parents' needs'. The intervening years have seen rapid strides in the development of integrated services and multidisciplinary provision and training. 'Joined up thinking' and 'wraparound' care and education are key words in government parlance and, in recent years, they have been central to developments at local and national levels.

Yet we can never afford to be complacent, as evidenced by tragic results for children when communication breaks down and services are not coordinated. This book marks a major breakthrough, not only in addressing the issues concerning the whole field of Childhood Studies, but in bringing together a range of authors with expertise and interests in key areas. The contributors to this book represent a range of disciplines and bring their own specialist perspectives to the study of childhood. They also provide a breadth of vision, extending their discussions to cover the whole period from birth to 18 years.

Much has happened, particularly in the field of Early Childhood, while the book was being written. Welcome recognition by the government of the importance of the very earliest stage – from birth to 3 years – led to the commissioning of a project to develop a framework of effective practice to support all those working with children within this age group. The resulting pack of materials, *Birth to Three Matters* (2002), has been distributed nationally to the vast range of practitioners who work with our youngest children. As director of this project it has been particularly heartening to experience the interest and support from all professions and disciplines concerned with the health, welfare and education of children and families. Paediatricians, health visitors and social workers have joined parents, childminders, teachers and private and voluntary sector workers in contributing their views and experiences in developing a framework which depicts children as strong, skilful communicators, competent learners and emotionally and physically healthy.

The study of childhood and children is complex and demanding, as is working with them. It is always changing and developing as new research challenges existing notions of how children learn and develop and as changes in policy and new initiatives influence and affect practice.

Those who work with children, in whatever role or capacity, are in a privileged position. They require both a breadth and a depth of knowledge which needs to be continually updated in order to ensure that practice is informed and effective. This book makes a valuable contribution to our knowledge about children and childhood. It highlights the multi-faceted and interdisciplinary nature of work with children, while keeping the child firmly at the centre of all discussions.

Childhood Studies has become increasingly important in recent years and will continue to do so as recognition is given to what the term encompasses. Students on Childhood Studies programmes, along with parents, experienced practitioners and trainers, will find this book an excellent resource.

Lesley Abbott
Institute of Education
Manchester Metropolitan University

Acknowledgements

Very grateful thanks to Sarah Bird and her team for coming to find us in the first place and managing the project so effectively. Thanks also to the anonymous reviewers whose suggestions added much to the final outcome.

I am particularly grateful to Professor Lesley Abbott for her foreword and to Wendy Jolliffe, Muriel O'Driscoll and Annie Woods, who kindly read the manuscript and offered their comments prior to publication.

I congratulate the team of writers for their insights and look forward to future projects!

This book is dedicated to Oliver Legolas, Esther Hermione and to Jackie, who is a very special person and a constant inspiration to me.

Introduction

Childhood as an area of study has been growing in importance over the last 30 years. Before that time it was not studied as a subject in its own right. Instead people would study aspects of childhood through different subjects. Psychologists would study child development; literature students might study children's fantasy and fiction; education departments would help trainee teachers understand how children learn; people on law courses would study the laws that affected children, and so on. However, the subject of sociology emerged as one of the strongest voices. It was here that the whole way that we understood childhood, including how we defined it, came under intense scrutiny. Even the meaning of the words *children* and *childhood* has been extensively explored. Childhood studies as a subject is now well established and at its best is interdisciplinary, which means that it is informed by a range of different subjects. It also has a multi-professional perspective, which means that as a student you should understand the different ways that people who work with children carry out their work. Two examples underline the importance of multi-professional understanding and collaboration: (1) the Victoria Climbié enquiry report highlights, not for the first time, the tragic circumstances that can occur if professionals do not share information about children with each other; (2) the move towards multi-professional early years centres has been seen as a positive way to improve children's life chances, particularly those in poverty.

The issue of how different subjects represent childhood is also reflected in publications. There is a growing amount of fascinating books and papers about childhood being written in the different subject areas which are mainly aimed at the students of that subject. They require a depth of knowledge of the particular subject that you as a childhood studies student do not need to acquire. However, it is certainly the case that you need to acquire a broad knowledge from a range of subjects in order to understand children and childhood in a holistic way. But the key thing is that you need to be able to synthesize this knowledge from a range of disciplines and transform it into something that is uniquely about childhood. Books in the field of childhood studies itself tend either to be written by single authors or are edited collections. Single authors face the challenge of interdisciplinary writing, which is difficult because their experience is usually rooted in one discipline, such as education, health, sociology, etc. The challenge for editors of books which feature a range of writers is that they tend not to be comprehensive because the contributors write in the specific areas of their individual expertise.

Many of the writers in this book were contributors to another book that attempted, for the first time, to present an account of childhood that was not only interdisciplinary in content but also in its structure and in the process of writing. The book was called *Children: A Multi-Professional Perspective* and was published by Edward Arnold. For the present book we have built on and adapted our previous experience. The overall aim of this book is to present the first *comprehensive* account of childhood in the twenty-first century. To do this we have expanded the original team of writers. The writers of this book are taken from two universities, a college of further education and a local authority social services department. We teach on childhood studies programmes (at further education, higher, master's, and doctorate levels) but also teach in other areas such as education and healthcare. We have worked with children in a wide variety of ways: as lawyers, teachers, midwives, nurses, social workers, children's charity workers, parents, musicians. The level of the book is aimed at students who are studying in further education colleges and for those who are in the early stages of their degree at university.

The book is organized into three large parts which progress from the individual child (Part I: Children and Childhood) through to the child in wider society (Part II: Children and Services; and Part III: Children and Society). We define childhood as spanning pre-birth through to 18 years of age. The structure of the book combines subject-based sections and chapters with interdisciplinary ones in order to give you a completely holistic picture of the subject. For example, in the first part of the book, called 'Children and Childhood', there is a chapter called 'Attachment' which draws strongly on psychological work. There is also a chapter called 'Parenting' which is more interdisciplinary in character. Most of the chapters in the book are about 2,000–3,000 words. This word limit was set deliberately to offer a reasonably succinct reading which could be used prior to or following a lecture. Three of the chapters are longer (up to 6,000 words), which allowed us to focus on some key issues in more depth. 'Histories of Childhood', 'Children's Rights' and 'The Demonization of Childhood' are essays which explore interdisciplinary themes that have exercised the minds of childhood scholars for some years. No book can ever be totally comprehensive and we recognize that 2,000 words can only offer the key points about the different topics that we address. Because of this you will find further reading recommendations at the end of each chapter. These usually include reference to a book, an article and a website. When you follow up these recommendations you will certainly be examining the topic in more depth.

Each chapter begins with a short abstract which explains the content. This is followed by the main text. At the end of the chapter you will find suggestions for further reading. In addition there is also a task which we think will help you to develop your knowledge even further. Having completed the task you will find, in the appendix at the end of the book, short reflections about some of the issues that we anticipated you would learn about. We have also tried to anticipate some of the technical terms that you might find difficult, so there is a glossary at the end of the book. The first occurrence of any words that are in the glossary are printed in **bold**, in addition to the G in the margin; cross-references to other chapters are printed in bold SMALL CAPITALS.

The lives and perspectives of children themselves are central to our philosophy of the subject. That is why Part I is called 'Children and Childhood'. In this section you will find case studies of children (such as the ones in chapter 10: 'The Development of Language and Literacy') and descriptions of how children establish concepts of their own identities (chapter 2: 'Self-Concept'). The overall philosophy of the book is hinted at in the opening chapter 'Histories of Childhood' and is the idea that just as children's socialization is a two-way process of negotiation between adults and children, so this book reflects a negotiation between adult perspectives and child perspectives. The book is unashamedly child-centred and its stance is that students of childhood should be advocates for children. The reflection of children's own views is one part of this and our research into children's participation rights in chapter 15 demonstrates our active commitment to these philosophies.

We hope that you will find as much of interest when you read the book as we did while we were writing!

Part *One*

Children and Childhood

Chapter *One*

Histories of Childhood

JOHN CLARKE

The history of childhood has become a particularly influential area of study in recent years. The chapter examines Philippe Ariès's claims that childhood didn't exist before the seventeenth century. Criticisms of Ariès's ideas are also explored, but it is concluded that while the detail of Ariès's views may be questioned, his overall idea is accurate.

I know a lot about children – I used to be one.
(Spike Milligan)

It goes without saying that Sam will not enjoy his childhood. That is not the point – childhood is not an end in itself, but a means to growing up.
(Roger Scruton, philosopher and conservative columnist, talking about his 4-year-old son. **Independent** *10 May 2002)*

The questions about childhood and its meaning are ones that have concerned historians in recent years, most obviously in the debate about whether or not our current idea of childhood is in fact just a recent invention – 'an artefact of modernity'. Some writers have argued that up to the modern period the current idea of childhood simply did not exist. This view holds that some time between 1600 and the twentieth century the idea of childhood was 'invented' and what we now think of as childhood would not have made sense to our ancestors. This view is most strongly associated with the French author Philippe Ariès, whose book *Centuries of Childhood*, first published in the 1960s, has dominated debates on the history of childhood ever since. The text of a number of Ariès's chapters is available on the web at http://www.socsci.kun.nl/ped/whp/histeduc/links09e.html.

Much of this debate has involved historians identifying evidence to show Ariès and his co-thinkers to be wrong about the historical facts. However, the debate has focused people's attention on previously neglected areas of history and allowed for the development of the history of childhood as a serious specialism.

Philippe Ariès: Childhood as a Modern Invention

Ariès is a French historian associated with a school of history which attempted to shift attention from what might be seen as traditional history, which described the actions of kings and statesmen, towards aspects of everyday life such as diet, family life or popular customs and practices. This perspective stresses the importance of understanding how people saw their own lives and how ideas and feelings (what the French call **sentiments**) change over time.

Ariès took the view that the modern world had seen a transition in people's ideas about childhood. Put simply, in medieval society young people about the age of seven moved out from the protection of the family into a broader adult society where they acted as smaller versions of the adults around them. By contrast, in modern society the age of seven marked a gradual move from infancy to childhood, which was a special state of transition, neither infant nor adult, around which the whole structure of the family revolved. The modern world was characterized by a separate isolated family unit which was centred on the needs of the child. This idea of the child-centred family is so familiar to us today that we find it hard to imagine that it is a recent invention, but Ariès argued that it is only modern changes, particularly the development of schooling prescribed and provided by the state, which brings about the phase we call childhood. In his most extreme and controversial claim, Ariès states: 'in medieval society the idea of childhood did not exist' (Aries 1960: 125).

Aries came to his conclusion in the following ways:

- He studied medieval writings on age and development, particularly those which talked about the 'ages of man [*sic*]', and attempted to show which things were appropriate at different phases of life.
- He looked at the portrayal of children and childhood in medieval art.
- He looked at ideas of how children should dress.
- He looked at the history of games and pastimes.
- He studied the way moralists and others wrote about the idea of childhood 'innocence'.

This led Ariès to develop his claim. For example, his study of medieval painting suggested that in early medieval art children tended to be portrayed as if they were small versions of adults. The most common portrayal of a child in medieval European art was of course the picture of Jesus in innumerable paintings of the Madonna and Child. You can find some examples at http://www.sjsu.edu/depts/te/cd/cd106/slide3.html.

Ariès argues that these portrayals show Jesus as a small version of an adult – the faces have very 'grown up' features and the bodies are elongated and developed like an adult. Only size indicated that a figure was that of a child. This suggests that medieval artists saw children as simply 'reduced' versions of adults. Ariès says: 'medieval art until the twelfth century did not know childhood or did not attempt to portray it' (Ariès 1960: 31). This view is reinforced, says Ariès, by the study of medieval children's clothing, which was generally simply smaller versions of what was fashionable for adults. Infants wore baby clothes which were generally the same for boys and girls, but at about the age of seven people moved on to smaller versions of adult outfits.

Perhaps most controversially, Ariès and other historians associated with his view have tended to see childhood in medieval times as having less emotional loading or significance to their parents. The suggestion is that parents, especially fathers, were less emotionally tied to children and were less affected by the impact of children's illness or death.

From the seventeenth century onwards, Ariès argues, our conception of childhood in the modern sense begins to develop. This is reflected in art; for example, by the beginning of the **representation** of *ordinary* children (i.e. not Jesus or angels) in everyday situations and even the portrayal of dead children. This is described as 'a very important point in the history of feelings' (Ariès 1960: 352). This change in sentiment takes two forms: firstly, within families children take on a more central role: 'parents begin to recognize pleasure from watching children's antics and "coddling" them' (Ariès 1960: 127). Secondly, among moralists and writers on social life there begins to emerge an idea of children as fragile beings who need to be safeguarded and reformed.

This implies that neither of these sentiments had been common before 1600. Their development in the seventeenth century lays the foundation for modern views of what childhood is. The crucial role in this development, for Ariès, is played by the development of schooling, initially for the (male) children of the aristocracy, but increasingly as the modern period develops for all children whatever their social origins. Schooling is seen here as providing a kind of 'quarantine' period for children between infancy and adult life and its gradual extension and intensification is the basis for defining a new idea of childhood.

It is important before moving on from Ariès to note that his work is essentially about ideas, not about the reality on the ground. He writes about childhood, not children, and what he is trying to do is to construct a history of the way people think about the idea of childhood rather than how individual children were reared or treated.

His work was extremely influential in generating new ideas about children in history. In particular, his ideas fed into a growing body of theory which saw the family as progressing from an institution based on practical needs and economic necessity, with little or no emotional content, to the modern idea of the family as the institution which meets the needs of its members, especially children, for love and affection. The French writer de Mause (1976), for example, portrayed the history of childhood as a progression from classical times, where children were frequently killed or abandoned, through medieval indifference, where wet-nursing and the 'farming out' of children were common, to the present-day emphasis on caring. Shorter (1976: 170) goes so far as to argue that 'good mothering is an invention of modernization' and that in traditional societies infants under the age of two were treated with emotional indifference because of the high possibility of infant mortality, while in the twentieth century the welfare of the small child has been given a dominant status in public discourse.

Lawrence Stone (1977) points out that as late as the seventeenth century relations within the family were remote and emotionally detached and that the **Puritans** held a negative view of the child as a sinful being whose will had to be broken by flogging and denial. Only with the growth of the middle classes and the stress on individualism which came with industrialization did a child-centred view emerge, gradually filtering down from the middle class to the rest of society.

While the above historians differed from Ariès in matters of chronology and detail, they shared a key perspective, what Anderson (1980) calls the *sentiments* approach. What they all argue is that the key change which arrived with modernity was a shift in the way people *felt* about children – an alteration in their emotional meaning and significance. This shift was broadly one from indifference or neutrality to high valuation. The twentieth-century family is seen as child centred and focused emotionally on the welfare of the child in ways that these writers claim would have been unrecognizable to people from previous centuries.

Criticisms of Ariès and his Co-thinkers: The Case for Continuity

Many writers agreed with Ariès's perspective, but his work also attracted a wide range of critiques. Other historians attempted to show that his central idea that 'in medieval society the idea of childhood did not exist' was wrong. Much of this work is summarized in Linda Pollock's book *Forgotten Children* (1983), which attacks Ariès and his co-thinkers on a number of grounds.

Essentially, these critics reject the view that childhood did not exist in medieval times, and criticize the idea of childhood as an invention of modernity. Ariès, de Mause, Shorter and Stone are all attacked for their methodologies and for the conclusions they draw from evidence. Pollock argues that there is a need to study *actual* parent–child relationships in history rather than generalized ideas about 'sentiments'. These are represented in diaries, autobiographies and other first-hand accounts, which she examined for the period 1500 to 1700. If we do that, Pollock argues, the strongest impression is one of *continuity*. For instance, she quotes examples of grief at infant death (from mothers and fathers), from throughout the period, to show that there was no pattern of indifference. Similarly, she shows that while there were examples of cruel and brutal child discipline practices these were by no means the norm and were frequently described by writers so as to condemn them as undesirable extremes.

Pollock argues that it is a mistake to base our image of what childhood was like on the texts of advice books, sermons and other documents removed from actual experience. It would be rather like assuming that we could describe what driving is actually like on the roads by a reading of the current edition of the Highway Code! It is better, says Pollock, to study what people actually did, what their experience actually was, and this suggests much more similarity between families of the past and those of the present day than Ariès and his colleagues would assert. It is important to note, of course, that the family lives described in diaries and autobiographies are generally restricted to the literate upper and middle classes.

In relation to Ariès's specific claims about the Middle Ages there have been a number of strong critiques. Shahar (1992: 1) argues that there was indeed a concept of childhood in medieval society. She claims that 'a concept of childhood existed' and 'that scholarly acknowledgement of the existence of different stages of childhood was not merely theoretical and that parents invested both material and emotional resources in their offspring'.

Ariès, of course, was not arguing that there was no affection for children in the Middle Ages. People having no idea about childhood is not the same as people not caring for their children, but Aries maintains that there was a much clearer sense that from about seven years old people moved out of the family into a broader adult world. What distinguishes modern society is the separation of a distinct childhood sphere, a distinct world of childhood with its own clothes, games, entertainments, etc.

In relation to Ariès's use of pictorial evidence critics have pointed out that there were in fact numerous medieval pictures showing the naturalistic portrayal of childhood and that the way in which religious paintings were constructed did not so much reflect the painter's idea of naturalistic truth as his idea of theological or religious truth. Jesus was depicted as older looking than his age and as larger than might be expected because of his significance as the Son of God, as 'God become human'. Spiritually he was seen as superior to all the adults around him and this was reflected in the painting.

In the same way, the spread of naturalistic images of Jesus later in history, such as Raphael's chubby little baby, reflects the fact that religious views were changing to stress more forcefully the humanity of Jesus (e.g. in displaying his genitals). It was theology which determined the treatment of Jesus and angels, not sentiments about childhood.

Critics have also rejected the view that in some sense children in earlier ages were not valued because of the likelihood of infant mortality. As we have seen, diaries and personal accounts suggest that the loss of a child was deeply felt by mothers and fathers despite the much greater probability of such bereavement, and that while pious families might see the death of a child as God's will it was nevertheless a source of enormous grief and pain.

The Middle-Class Family: Ideology of Child-Centredness

Despite the critiques there is a general agreement that something about the role of children in families and in the broader society changed between the seventeenth century and the present day. This is best described as the emergence and then the spread of a middle-class model or ideology of the family. This model is associated with the newly emerging commercial classes in Western Europe and is based on the idea of the self-contained family led by a strong father with a central focus on the upbringing of children. Children are seen as the central part of the family's purpose. There are mechanisms for the proper upbringing of children and their key function is education. In some cases this version of the family was derived from religious faith. The Puritan family in England or the American colonies was seen as an institution based on ensuring the salvation of family members by proper education in the rules of good behaviour and the importance of faith. This responsibility was seen as resting primarily with the father, who was seen as the head of the household in religious as well as economic terms. The need was to 'school' the child in correct behaviour using appropriate punishments (including regular beatings) to enforce discipline. Children were seen as inherently sinful and in need of guidance. At the extreme they were compared to wild animals whose spirit needed to be broken in order that they might develop the humility and obedience which would lead them to be good Christians (Ozment 1983). Not all families followed this extreme model, even in Protestant communities. Simon Schama describes seventeenth-century (Protestant) Holland as a society 'besotted with the children', where the idea of children and their pastimes played a major part in family life and in art (Schama 1987: 495).

What both models of the family share though, is a focus on the child and the importance of education. This emphasis was widespread among the new middle classes and was re-emphasized in the eighteenth century by the Enlightenment view that children were 'naturally innocent' and needed to be directed by appropriate care and education to become good citizens. This view is best expressed in Rousseau's classic book *Emile* (1758), which sets out a plan for the education of a boy to allow natural curiosity and virtue to flower.

This benign child-centredness became popular and was associated with the growth of **Romanticism** (CHAPTER 33), which saw children as close to nature and in some sense uncorrupted and pure. A fashion developed for child portraits by artists such as Reynolds which stressed innocence and 'cuteness' (Porter 1990: 247). However, the view was largely confined to the enlightened aristocracy and the new middle classes. For the great mass of the population of Western European countries like Britain and France, children's lives were characterized by poverty, hard labour and **exploitation**. This set up a contradiction which was to dominate writing and thinking about childhood through the nineteenth century and into the twentieth. There was a contradiction between a romantic idealized view of childhood rooted in eighteenth-century Enlightenment and the brutal reality of most children's lives. We only need to think of the works of Charles Dickens to see this contradiction constantly addressed. In *Oliver Twist*, for example, the simplicity and naivety of Oliver is contrasted with the adult corrupt lives of the Artful Dodger and Fagin's gang. Similarly, in Kingsley's *Water Babies* the chimney boys are shown to be really innocent babies. This view of childhood purity (which contrasted with the Puritan view of children's inherently sinful nature) paralleled the nineteenth-century concern to 'save' children from labour and exploitation (CHAPTER 39).

Nineteenth-Century Children and Social Policy: Children Without Childhood

While the newly emergent middle classes were developing a child-centred ideology of the family, the impact of industrialization on the rest of the population had been to intensify the exploitation and wretchedness of many children's lives. In pre-industrial societies children always worked in farming or in cottage crafts, but the emergence of the factory system introduced the idea of going out to work. For the first time the workplace was separate from the family and children who worked in mines and cotton mills had to travel to their workplaces. Their working day was frequently longer than 14 hours, in addition to the time for travel.

G **Child labour** was not just an accidental side effect of industrialization. Child workers were often preferred to men or women because of their flexibility, their docility and above all their low cost. Child workers were generally economically essential to their families and made a major contribution to household incomes.

The exploitation of child labour by industrialism stood as a stark contrast to the idealization of childhood being spread among the new middle classes. This contradiction became the basis for the campaigns to limit and eventually to abolish child labour which ran through the century. The various **Factory Acts** limited working hours and set minimum ages. The idea was spreading that childhood was a period of life in need of protection, where even in the **laissez-faire** atmosphere of Victorian Britain it was appropriate for the state to intervene (Briggs 1999).

G This enthusiasm for saving children paralleled a growth in **philanthropic** and charitable initiatives which laid many of the foundations for the twentieth-century Welfare State. The massive movements of population which preceded and accompanied the industrial revolution had led to a growth in the numbers of abandoned children. **Foundling hospitals** became a major focus of humanitarian concern and the Poor Laws began to focus on the needs of 'lost children' or 'children without childhood' (McClure 1981). Later in the century the ideology of child innocence was most starkly challenged by the growing awareness of child prostitution, and campaigners like Josephine Butler demonstrated the hypocrisy of a society which turned a blind eye to such practices.

This idea of childhood as a special phase was even more strongly reinforced by the development of compulsory state schooling. This came late in the day in Britain as compared with continental rivals like Germany, and at first was not taken very seriously in parts of the country which saw child labour as essential. However, as the century progressed it was the need to attend school rather than the illegality of employment which ended the worst excesses of child labour (Hendrick 1997).

By the end of the nineteenth century, while the lives of most children were still dominated by poverty, ignorance and illness (see, for example, Robert Roberts's autobiographical accounts of his life in turn-of-the-century Salford: *The Classic Slum* and *A Ragged Schooling*), the idea of child-centredness as a key focus for policy development had firmly taken root, paving the way for the twentieth century – described by many commentators as 'the century of the child'.

The Twentieth Century: Century of the Child

The first change in thinking about childhood during this century was the growth of deliberate limitation of family size (Banks 1968). The spread of family limitation from the Victorian middle class to the rest of the population was a gradual process which extended throughout the period up to the 1970s. What it led to was the decline in the average number of children per family from five or six in the 1870s to below two in the 1970s. This also needs to be considered in the light of the dramatic decline in infant mortality. A family of five or six children in Victorian times would generally have involved a higher number of pregnancies which resulted in the loss of the children involved. The decline in average family size obviously has an influence on the extent to which time, effort and attention are devoted to individual children. One or two children are easier to focus on and idealize than eight or nine.

The development and gradual extension of compulsory schooling (along with the corresponding decline in child labour) changed children from being an economic asset to be coolly valued as part of a family strategy for survival. Children were being seen as a 'liability', something into which the parents had to pour resources in the hope of receiving emotional and expressive rewards (affection, pride, etc.) rather than financial returns, as Anderson's (1972) study of nineteenth-century family life in Preston suggests.

Schooling also creates a period of ambiguous status for children. The period of compulsory schooling (gradually extended throughout this century) is a time when children are not physically dependent (breastfeeding, nappy changing, etc.) on adults, yet they are not adults themselves. From nursery school to their late teens they occupy a kind of limbo status with confused signals about rights and responsibilities offered at every turn. What is implicit in the provision of schooling though is the fact that this is a time when they are in need of protection, nurturing and guidance. Further, it is clear in the twentieth century that the welfare of children is not just a family responsibility. Children are seen as increasingly the responsibility of the state, which intervenes in their education, their health, their diet and their upbringing in ways designed to improve the national well-being by developing its future citizens. In some countries like France this reflects a concern with population size and the need to 'keep pace' with rival nations; in other countries the concern arises from a sense that families and in particular mothers are not to be trusted to act always in the child's and the nation's best interests.

A further development in the twentieth century is the idea of the child and their development as a proper subject for scientific study. The growth of psychology as a discipline is closely tied to the role it played in the increased surveillance and control of childhood, from IQ testing to identifying the origins of **delinquency**. As the century went on parents were bombarded with advice, often contradictory, on the appropriate ways to look after children. From Truby-King's regimented view of the importance of routine to the more relaxed perspectives of Benjamin Spock there was a general view that the care and nurturing of children was a skilled task and not one which came naturally to parents through instinct (Hardyment 1983).

In this sense, whatever the criticisms levelled at Ariès and his colleagues, it does make sense to see our current notion of childhood as a modern invention. Primarily because of the spread of the middle-class ideology of the child-centred family, the development of compulsory universal schooling and the preoccupation of policy makers and welfare institutions with the interests of the child, there did come into being in the late twentieth century in the affluent West a new idea of childhood. This separate conception of childhood would have made little sense to our ancestors.

This is not to say of course that children are not still abused, exploited and brutalized in the affluent West as well as elsewhere. Millions of children still live in poverty in the heart of affluent Europe and America. For much of the developing world the realities of child labour, high infant mortality and abandonment remain facts of everyday life. However, these failures and abuses are seen as contradicting the central value systems of the societies where they happen. Groups like the Child Poverty Action Group or Save the Children (CHAPTER 38) can appeal to the public's sense of what childhood ought to be like when they try to combat these problems. In this sense our idea of what it is to be a child is a social construct of modernity and one that affects all who are involved with children.

Activity

Collect the childhood memories of some friends and relatives. Choose people who represent different generations.

REFERENCES

Anderson, M. (1972) *Family Structure in Nineteenth-Century Lancashire.* Cambridge: Cambridge University Press.

Anderson, M. (1980) *Approaches to the History of the Western Family 1500–1914.* Cambridge: Cambridge University Press.

Banks, J. A. (1968) *Prosperity and Parenthood.* London: Routledge and Kegan Paul.

Briggs, A. (1999) *England in the Age of Improvement.* London: Folio.

Cunningham, H. (1991) *The Children of the Poor: Representations of Childhood since the Seventeenth Century.* Oxford: Blackwell.

De Mause, L. (ed.) (1976) *The History of Childhood.* London: Bellew.

Dickens, C. (1971) [1837] *Oliver Twist.* Harmondsworth: Penguin Books.

Hendrick, H. (1994) *Child Welfare: England 1872–1989.* London: Longman.

Hendrick, H. (1997) *Children, Childhood and English Society, 1880–1990.* Cambridge: Cambridge University Press.

Kingsley, C. (1984) [1863] *The Water Babies.* Harmondsworth: Penguin Books.
McClure, R. K. (1981) *Coram's Children: The London Foundling Hospital in the Eighteenth Century.* London: Routledge.
Ozment, S. (1983) *When Fathers Ruled: Family Life in Reformation Europe.* Cambridge, MA: Harvard University Press.
Pollock L. H. (1983) *Forgotten Children: Parent–Child Relations from 1500 to 1900.* Cambridge: Cambridge University Press.
Porter, R. (1990) *England in the Eighteenth Century.* London: Folio.
Roberts, R. (1992) *The Classic Slum.* Harmondsworth: Penguin Books.
Roberts, R. (1994) *A Ragged Schooling.* Manchester: Mandolin.
Rousseau, J.-J. (1979) [1762] *Emile.* Translated by Allan Bloom. New York: Basic Books.
Schama, S. (1987) *The Embarrassment of Riches: An Interpretation of Dutch Culture in the Golden Age.* London: Fontana.
Shahar, S. (1992) *Childhood in the Middle Ages.* London: Routledge.
Shorter, E. (1976) *The Making of the Modern Family.* London: Fontana.
Stone, L. (1977) *The Family, Sex and Marriage in England 1500–1800.* London: Weidenfeld.

FURTHER READING

Ariès, P. (1960) *Centuries of Childhood.* Harmondsworth: Penguin Books. This is obviously the key work and it is certainly worth browsing to get a sense of Ariès's arguments.

Cunningham, H. (1995) *Children and Childhood in Western Society since 1500.* London: Longman. This is a very accessible, readable introduction to the whole area. It includes a clear discussion of Ariès and his critics as well as good descriptions of the changing attitudes to children in the last three centuries.

Hardyment, C. (1983) *Dream Babies: Child Care from Locke to Spock.* Oxford: Oxford Paperbacks. A clear, well-written account of the 'advice to parents' industry.

Rousseau, J.-J. (1762) *Emile.* Web version at http://projects.ilt.columbia.edu/pedagogies/Rousseau/Contents2.html. The classic portrayal of a child-centred education. Compare Rousseau's plans for Emile with those for Sophie, who he sees as a helper and servant of the 'ideal (male) citizen'.

Chapter *Two*

Self-Concept

NICOLA LEATHER

The components of self-concept are described. Examples are offered in relation to the early years, the primary years and during adolescence. The chapter concludes by summarizing four identity statuses.

Show me the sensible person who likes him or herself?
I know myself too well to like what I see.
I know but too well that I'm not what I'd like to be.
(Golda Meir, Prime Minister of Israel, 1969)

The Western concept of the 'self' as an individual, that is entirely separate from its social context and relationships, is a relatively recent development. It first began to emerge with the work of the seventeenth- and eighteenth-century philosophers Descartes, Locke and Hume. Gradually the concept of the individual rather than the community became dominant in society, and the idea of the 'self' continued to develop until it was regarded by people in Western societies as self-evident.

Psychological theories of the self have always recognized the importance of other people in influencing the ideas that we develop of ourselves. In 1890 William James argued that **self-concept** develops from social comparisons: we compare ourselves with significant others and use this information to develop an idea of what we are like. Cooley in 1902 saw feedback from others as crucially important. Mead in 1934 emphasized the importance of social interaction in the development of our ideas about us.

Before you read any further, you may like to try the following exercise. Write down 20 answers to the question 'Who am I?' and then look at the list and think about what you wrote and where the ideas came from. My list would include things like these:

I am a person with many roles: mother, wife, daughter, sister, friend, manager, lecturer, student.
I am small in height and petite.
I am logical in thought.
I am a good cook and like entertaining.

My list, and probably yours, contains ideas about how I look, my roles in life and something about my beliefs, attitudes and qualities. These are all aspects of our self-concept.

Components of Self-Concept

G There are many ways of looking at the make-up of self-concept, but it can be regarded as having two main components, namely self-image and **self-esteem**, and can be described as being made up of the subjective self and the objective self. Self-image is a factual self-portrait, which includes information about the body, likes and dislikes, past experiences and many other facets. It is how we see ourselves and is developed from a collection of life experiences. Self-esteem is the evaluative component of the self-concept, and is concerned with internalized social judgements and ideas about how worthwhile a characteristic or personal quality is. Coppersmith in 1968 concluded that positive self-esteem is an important aspect of good psychological health, and that parenting can be influential in the development of self-esteem. Self-esteem is thought to develop throughout childhood as we internalize social standards through social interaction.

Subjective and objective self is an idea developed by Michael Lewis to describe how the self-concept emerges during childhood. The first task that the child faces is to find out that he or she is separate from others and that this separate self endures over time. This is what he calls the subjective self. I will look at the timescale in relation to this development later. Objective self is thought to mean the development of understanding of our objective qualities, in relation to things such as gender, age, size, name and other characteristics. It is the idea that we all have properties and are objects in the world.

Early Self-Awareness

Recognition of self

Current ideas about how the child develops a sense of self are still strongly influenced by the work of Freud and Piaget, both of whom assumed that the infant starts life with no sense of being separate. Piaget's work emphasizes that in order for the infant to start to develop a sense of self there first needs to develop the concept of object permanence. This is thought to develop between the ages of nine and twelve months, when the child understands that something still exists even when out of view. Thus, the child understands that mum and dad continue to exist when out of sight and can begin to understand that he or she exists as a separate being from them. Lewis described this as the development of the subjective self. The most frequent method used to look at the emergence of the idea of self with young children involves the use of a mirror. First the infant (aged 9–12 months) is placed in front of the mirror to see how they react. Most will look at their reflection, make faces and try to interact with the reflected baby in some way. An adult then puts a spot of rouge on the infant's nose and again lets them look in the mirror. The important question here is whether the infant reaches for their own nose rather than the reflected image in the mirror. At the ages of 9–12 months, none of the infants reached for their own nose, but by age 21 months 75 per cent did so, demonstrating the development of self-recognition. Once this is established the young child begins to do more for themselves and recognizes that 'mine' is meaningful.

Demonstration of self-concept in emotions

As you will see further in chapter 3, infants are able to read emotions in others to some extent, in that they respond differently to different expressions and by ten months show social referencing. During the early months of life the infant will develop a selection of different and individual emotional expressions. These will convey things such as pain, interest, enjoyment and discomfort. Expressions of anger and sadness are thought to develop by age 2–3 months, and fear by 6–7 months. But only once the infant has developed recognition of self can they begin to recognize these expressions in themselves, via self-evaluation.

Concrete examples

Once the initial self-concept has developed, the preschool child will begin to define 'who I am' in relation to their own roles and qualities. They begin to use the world around them to relate to their play and stories. At this point the preschool child will still be using concrete examples in order to categorize themselves. So they may describe themselves: 'I'm good at jumping', 'like playing with cars', 'being a big boy', with their examples being very specific and relating to visible characteristics.

Self-Concept at School Age

Over the years in primary school the concept of self develops from this concrete concept to a more comparative and abstract concept. So at the start of primary school the child may use words such as 'good' and 'small' to describe themselves as they do in the preschool years, but by the time they reach junior school age, at about age eight, they are more likely to use comparative terms such as 'cleverer than most of the class' or 'not good at PE'. At the same time the child's self-concept becomes less focused on external characteristics and more focused on internal qualities and beliefs. The child understands that some of their qualities are stable and unlikely to change over time.

These changes are reflected in the way that teachers interact with children. During the early school years the emphasis is on the effort the child makes and their application to the task in hand, rather than comparison with their peers. Gradually the teachers make more comparative judgements about the child and use not only other children, but also external standards, to compare them.

Self-Concept in Adolescence

Self-definitions

During the period of change from childhood to adulthood, the young person is more likely to use abstract concepts to define themselves, rather than rely upon physical characteristics. This is not to say that they abandon the use of physical criteria, but that beliefs, values and qualities become more dominant in describing the individual.

Identity

Erik Erikson (1980) describes the establishment of identity as one of the central tasks of the adolescent phase of life. He argues that the young person needs to establish who they are and what values they hold in relation to occupational roles, religious roles, sexual roles and educational roles. The early self-concept that the child developed needs to adapt to the changes that are taking place in both body and mind. The young person needs to evaluate their own beliefs and those of their parents in order to become an independent individual with a separate identity. The most important researcher to look at identity was James Marcia, who described four identity statuses, which were based on Erikson's theoretical principles. Marcia (1980) considers that the formation of identity has two parts: a crisis and a commitment. By the term 'crisis' he meant a period of time when the values and beliefs held in childhood are re-evaluated. He describes 'commitment' as the outcome of this re-evaluation. In conclusion, by putting the two parts together it is possible to create a matrix of four different 'identity statuses' (table 2.1).

Table 2.1 can be explained as follows:

- Identity achievement is when the person has been through a crisis and has reached a commitment.
- Moratorium is when a crisis is in progress and the person has not yet reached a commitment.

Table 2.1 An adaptation of the four identity statuses proposed by Marcia (1980)

		Degree of crisis	
		High	*Low*
Degree of commitment to a particular role or value	High	Identity achievement status – crisis passed	Foreclosure status
	Low	Moratorium status – in midst of crisis	Identity diffusion status

- Foreclosure is when a commitment has been made without a crisis having occurred: positions are simply accepted and unchanged.
- Identity diffusion can be the time before a crisis occurs or following a crisis when no commitment has been made.

Activity

Think about situations in which you are tested: these could be SATs, GCSEs, 'A' Levels, a driving test, etc. How did the process of being tested affect your self-concept? Is the relationship dependent upon the outcome of the test? How do teachers, parents, peers and test results interact to form your self-concept?

REFERENCES

Erikson, E. H. (1980) *Identity and the Life Cycle.* New York: Norton.

Lewis, M. (1994) Myself and me. In S. T. Parker, R. W. Mitchell and M. L. Boccia (eds) *Self-Awareness in Animals and Humans: Developmental Perspectives.* New York: Cambridge University Press.

Marcia, J. E. (1980) Identity in adolescence. In J. Adelson (ed.) *Handbook of Adolescent Psychology.* New York: Wiley.

FURTHER READING

Harter, S. (1987) The determinants and mediational role of global self-worth in children. In N. Eisenberg (ed.) *Contemporary Topics in Developmental Psychology.* New York: Wiley-Interscience. Harter's work on self-esteem is clearly introduced in this paper.

http://www.kidshealth.org/kid/feeling/emotion/self_esteem.html. A useful website of information and ideas for children, aimed at enhancing their self-esteem.

http://www.self-esteem-nase.org. A website looking at the research into self-esteem.

Relationships

Chapter *Three*

Attachment

NICOLA LEATHER

The development of the relationship between two or more people is something that we all consider at many times throughout our lives. This chapter looks closely at the relationship between the child and its carers from the earliest days of life. Secure and insecure attachment behaviour is described and the chapter concludes with a short summary of research on the effects that mothers' employment has on children.

The strongest theoretical influence on current studies of caring relationships is attachment theory, particularly the work of John Bowlby (1907–90). In the writings of John Bowlby and another influential researcher, Mary Ainsworth (1913–99), the key concepts are those of **attachment** and **affectional bonds**. Ainsworth describes an affectional bond as a long enduring emotional tie to a specific individual. An attachment is seen as a type of affectional bond which is characterized by the following features: physical proximity seeking, comfort and security, separation upset and **reciprocity**.

Attachments can form at any age, but the earliest relationships are the ones that have received the most attention from psychologists. The assumption is often made that the very first relationship formed by a child is a prototype for all subsequent relationships formed by that individual. Bowlby described attachment as being based upon a number of inborn action patterns, such as crying, sucking, babbling, smiling and clinging. These actions have emerged in the course of evolution because they increase the survival chances of the young of the species by promoting proximity to and interaction with the carer. The original work by Bowlby described this relationship as primarily with the mother, although subsequent work acknowledged that any significant carer or frequent presence near the infant might promote an attachment relationship. For ease of writing, 'parent' will be used in this chapter to cover all possible carers.

In the first year or two of life the child's attachment is very much a case of seeking the physical presence of the parent in order to gain the comfort, security and caregiving required. In time, however, children come to form what Bowlby referred to as an 'internal working model' of their attachment figure. That is, they develop an inner sense of the nature of the individual, their behaviour patterns and the relationship that the child has formed with them. Separation, for example, is tolerated much more easily when children are able to form an internal representation of their parents – they can relate to them in their absence without needing the constant reassurance of their physical presence.

Formation and Features of Attachment

Bowlby outlined four phases in the development of attachment and similar outlines have been developed by Mary Ainsworth and others. Table 3.1 (adapted from Bowlby 1969) provides a summary of the characteristics of these phases.

The usual method of detecting whether a child has developed an attachment to a specific individual is to observe the child's behaviour when the individual is present and when they depart. Separation distress combined with evidence that people are not interchangeable as caregivers highlights the existence of a clear-cut attachment to a particular individual. This is an important milestone of development, as up to this point (around the age of seven or eight months) infants are by and large indiscriminate about who cares for them. Caregivers are to a large extent interchangeable and the degree of comfort obtained by the infant is more related to competence of care rather than attachment relationship. It is only from about seven months that infants seek the proximity of certain individuals and show wariness and proximity avoidance to others.

Table 3.1 Phases of attachment and principal features of the child's behaviour

Phase	*Average age range*	*Principal features*
Indiscriminate social responsiveness	0–2 months	Respond to human interaction, but not selective about whom they respond to.
Attachment in the making – focusing on familiar people	3–6 months	Recognition of familiar people, more selective and responsive to familiars.
Intense attachment and active proximity seeking	8–35 months	Separation fear, wariness of strangers, intentional communication, security in routine, uses carer as safe base.
Goal corrected attachment – partnership behaviour	24 months on	Two-sided relationships develop; children begin to understand parents' needs.

Over the next few months infants become strongly attached to specific individuals and learn to recognize usual behaviour patterns and routines. Those of you who have children, or who babysit for others, may recognize the following scenario. The parents have decided to have a special night out. They try to maintain the infant's routine of feeding, bathing and bedtime while getting ready for the night out (so the infant may see one parent in a dressing gown following a shower, or one parent taking over from another to enable them to get ready). The infant is aware that something different is happening, so instead of cooperating as they normally would do, they become 'difficult' and refuse to settle. It appears to an outsider that the infant is unsettled by the change of routine, but perhaps they are also interested in what is happening and want to stay awake to find out more!

Social referencing

By about the age of ten months the infant has learned to use the attachment figure(s) to obtain clues about any novel situations encountered. When confronted, for example, with new toys, new surroundings, strangers, the infant first looks at the parent's facial expression. By 'reading' the expression, the infant can judge whether this 'novel' experience is supposed to be fearful, delightful or neutral. The infant is therefore more likely to accept a novel situation if the parent looks positive about it.

Separation anxiety and protest

Once the child has developed an attachment they will protest at separation from that preferred person and will also show fear of strangers. A young child is likely to experience severance of this bond with the parent as devastating, especially if it occurs under stressful situations and involves a strange place or people. In the 1960s James and Joyce Robertson undertook detailed observation of how young children behave in this type of situation, using the technique of non-participant observation. This revealed three stages that the child may go through in these circumstances (table 3.2).

Table 3.2 Stages of separation behaviour as observed by Robertson and Robertson

Distress	A period of protest when the child cries for parent and refuses to be comforted by others.
Despair	The child becomes quiet and apathetic: overt protest is less; the child accepts care passively; appears to be in a state of hopelessness.
Detachment	The child appears to have come to terms with the loss of the parent and the situation; begins to develop other relationships; may be unable or unwilling to trust parent if/when they return, or may become very 'clingy' and refuse to let parent leave them in any situation.

From the age of about two years old children start to understand that parents have needs as well. They begin to move from seeing themselves at the centre of the family, to seeing themselves as part of the family. Children begin to develop further techniques for controlling the behaviour of their parents and getting what they want. This type of behaviour continues throughout childhood and adolescence. Think about how you got what you wanted from your parents, or how your children control you. Behaviours typically include helping, pleading and pestering, asking one parent then another, tone of voice, and many others.

Secure and Insecure Attachments

The assumption that the first relationship the child forms is a prototype for subsequent relationships has prompted the examination of the nature of infants' attachments, with particular reference to the sense of security they obtain from the adult carer. Ainsworth developed a procedure for looking at this relationship, which has become known as 'the strange situation'. It consists of a series of episodes, which take place in a laboratory situation, typically undertaken when the child is between 12 and 18 months old:

1. Child with its mother.
2. Child with mother and a stranger.
3. Child left with the stranger for a few minutes.
4. Reunited with mother.
5. Left completely alone.
6. Reunited with stranger.
7. Reunited with mother.

The behaviour of the child during these episodes can be classified into a number of types, as described by Ainsworth and colleagues (see table 3.3 for a summary).

Mary Ainsworth felt that the degree of attachment security could be influenced by parenting style, with the principal cause being differences in parental responsiveness to the needs of the child. An insecure relationship with an attachment figure which is full of uncertainty and doubt about being loved is regarded as setting the tone for future relationships, which the individual may also approach with doubt and lack of confidence.

Parental deprivation is the current term for what used to be called maternal deprivation, and basically refers to an insufficiency of parental care. A lack of psychological care is usually noted as the key component which may be linked to a lack of physical care. The most frequently seen deprivation happens to children in institutions where, in the worst cases, the environment can be impersonal and one of neglect, but deprivation can also be experienced in the home. The effects can be wide-ranging and include physical, intellectual and social harm. These cases result in referral to social services departments as part of child protection legislation (CHAPTER 17).

Table 3.3 Categorization of secure and insecure attachment in Ainsworth's strange situation

Securely attached	Child explores environment, but returns to mother when upset. Actively seeks contact and is easily consoled. Upset by mother's departure; greets her positively on return.
Insecurely attached: Detached/avoidant	Child avoids contact with mother, especially on reunion. Does not resist contact when offered, but shows no preference for mother over stranger.
Insecurely attached: Resistant/ambivalent	Child's tendency to explore is inhibited and they are wary of stranger. Greatly upset when separated from mother, but difficult to console on reunion. Seeks and resists comfort.
Insecurely attached: Disorganized/disorientated	Child displays confused mixture of behaviour, such as appearing to seek comfort while avoiding gaze.

Attachment security appears to be helpful in predicting a range of behaviours in childhood. One question that many people have attempted to address over recent years has been whether attachment security remains stable throughout childhood. The answer seems to be that while under certain circumstances security may change, it is more likely to remain stable over time. Some of the reasons for change will relate to changes in family circumstances, including separation and illness. Behaviour patterns that may be predicted by attachment security can include the following: sociability, self-esteem, behaviour problems and task-related behaviours. The securely attached infant will (a) subsequently get along better with peers, have more friends and be more confident with adults; (b) be more likely to develop into a child with higher self-esteem; (c) be less likely to show behaviour difficulties in later life; and (d) tend to be more confident and independent in play and work.

Clearly, separation experiences can be intensely upsetting for young children, but does this mean that children in the early years need the constant reassurance of the parents' presence? There is now a large body of evidence on the effects on young children of maternal employment and consequent day care. This can be summarized as follows:

- The majority of studies have found no differences in any aspect of behaviour between children of employed mothers and those who stay at home.
- There are no indications that attachment is diluted by not being together all day.
- Children in day care may be at an advantage in relation to the development of sociability and independence.
- Outcome depends upon the quality of care arrangements and the quality of parenting.

Activity

Think about all the people you are close to. Pick out one or more of these attachment relationships and make a list of all the attachment behaviours that you show towards that person. How are these similar or different to those shown by an infant to its parent or primary carer?

REFERENCES

Ainsworth, M. and Bell, S. (1970) Attachment, exploration and separation: Illustrated by the behaviour of one-year-olds in a strange situation. *Child Development*, Vol. 41: 49–67.

Bowlby, J. (1969) *Attachment and Loss: Vol. 1*. Harmondsworth: Penguin Books.

FURTHER READING

Bee, H. (2000) *The Developing Child* (9th edn). Needham Heights, MA: Allyn and Bacon. Contains a comprehensive but easy-to-read analysis of attachment behaviour and its effects on the child throughout its life.

International Attachment Network: http://www.attachmentnetwork.org.

Steele, H. (2002) State of the art: Attachment theory. *The Psychologist*, Vol. 15 (10): 518–22. An up-to-date analysis of attachment theory from the original works to the present day. Looks at whether attachment theory has kept pace with the changing family.

Chapter *Four*

Peers

DOMINIC WYSE

The distinction between vertical and horizontal relationships is established. The characteristics of peer relationships at different ages are described. The social and cognitive dimensions are considered and the chapter concludes with some thoughts about acceptance and rejection.

Part of the way that we judge ourselves is to think about how we are regarded by our peers. An important aspect of this is the nature of friendships that we have. As we become reflective adults we learn that if you base your views of yourself too much on other people's reaction then this could be a negative trait reflecting insecurity. However, for children, psychological research in particular has shown the important influence of peers. One of the reasons that peers are important to children's development is that they offer a different kind of relationship to the one experienced with parents.

The two main kinds of relationship are often described as vertical or horizontal. Vertical relationships are ones that are based on an unequal distribution of power. Parents are in a vertical relationship to their children because they have to exert varying degrees of control. However, over the years this will change and if parents become very old sometimes the roles are reversed, with the children having to make decisions for the parent. Horizontal relationships are based on an equal distribution of power. This is important because genuine cooperation and competition can be experienced. Cooperation with parents is different because the parent will often make allowances for the child and will also cooperate for reasons of enhancing the child's development. Cooperation with peers involves negotiation and the sharing of ideas to reach a goal that two or more children have decided that they want to achieve.

UNIVERSITY OF WINCHESTER
LIBRARY

Social Features of Peer Relationships

Children at different stages of development have different ways of interacting with their peers:

Birth to 2 years
- Growing interest in other babies
- Starting to share toys
- Attempts to approach another child
- Social contact tends to be one-way: not reciprocated

2–4 years
- Solitary play decreases
- Parallel play still important
- Able to communicate meaning through speech
- Shared role play begins
- Negotiation of rules for play
- Play with more than one other child

4–11 years
- Cooperative and sharing skills develop
- Better understanding of others' feelings
- Same-sex friendships develop strongly
- Social groups formed with more thought

11 years and older
- Quality of relationships is significantly linked to quality of relationships during adulthood
- Mixed-sex friendships and couples established
- Support about uncertainties of life sought for in peers
- Conformity to peer culture is stronger
- Peer group supports feelings of self-worth

The peer group also develops its own distinct values and customs. One study that broke new ground in showing the nature and importance of the customs of childhood was the Opies' work on the 'lore and language of school children'. This seminal work was one of the first to regard childhood as an important area of study for research. The Opies collected examples of children chants and rhymes by liaising with teachers and children throughout the United Kingdom. The chants emerged from children interacting with their peers in the playground or when playing outside their homes.

> It is a record of his [*sic*] strange and primitive culture, including seasonal customs, initiation rites, superstitious practices and beliefs, innumerable rhymes and chants (800 are given here in full), catcalls and retorts, stock jokes, ruderies, riddles, slang-epithets, nicknames, and the traditional juvenile argot which continues to flourish in street and

> playground, largely unknown and certainly unheeded by the adult world. (*Opie and Opie 1959*)

In their book the Opies provide thousands of examples of rhymes and chants that children develop in the course of their play with each other. These serve to cement relationships with peers. A couple of examples: the first deals explicitly with friendship. The children have to link their little fingers and say:

> *Make friends, make friends,*
> *Never, never break friends.*
> *(Ibid.: 324)*

The second example emphasizes the importance of telling the truth. The child has to lick their finger and show it, then say: 'My finger's wet.' Then the child wipes the finger in their armpit and says: 'My finger's dry.' Finally, they tilt their head back and draw their finger across their throat and say: 'Cut my throat if I tell a lie' (ibid.: 127).

The Opies clearly saw children rather like an unexplored 'tribe' and part of the evidence for this theory was the ways that children establish their own customs. This can have both positive and negative consequences. One positive consequence is that children are able to gain some elements of control by denying adults access to some aspects of their lives. This can even be a survival strategy for some children. For example, across the world there are street children who have developed support networks in order to protect themselves from abuse and exploitation. One negative consequence of identifying children as a tribe and as something very different from adults is that they can be denied all kinds of rights by virtue of their 'special' status as weak, immature, etc. Work like that of the Opies shows that peer group relationships clearly have a social dimension, but they also have a cognitive one.

Cognitive Features

There are strong assumptions that children can only learn from more experienced teachers, whether these are teachers in the professional sense or just people who in the course of everyday life teach them things by virtue of the fact that they have advanced knowledge of something. There is no doubt that children do learn much from these people, but there is also evidence that they can learn from their peers even when they are not particularly knowledgeable. Imagine a situation where children have to tackle a problem. Research has shown that when peers collaborate on tackling the problem their understanding develops more than it would have done had they worked alone.

> Just why peer collaboration can, under certain circumstances at least, be so effective a tool for learning, whether the essential process involves the children's cooperation or,

> on the contrary, the conflict of different ideas, is not yet established. What is certain is that relatively free-wheeling discussion among equally ignorant children of the problem facing them and the various solutions they might adopt generates new insights and promotes learning in the individual participants. (*Schaffer 2004*)

The education system in England has developed in recent years into one that emphasizes individual achievement. This is most obvious in the heavy emphasis on testing of children, which is designed to make schools accountable. But it is also evident from the fact that schools have rarely encouraged collaborative learning effectively. Given that there is evidence for the value of peer collaboration it is a shame that such collaboration is not more of a priority in the education system.

Acceptance and Rejection

An early concern of parents is about whether their child is settling in well at the various **settings** that they will encounter during their childhood years. They want to know if their child gets on with other children and makes friends. This instinctive regard for their children is supported by research which has underlined the importance of acceptance by peers and the potentially damaging effects of rejection. It is now known that in addition to the immediate effects of rejection there can also be longer-term effects.

One of the questions about rejection concerns whether it is caused by particular personality traits or whether the experience of being rejected leads to the development of such characteristics. Schaffer (1996) argues that rejected children bring with them characteristics which lead to their rejection. Aggressiveness, uncooperativeness and social ineptness are all characteristics of rejected children. By contrast, the case for popular children shows

> From the beginning they display skilful behaviour in group entry and in the management of social interactions; this makes them generally acceptable and quickly establishes their popular status. (*Ibid.: 321*)

We suspect that both previous characteristics and the experience of being rejected reinforce each other. Whatever the case, there is growing recognition that rejection can lead to a number of undesirable characteristics, in particular aggressive behaviour and withdrawal. In severe cases these characteristics can result in lower academic achievement, criminality, loneliness and depression. However, Hymel et al. (2002) point out that there is a lack of longitudinal research on the impacts of rejection. It is important that research considers the impact on individuals as well as on groups and that it tracks the connections between poor peer relationships and the characteristics of the child across time.

Although genetic characteristics have an influence on whether a child will become rejected, there are programmes that have been developed to counteract this. These programmes use various techniques to help children become more aware of their behaviour:

- Diagnose the child's behaviour patterns.
- Watch films showing models of more acceptable behaviour.
- Practise appropriate behaviour in role play situation.
- Comment on behaviour.
- Use positive and negative feedback for different kinds of behaviour.
- Discuss the behaviour and provide coaching.

> The indications are that those [programmes] based on a combination of modelling, reinforcement, practice, and cognitive approaches are most effective . . . A great deal still needs to be learned about how to produce change in established social patterns; in the meantime there is at least enough promise in existing work to regard this as an enterprise well worth the effort. (*Schaffer 1996: 324*)

For nearly all children, positive peer interaction results in friendships which are marked by subtle changes as children grow older. The idea of giving and taking fairly is part of friendships at all ages. Preschool children tend to describe friendships in terms of what they do together. Primary-age children emphasize loyalty and trustworthiness. Pre-adolescent children emphasize sympathy, self-disclosure and other aspects of social intimacy (Hartrup and Abecassis 2002: 286). There are also differences in the ways that the interaction between boys and girls who are friends is characterized. Girls anticipate greater affection, intimacy and help from their friends than boys do, although the research used to test these things has tended to regard intimacy in the context of empathy and self-disclosure rather than task mastery and camaraderie (ibid.: 292).

It is clear then that peers are a very important part of children's development. In future it will be necessary for adults to take a more positive interest in the kinds of peer relationships that children form and the characteristics of those relationships. It is perhaps in the area of education that much needs to be learned about the positive potential of peer collaboration as a powerful tool to support learning.

Activity

On a scale of 1–10, with 1 as a horizontal relationship and 10 as a vertical relationship, score some of your relationships with peers and others. Discuss two of these with one of your peers.

REFERENCES

Hartrup, W. W. and Abecassis, M. (2002) Friends and enemies. In P. K. Smith and C. H. Hart (eds) *Childhood Social Development.* Oxford: Blackwell.

Hymel, S., Vaillancourt, T., McDougall, P. and Renshaw, P. D. (2002) Peer acceptance and rejection in childhood. In P. K. Smith and C. H. Hart (eds) *Childhood Social Development.* Oxford: Blackwell.

Opie, I. and Opie, P. (1959) *The Lore and Language of School Children.* Oxford: Oxford University Press.

Schaffer, R. (2004) *Introducing Child Psychology.* Oxford: Blackwell.

FURTHER READING

Boyes, G. (1995) *The Legacy of the Work of Iona and Peter Opie: The Lore and Language of Today's Children.* London: Hodder and Stoughton. More recent evidence that children's chants and rhymes are alive and well.

Read On – Paired reading site: http://www.dundee.ac.uk/psychology/ReadOn/. An example of how peer tutoring can support the teaching of reading.

Schaffer, R. (1996) *Social Development.* Oxford: Blackwell. In addition to a wide range of topics relevant to the study of childhood this book includes a more extensive treatment of psychological research on peers.

Chapter *Five*

Family Structures

ROBERT BANTON

The notion of the 'nuclear family' and the idea that it is both biologically natural and universal is explored. Statistics showing changes in the structures and occurrence of different family groups are presented. The chapter concludes with a brief discussion of the two main arguments about the implications of these family changes.

What images spring to mind when you hear the word 'family'? Do you think of mother, father, brothers and sisters? Maybe you think of home, growing up, feeling loved and secure. Perhaps family for you brings images of arguing, discord, fighting and people shouting. For many people, the definition of the family is an image of two married biological parents with their children: this is called the nuclear family. The nuclear family also has particular roles for men and women. The woman is expected to look after the children and to ensure that the home is comfortable; the man is expected to bring home money for the family to live on. In spite of the major changes in family structures in recent years this traditional image of the family with stereotypical roles for men and women is still very strong in many people's minds. In fact, according to Muncie and Sapsford (1997) it is so strong that all other types of family are judged against it.

There are many families that cannot be described as nuclear. You will be aware of lone-parent families, single-sex partnerships, families that have adopted children and families that have no young children at all. Just about every conceivable variation of adults with or without children exists within contemporary British society, and has for some time. Although you might think that these variations are only a modern phenomenon, work from writers such as Bowley and Hogg writing in 1925 showed that the conventional family accounted for only 5 per cent of all households in the northern counties. Rimmer and Wicks writing in 1981 noted that single-breadwinner families were only 15 per cent of all households.

This array of living arrangements leads some writers to avoid the term 'family' altogether. Lorraine Fox-Harding (1996) argues that the term is not a unitary concept with a single accepted meaning or reference point. The meanings tend to overlap with other concepts such as household, kinship, marriage and parenthood. Perhaps more importantly the term may also carry judgemental ideas about what constitutes a 'proper' family.

Many people point to the fact that the family is biologically natural. After all, you need both male and female to produce a baby and then to adequately nurture the child. However, contemporary developments in medical science have eliminated the need for a couple to have sexual intercourse together to produce a child. Developments in *in vitro* fertilization (IVF) mean that a woman's ova can be fertilized by sperm from a man she has never and will never meet. Indeed, today a woman may have a child for which she has not contributed any genetic material by using ova from another woman. Developments in the science of genetics mean that the possibilities of cloning a baby from the cells of an adult are already raising ethical, moral and medical concerns. All of this means that the old certainties surrounding the creating and nurturing of children will continue to undergo considerable change.

There are other indications that the nuclear family is far from the norm. If we look briefly at other societies and **cultures** we find further variety. One example is the Nayar people of southwest India. The men are full-time soldiers and so are often away from home. Once Nayar women are married there is no obligation to have any contact with their husband until his death, when there is a duty to attend his funeral and mourn for him. The women are also free to take a number of visiting husbands (*Sandbanham* husbands), who may spend the night with them.

Changes in Family Structures

According to data from the National Family and Parenting Institute (NFPI 2001) there are just over 16 million families and 12 million children in the UK today. The NFPI points to a series of changes over time that have affected the dominance of the nuclear family. These changes affect both the type of family as well as their composition. These changes include the reduction in the number of marriages and the increase in the rates of divorce. Another striking feature is the rapid growth of lone-parent families as well as the growth of reconstituted families. Family size has also changed, with smaller families containing fewer children. Family structure is now characterized by increasing diversity and change.

Marriage and divorce

In general the trend is for fewer individuals to marry. Since 1976 the marriage rate for individuals over 16 years of age has reduced by more than half. In 1999 there were just over a quarter of a million (293,000) marriages in the UK: one of the lowest annual figures recorded in the twentieth century. However, within this general downward trend there was an increase in weddings in 2000 for the first time since 1992. Data from the 2001 census showed that there were 305,900 weddings in the UK – 1.6 per cent more than in 1999. Although marriage may be less popular generally, many individuals who do get married and then divorced will remarry. Just over 40 per cent of weddings in 1999 and 2000 were remarriages for one or both partners.

Additionally, those who do choose to marry are doing so later in life. Since 1961 the mean age for first marriages has risen in both sexes by 5 years to just over 30 for men and to just over 28 for women. A variety of explanations may account for this, including increased and longer participation in further and higher education, particularly among women (Office for National Statistics 2002).

Of the people who do choose to marry, more will become divorced. Since 1976 the divorce rate has risen by over a third. The number of divorces granted in England and Wales fell by more than 2 per cent in 2000 to 141,135, compared with 144,556 in 1999. Although the divorce rate peaked in 1993, 40 per cent of marriages will still ultimately end in divorce.

Cohabitation

More couples are choosing to cohabit, that is to live together but not marry. This may be a choice for life or as a prelude to marriage. In 1998 more than 10 per cent of adults had cohabited in a relationship that did not lead to marriage. For young people aged between 25 and 29 years, this figure rises to 25 per cent.

Single-parent families

Not all families are headed by two adults, whether they are married or not. The proportion of single-parent families has grown steadily from 14 per cent in 1986 to 20 per cent in 1991. This substantial rate of growth in lone-parent families over the last 25 years appears to have stabilized in recent years. The number of one-parent families in Great Britain in 2000 was provisionally estimated at 1.75 million, 25 per cent of all families with dependent children (Office for National Statistics 2002). A large part of the increase up to the mid-1980s was due to divorce, while after 1986 the number of single lone mothers grew at a faster rate consistent with the growth in the proportion of live births outside marriage. A lone mother heads the majority of lone-parent families; 90 per cent of lone parents are women. A lone father heads around 10 per cent of lone-parent families (Office for National Statistics 2001).

Later childbearing and fewer children

If we look back in history we can see that in general family size was larger. Today the trend is for women to have children much later in life. Over the past decade the mean age for women having a baby has risen from 27.7 years to nearly 29 years of age. Births to women between the ages of 25 and 29 accounted for nearly 92 per cent of all births in 2001.

As well as having children later in life women seem to be having fewer children. In the US, almost 14 per cent of women aged 18–34 plan to have just one child and this figure is rising. This figure is backed by the Family Policy Studies Centre, which claims that women in the UK are having fewer children when they embark on motherhood, and that we are seeing a decline overall in the number of children being born. G The **total fertility rate** for women in the UK has fallen for all ages up to 30 years of age. This rate has risen in women over the age of 30.

The Impact of Family Changes

There are two opposing views about the changes in family structures. There are those who feel that the changes described above are negative and are causing many of the social problems we see around us in society. The counter-argument is that we are simply seeing the natural evolution of the family reflecting changing patterns within society. For example, many women no longer expect that working in the home and caring for children will be their only role. Women not only have to work to support the family finances, but they also want the same kinds of freedom that men have enjoyed for many years. Societal views about marriage have changed. There is less pressure for men and women to put up with unhappy marriages for the sake of the children or because it is the respectable thing to do. Many people reject the traditional teachings of the church and state and feel that marriage itself is an outdated institution and prefer the freedom of cohabitation. Many couples choose not to have children at all in favour of developing their careers or enjoying greater financial and social freedom.

Some politicians and academics even talk about the *death* of the family. Patricia Morgan, in her book *Farewell to the Family?* (1995), sums up the main argument by saying that the changes in family structure are damaging to children and society as a whole. Morgan asserts that two-parent families are necessary for a stable society. With regard to the changes mentioned above, Morgan argues that they remove men from the household, which in turn leads to consequences such as poverty and hence a need to rely heavily on state welfare. Boys lack effective male role models and this may lead to the development of anti-social tendencies. Morgan also points to the lower educational attainment of children from non-traditional families. She is certainly not the only person to voice these views.

In 1998 the government published a consultation document called *Supporting Families*. In the document the home secretary Jack Straw argued that society needs strong families and that marriage is still the best family structure within which to raise children. He talked in terms of families having two parents and those parents being married, and went on to say: 'families are also under considerable stress. As ever it is a hard job to be a parent. More marriages end in divorce. More children are brought up in lone-parent families' (Home Office 1998: 2). The significant point here was that in spite of the arguments suggesting that the changes in family structure were a natural process, Straw saw these as signs of families 'under stress'. The document went on to state that 'there is more child poverty, often as a direct consequence of family breakdown. Rising crime and drug abuse are indirect symptoms of problems in the family' (p. 4). Straw made a questionable causal link between the changing nature of families and the problems of wider society.

In order to try to reverse these changes Straw introduced a number of new strategies aimed at helping parents with the 'hard job' of raising children. These new initiatives included the creation of a National Family and Parenting Institute, which provides support that includes a national parenting helpline to offer advice to parents and refer people to local sources of help. Health visitors were given an enhanced role to look after the health of both parents and children. The most significant initiative (which cost £540 million) was called Sure Start (CHAPTERS 19, 37).

Is there evidence that the changes in family organization we have mentioned are really linked to the social problems that Jack Straw identified? Many of the arguments presented above can and have been attacked. The presence of two parents is not a guarantee of positive outcomes, as the data for child abuse and domestic violence show. On average, social services receive 160,000 referrals concerning child abuse every year. The majority of child abuse is carried out within the family. The Women's Aid Federation (2002) cite an analysis of ten separate domestic violence prevalence studies by the Council of Europe that showed consistent findings: 1 in 4 women experience domestic violence over their lifetimes and between 6 and 10 per cent of women suffer domestic violence in a given year. The 2001/2 British Crime Survey (BCS) found that there were an estimated 635,000 incidents of domestic violence in England and Wales: 81 per cent of the victims were women and 19 per cent were men (Women's Aid Federation 2002). Keeping families together where there are high levels of conflict may actually be more harmful for children in the long run. Divorce and separation can be managed to make the experience less traumatic for children. If this is done there is evidence that the long-term outcomes are usually positive.

While it may be true that children from non-traditional households do experience poorer health and lower educational attainments, the question must be asked, is this the result of the family structure or the poverty that many of these families live in? Many single-parent families in poverty actually started out as two-parent families living in poverty. Morgan and Straw place the responsibility for many anti-social acts at the door of non-traditional families. It is likely that other possible causes – such as unemployment and inequalities in income – are of equal or even greater significance. Action to make life in families positive is always welcome, but this should also be accompanied by a more concerted attempt to tackle poverty and social exclusion.

Activity

Compile a montage of images of the family from the press. You can include newspapers, magazines, advertisements and even images from the television. What image of the family do they present?

REFERENCES

Bowley, A. L. and Hogg, M. H. (1997) [1925] *Has Poverty Diminished?* In J. Bernardes (1997) *Family Studies: An Introduction.* London: Routledge.

Fox-Harding, L. (1996) *Family, State and Social Policy.* London: Macmillan.

Home Office (1998) *Supporting Families: A Consultation Document.* London: HMSO.

Morgan, P. (1995) *Farewell to the Family?* London: IEA Health and Welfare Unit.

Muncie, J. and Sapsford, R. (1997) *Understanding the Family.* London: Sage.

National Family and Parenting Institute (NFPI) (2001) *The Family Today: An At A Glance Guide. Factsheet 1* [online] 2nd edn, September 2001. London. Available at http://www.nfpi.org/data/publications [accessed November 2002].

Office for National Statistics (2002) *Homepage: Census 2001* [online]. Available at http://www.statistics.gov.uk/census2001/default.asp [accessed February 2002].

Office for National Statistics (2001) *Families with Dependent Children Headed by Lone Parents* [online]. Social Trends 32. Available at http://www.statistics.gov.uk/statbase/ssdataset.asp?vlnk=4992&more=Y [accessed February 2002].

Rimmer, L. and Wicks, M. (1981) The family today. *MOST: Journal of Modern Studies Association*, 27 (autumn): 1–4. Quoted in J. Bernardes (1997) *Family Studies: An Introduction.* London: Routledge.

Women's Aid Federation (2002) *Domestic Violence Statistics Factsheet – 2002* [online]. Available at http://www.womensaid.org.uk/dv/dvfacysh2002.htm [accessed January 2002].

FURTHER READING

Bernardes, J. (1997) *Family Studies: An Introduction.* London: Routledge. A readable book which provides a good introduction to the study of the family. The book covers the argument that variation and diversity are increasingly the hallmarks of contemporary family structure.

National Families and Parenting Institute: http://www.nfpi.org/. The Institute's role is to share knowledge and unite different organizations to enhance the value and quality of family life.

Smith, R. S. (1997) Parent education: Empowerment or control? *Children and Society,* Vol. 11: 108–11. This article describes the recent growth of interest in both government circles and elsewhere in the subject of education for parenthood.

Chapter Six

Parenting

JANE BAKER

The changing nature of families has resulted in different experiences for parents and their children. This chapter considers parenting from the perspectives of different families, the law and society. One theory of parenting styles is applied to the writer's own experiences of being a parent.

In chapter 5 we provided statistics to show how the traditional family structure has undergone many changes. The concept of the traditional family has radically altered in the past 40 years. The higher divorce rate of recent times, the impact of parents who form relationships with new partners, and the place of extended families, including step-families, has meant that children are much more likely to be cared for by more people than their two biological parents. The subject of whether such changes are harmful or beneficial to children has been covered in the media. For a long time divorce and family breakup was regarded as entirely negative. However, in recent times, although it is recognized that relationship breakdown is always stressful in the short term, the way that this is handled by parents is important if the long-term outcomes are to be more beneficial for the child. Inevitably these changes have meant that parenting roles have changed.

If we think about some of the family structures that were identified in chapter 5 it is clear that each has implications for parenting.

Nuclear family

The work involved in parenting children is so extensive that having two people to share the workload is often good for the child. In happy families this structure can work well. However, if the parents see this as the only appropriate way to bring up children then there can be intolerance to other family structures. Any separation process could also be more traumatic for the children if the parents are unable to see the positive aspects of more diverse family structures.

Extended family

Grandparents often have an important role in caring for their grandchildren. If the family still lives together in one local area then grandparents' role can sometimes involve regular times when they look after the children. One of the potential problems here is that the grandparents may not want to become 'cheap' child-minders and might want what they see as a more enjoyable relationship with their grandchildren.

Reconstituted families

This family is made up of a natural parent and a step-parent. One of the benefits of this structure is that both parents may bring children from a previous relationship. The interaction with a wider range of people that this offers can provide alternative support networks. The negative side can be difficulties for children forming positive relationships with step-parents. For step-parents, discipline can also be a problem in the short term which may require them to defer to the biological parent.

Lone parents

In many people's eyes this is a negative family structure. All kinds of societal problems with children have been questionably linked to one-parent families. One of the positive aspects of lone parenting is that the children get a consistent approach. With two parents there can be many disagreements about rearing children and this can result in children exploiting these differences, exacerbating family tensions. The other advantage is often one of necessity: the children's lives would have been much worse had they remained with their two parents.

Adoptive families

The role of parents who adopt is a very important one in society. Most adoptive parents approach their role as seriously as biological parents. The advantage can be that a great deal of thought and preparation has preceded the decision to adopt. Some of the difficulties centre on the fact that biological parents will exist and the children will have all kinds of conflicting emotions about this.

Parental Responsibility

Society has expectations about appropriate parental responsibility, which are reflected in the law. Parents have rights and responsibilities just as their children do. Parental responsibilities include the need to ensure that children are appropriately cared for and in particular to ensure that the child is not neglected and abused. Parental rights include:

- Naming children.
- Giving consent for medical treatment.
- Allowing marriage for children aged 16–17.
- Making sure that children attend school.

The permanence of the responsibilities and their reflection in law are summarized by Bainham and Cretney (1993: 109):

> It is not open to a parent to pick and choose between the various responsibilities attaching to his [*sic*] status. Parenthood in this respect, like marriage itself, is the condition of belonging to a class of persons in relation to whom the law assigns particular rights and obligations. This status is not lost except though the ultimate step of adoption – a position neatly encapsulated in the catchphrase 'parenthood is for life'.

The Children Act 1989 defines parental responsibility as 'all the rights, duties, powers and responsibility and authority which, by law, a parent has in relation to a child and his property'. While the act clearly establishes rights and responsibilities for parents it also went some way in strengthening children's rights. The idea that children have rights of their own can be a challenge for some parents.

Sometimes it can be unclear whose rights are paramount. An example of this was the Gillick case in the 1980s (Gillick vs. West Norfolk and Wisbech Area Health Authority, 1986). The case involved a judgement on whether a girl under 16 had the right to contraception advice without parental consent. One of the key issues that arose was the extent to which the child fully understood the consequences of the advice. It was judged that she did and so the case found in favour of the rights of the child:

> Parental rights to control a child do not exist for the benefit of the parent. They exist for the benefit of the child and are justified only in so far as they enable the parent to perform his duties towards the child.

Linking the Practice and Theory of Parenting

Children do have powerful rights of their own which are enshrined in human rights and child rights legislation (CHAPTER 15). However, during day-to-day parenting the attitudes of parents will have a strong bearing on the extent to which the balance between rights and responsibilities is struck. At the very least there should be much negotiation with children in order to make decisions about their lives.

> As a parent myself I have become aware of the way that my own attitudes have changed. When I became pregnant with my first child, I had the vision of being the perfect mother who would spend her days in pure white chiffon with a baby who never cried! As they grew up I expected that they would look at me lovingly and be in awe of my wisdom and knowledge. This image began to fade about the Tuesday after his arrival and finally ended when he hit the toddler stage! My approach to parenting has changed over the years and depending on specific incidents I have used different strategies. Now, as a mother of three children, I am still learning, still making mistakes, and still living in hope that it will all turn out OK.

But is parenting really just down to hope? Research has attempted to link specific parenting styles to the development of the child. Baumrind (1971) looked at the type of relationship between parents and their children in an influential piece of research. She identified three different styles of parenting: permissive, authoritarian and authoritative. The *permissive* parents were often inconsistent and emphasized the child's own independence and ability to express themselves without restriction. The result of this approach was that the children often showed signs of aggression to others, impulsive behaviour and little sense of direction. The *authoritarian* parent, in contrast, had very strict rules and regulations and showed little affection. The children of this parenting style were irritable and sometimes deceitful. They tended to be withdrawn or at times aggressive. The *authoritative* parents were described as ones that found a balanced style. This style takes into consideration the child's views while providing clear boundaries. It is argued that this approach has a positive effect on the children, resulting in appropriate behaviour.

Many people agree that the authoritative style is one that they aspire to, although there are a number of practical issues that affect the ability of parents to achieve this. Looking again at my own experiences as a parent, I questioned this because each of my three children responded in a different way and required subtly different styles of parenting. Also, the styles that were required when the children were aged 3 were different for those that were required when they were 13, and will be different when they are 23. Although Baumrind's model could be a useful way of crudely categorizing parenting styles, it is not sensitive enough to allow for the many factors that differentiate the millions of different parent–child relationships that exist.

The job of parenting is one that carries huge responsibility and requires much thought. Although this knowledge is often passed down from generation to generation, wider society also has a responsibility.

> Just as children are absolutely dependent on their parents' sustenance, so . . . are parents . . . dependent on a greater society for economic provision. If a community values its children it must cherish their parents. (*Bowlby 1951: 84*)

The current government has begun to recognize the importance of supporting parents in bringing up children. Initiatives such as the Child Tax Credit are among the strategies that have been put into place. Parents need to feel valued and supported: economic support is just one way this can be achieved.

Activity

Work in groups of three. Take on the roles of a 15-year-old child, her mother and a judge. Devise a role play that illustrates the conversation between mother and daughter when the mother discovers that her daughter is on the contraceptive pill. Then illustrate the kind of conversation that a judge might have with the daughter to ascertain if she is Gillick Competent (see CHAPTER 28).

REFERENCES

Bainham, A. and Cretney, S. (1993) *Children: The Modern Law*. London: Family Law.

Baumrind, D. (1971) Current patterns of parental authority. *Developmental Psychology Monographs*, Vol. 4: 1–103.

Bowlby, J. (1951) *Maternal Care and Mental Health*. World Health Organization (WHO) Monograph (Serial No. 2). Geneva: WHO.

FURTHER READING

Department for Education and Skills (n.d.) *The Parents' Centre*: http://www.dfes.gov.uk/parents/ [retrieved 6 November 2002]. This site focuses on educational help for parents to support their children. The links to other useful resources are also helpful.

Nolan, Y. (ed.) (2002) *BTEC National Early Years*. Oxford: Heinemann. A useful resource for the early years student practitioner. The role of the practitioner in supporting the parent is just one of the areas that it considers. It briefly describes the different types of family structure and the impact of this on the child.

Taylor, J. and Woods, M. (eds) (1998) *Early Childhood Studies: An Holistic Introduction*. London: Arnold. This book notes the importance of relationships within a child's life. It charts the many changes that have occurred in the structure of the family. The discussions surrounding the relationships that children experience throughout their lives provide some worthwhile commentary from the child's perspective.

Chapter Seven

Parental Separation

ROBERT BANTON

The general effects of divorce on children are explained. The specific ways that girls and boys respond differently and the ways that the age of the child results in different responses are explored. The damaging effect of parental conflict is highlighted.

The incidence of divorce and parental separation has risen dramatically in the last 30 years. Many people would argue that family disruption can have repercussions for children once they are adults and that children whose parents have divorced or separated are prone to a series of emotional, psychological and social problems. The central question we wish to ask in this chapter is: what are the consequences for children of parental separation?

The General Effects of Separation on Children

Divorce is a very stressful experience for children. The result of divorce may be negative due to escalating conflict between parents, decline in authoritative parenting and lack of contact with a parent who moves out of the family home. Additionally, economic hardship, residential instability and additional family transitions may lead to problems for the child.

Research by Ermisch and Francesconi (2000) based on data from 80,000 adults suggests that parental divorce has an adverse effect on children's lives compared with those raised in intact two-parent families. Adults who experienced a parental divorce had lower psychological well-being, more behavioural problems, less education, lower job status, a lower standard of living, lower marital satisfaction, a heightened risk of divorce, a heightened risk of being a single parent, and poorer physical health. Rodgers and Pryor (1998) argue that children whose parents separate are likely to show signs of unhappiness that can include worry, bedwetting, low self-esteem and difficulties with behaviour and friendships. In the longer term, as the immediate distress of divorce starts to fade, most children settle into a pattern of normal development. Research has nevertheless shown that there is a greater probability of poor outcomes among children whose parents have separated than among others, and that some can be observed many years later during adulthood. Longer-term disadvantages, including employment, health and behaviour problems, occur more often than among children whose parents have stayed together, but they are typically found in no more than a minority of those whose parents have divorced.

For the minority of children from separated families the outcomes are twice as likely to be negative as they are among children whose parents have stayed together. Areas where children of separated families are at increased risk include: growing up in households with lower income; poorer housing and greater financial hardship; leaving school with fewer educational qualifications; experiencing low pay and unemployment as adults; withdrawn behaviour; aggression and delinquency; health problems and admission to hospital following accidents; leaving home when young, early sexual activity, teenage pregnancy and giving birth outside marriage.

Effects of Divorce by Gender and Age

Social adjustment includes measures of popularity, loneliness and cooperativeness. The negative effects of divorce in relation to social adjustment are stronger for boys than for girls. However, in other areas such as academic achievement, conduct or psychological adjustment, no differences between boys and girls are apparent. The research examining the effects of divorce on adults also shows very little difference between the effects on men and women, with one exception. Although both men and women from divorced families obtain less education than do those from continuously intact two-parent families, this difference is larger for women than for men.

Preschool children find it difficult to understand the meaning of divorce. Because they do not understand what is happening many of them become fearful. Young children may also blame themselves for their parents' divorce. For example, they may think, 'Daddy left because I was bad'. Additionally, regression to earlier stages of behaviour is also common among very young children. Primary school age children have greater maturity and can grasp the meaning of divorce more clearly. They may still grieve for the loss of the family as it was, and feelings of sadness and depression are common. Some children may see the divorce as a personal rejection. At the adolescent stage the young person is less dependent on the family than younger children and they may be affected less directly by the divorce. However, adolescents may still feel a considerable amount of anger toward one or both parents and this may lead them to question their own ability to maintain a long-term relationship with a partner.

There is evidence that children affected by divorce in recent times may be showing less severe effects of divorce than previous generations. There may be a number of explanations for this. Firstly, as divorce has become more common, attitudes toward divorce have become more accepting, so children probably feel less stigmatized and will find it easier to obtain support from others in similar circumstances. Secondly, because the legal and social barriers to divorce were stronger in the past, couples who obtained a divorce several decades ago probably had more serious problems and experienced more conflict prior to separation than today.

Many authors emphasize that poor outcomes are far from inevitable and that there is no direct or simple link between parental separation and the way that different children adjust. Although differences in outcomes are clear, it cannot be assumed that parental separation is the only underlying cause.

Factors Influencing the Reactions of Children

Conflict and poor parent–child relationships are among the major risk factors linked to long-term problems. In many cases confusion and misunderstanding have been caused by a failure to view parental separation as a process beginning with family circumstances before divorce and continuing long after. Pre-divorce family factors appear to be important in determining the effects of divorce on children. A longitudinal study followed over 2,000 individuals in detail for 20 years. Analysis revealed two main types of marriage that ended in divorce. Type A marriages are consistently unhappy and divorce occurs because of serious difficulties. Type B marriages are in many ways average and very similar to marriages that remain intact. You may assume that Type A marriages would always result in more damage to children. However, it seems to be the nature of conflict that is more important than the type of marriage overall. High-conflict marriages that remain intact have strong negative outcomes for children but have average outcomes when they end in divorce.

Research seeking explanations for the links between divorce and the adverse outcomes experienced by some children has found that financial hardship and other family circumstances that pre-date as well as follow separation play an important part in limiting children's educational achievement. Additionally, family conflict before, during and after separation is stressful for children, who may respond by becoming anxious, aggressive or withdrawn. The ability of parents to recover from the distress associated with separation is important for children's own ability to adjust.

Children and parents should have access to professional support at the time of separation. Help for parents in coping with distress will make it easier for them to help their children. In recent years there have been moves to encourage parents who are going through divorce to use non-adversarial forms of mediation. Unfortunately, once the divorce process ends up with solicitors the likelihood of conflict is much greater, with the consequent negative impact on children. Both children and parents will need better information and support before, during and after separation. It is important that parents appreciate the possible damage caused by conflict and the inappropriate involvement of children in their disputes, such as restricting access to children for reasons of revenge. If they are able to minimize such behaviour, then they will improve their children's chances for better adjustment. Support for parents should allay their fears that separation itself will always do permanent damage to children, but they should be made aware of the detrimental effects of continuing conflict.

There are likely to be benefits from enabling children to maintain contact with both their parents. Aside from circumstances where it is necessary to protect children from family violence or abuse, support services should enable non-resident parents to remain involved in their children's lives. If families are to be helped to function in ways that are best for the health and well-being of children, it is also vital that policy makers recognize the growing diversity of family structures – in particular, the numbers of children living in lone-parent families, cohabiting families and step-families. Support for parents and children is important at all times, not just during periods of separation. What is needed is a focus on parenting rather than on marital status.

Activity

Work in a group of four. Use role play to enact two different divorce scenarios. In the first, the parents should act to minimize conflict in the best interests of the children. In the second, the effect of conflict should be illustrated by the children's responses, which should reflect some of the negative outcomes explained in this chapter.

REFERENCES

Ermisch, J. and Francesconi, M. (2000) Patterns of household and family formation. In R. Berthoud and J. Gershuny (eds) *Seven Years in the Lives of British Families*. London: Policy Press.

One Parent Families Scotland (2002) *Children in One Parent Families*. http://www.opfs.org.uk/factfile/children.html [retrieved 28 October 2002].

Rodgers, B. and Pryor, J. (1998) *Divorce and Separation: The Outcomes for Children*. York: Joseph Rowntree Foundation.

FURTHER READING

Berthoud, R. and Gershuny, J. (2000) *Seven Years in the Lives of British Families*. London: Policy Press. This book represents a collaboration between members of the University of Essex's Institute for Social and Economic Research. It reviews existing findings and presents new analysis of data from the British Household Panel Survey.

Butler, I., Scanlan, L., Robinson, M., Douglas, G. and Murch, M. (2002) Children's involvement in their parents' divorce: Implications for practice. *Children and Society*, Vol. 16 (2): 89–102. Reports findings from a research study that explored children's experience of divorce. It shows that children experience parental divorce as a crisis in their lives, but that they are able to mobilize internal and external resources to regain a new point of balance.

Joseph Rowntree Foundation: http://www.jrf.org.uk. Contains many research reports dealing with issues related to families and children. The Joseph Rowntree Foundation is one of the largest social policy research and development charities in the UK. It spends about £7 million a year on a research and development programme that seeks to understand better the causes of social difficulties and explore ways of better overcoming them.

Psychology

Chapter *Eight*

The Nature/Nurture Debate

NICOLA LEATHER

The extent to which genetic or environmental factors are the most important contribution to human development has been the subject of much debate. This chapter defines a number of concepts that are relevant to the debate. It is concluded that the interaction between nature and nurture is one of the most interesting aspects of current thought on the issue.

Of all mammals, humans are the most immature at birth, needing the longest period of development, learning and interactions with others before becoming independent. Physical maturity develops by the end of adolescence, while development continues throughout life. Aspects of both growth and development seem to fascinate humans, as we often talk about physical attributes. Adults are especially likely to do this to children and almost all children will have experienced someone saying, 'haven't you grown since I last saw you' or 'you look just like your mother/father'. To children, these remarks probably appear to be 'silly' things to say, as people are worried if children do not grow.

Professionals, such as developmental psychologists, often study the average or typical rate of development. This information can be used to evaluate the development of an individual child and to plan educational programmes for children of different ages. Psychologists are most interested in how certain behaviours develop, why they develop, when they develop, and how the environment may influence the development. Many theories seek to explain human behaviour either in terms of inherited factors or life experiences. In order to consider how children develop we need to look at both the *nature* and the *nurture* sides of development.

It is useful to start with a consideration of the major theoretical approaches that are thought to govern development, and then move on to look at how they interact to explain development. The argument is about the degree of influence of the two viewpoints, and is usually described as nature vs. nurture, or heredity vs. environment, and has been debated over the centuries. It is one of the oldest and most controversial issues in child development and influences many other areas of research.

Nature

Historically the nature or heredity side of the debate is represented by the work of the ancient scholar Plato and more recently (in the 1600s) by the work of René Descartes (a French philosopher), both of whom believed that at least some things were innate. The advent of Charles Darwin's theory of evolution also led to an increase in interest in the nature side of development. In order to look at this in more detail it is useful to break it down into three areas: (1) genetic differences, (2) the role of **maturation** and (3) inborn strategies at birth.

Genetic differences

As a human takes half of its genetic inheritance from its mother and half from its father, all children have a unique genetic inheritance. This accounts for things like eye colour, aspects of size, likelihood of developing particular illnesses, etc. The only times when genetic inheritance is shared is between identical twins and between cloned individuals.

Role of maturation

Genetic differences are affected by the process of maturation – innately determined sequences of growth and change that are relatively free of environmental influence. In 1925 Arnold Gessell used the term 'maturation' to describe the general sequences of change that take place in all children, including increase in body size, change in body shape, puberty and change in general behaviour. These things are not generally under the control of the individual, although some people go to some lengths to try to influence them.

Inborn strategies at birth

The concept here is that each baby is programmed in some way to take greater account of certain kinds of information, or respond in particular ways to certain objects. These are usually described as inborn biases or constraints. The linguist Noam Chomsky proposed that all children are born with a Language Acquisition Device (LAD), which enables them to learn to talk seemingly effortlessly.

Nurture

John Locke (a seventeenth-century British philosopher) rejected the prevailing notion of the time – that infants were miniature adults who arrived in the world fully equipped with abilities and knowledge and who simply had to grow to enable these abilities to appear. He insisted that at birth the mind is a blank slate (or *tabula rasa*), which is built up by experiences: what the baby sees, hears, smells, tastes and feels. The beginning of the twentieth century saw the start of a behaviourist movement and the re-emergence of the nurture debate. Behaviourists such as John B. Watson and B. F. Skinner argued that human nature is completely malleable, suggesting that early training can turn a child into any type of adult, regardless of his or her heredity. If experience has such a profound effect on development we need to look at some important features: the timing of experiences; interpretation of experiences; ecological aspects; and culture.

Timing of experiences

The time at which an experience happens to a child will affect the amount of influence this has on his or her development. We all realize that the age we do something dictates what we get out of the experience and how much we learn or remember of it. There are thought to be 'critical periods' when it is important for the child to develop certain characteristics, and that if they do not develop at that time then they may never develop to the extent they would have.

Interpretation of experiences

The effect of an experience on an individual relates to the interpretation or meaning of that experience by the individual, rather than any properties of the experience itself. This is based upon our own self-concept, the reactions of others, and **theory of mind**. For example, a friend may say that your hair looks better in a new style. Your friend is giving you a compliment, but you may only hear the implied criticism (your hair used to look awful). This is why people sometimes say that the glass is either 'half full' (emphasizing the positive aspect of the situation) or 'half empty' (emphasizing the negative aspect of the situation). Theorists have argued that each child creates a set of internal models (assumptions or conclusions) about the world, self and relationships, through which all subsequent ideas and experiences are filtered and measured.

Ecological aspects, including culture

This refers to the wider environmental network that includes family, friends, toys and possessions, and wealth in general. Until the 1970s most research on environmental aspects focused on the child's family (frequently only the mother was considered), with some consideration of playmates and toys. Research since then has widened to include the ecology or context in which each child develops. Some of this emphasizes that each child grows up in a complex social environment (a social ecology), which includes family, extended family, friends, pets, teachers and childminders within the larger social environment of society as a whole.

In addition to this description it is important to add the concept of culture, which describes a system of meanings and customs related to particular groups. For example, the ecological factors for a middle-class British white family will be different to those for a middle-class British Asian family. We often make assumptions that the way we do things in our society is the only way and the best way that things should be done. As a consequence of this we can make negative judgements about people and events. In these judgements we are inclined to use certain ways of thinking, described as G **egocentrism** and ethnocentrism. Egocentrism is described as seeing things from our own particular viewpoint, to the exclusion of others. Ethnocentrism is described as seeing things from the viewpoint of our own cultural group and rejecting the viewpoints of different cultural groups.

Interactionist

Nowadays it is broadly agreed that every facet of a child's development is a product of some pattern of interaction between nature and nurture. If this pattern is disrupted or altered in some way there may be negative consequences. For example, the human foetus develops within the mother's body according to a fairly fixed schedule, with development occurring in an orderly sequence. However, if the uterine environment is seriously abnormal in some way, *maturational processes* can be disrupted. Thus, if the mother contracts rubella in the first three months of pregnancy (when the foetus's basic organ systems are developing), the infant may be born deaf, blind, brain-damaged, or with heart defects (depending upon which body system is developing at the time of infection). Maternal malnutrition, smoking, drug and alcohol ingestion will all affect the *environment* in which the foetus matures.

G **Motor development** after birth also illustrates the interaction between nature and nurture. All children go through the same sequence of motor behaviours in about the same order, thus we must assume that the innate timetable is governed by maturation. But not all children develop at the same rate, so the degree of influence of environment, learning and experience is seen to be important. Some studies appeared to show that basic motor skill development was not governed by practice, but more recent studies do indicate that practice or extra stimulation can accelerate the appearance of motor behaviours to some extent. A study in the 1970s looked at the relationship between the stepping reflex of newborn infants and the development of walking. A group of infants who were given stepping practice for a few minutes several times each day in the first two months of life, began walking five to seven weeks earlier than the control group. Thus the conclusion may be that earlier development is the result of practice.

Activity

See if you can identify one of your own characteristics or behaviour patterns that has been strongly affected by 'nature' and one that you think is strongly a result of your upbringing or 'nurture'.

FURTHER READING

Cole, M. (1992) Culture in development. In M. H. Bornstein and M. E. Lamb (eds) *Developmental Psychology: An Advanced Textbook*, 3rd edn. Hillsdale, NJ: Lawrence Erlbaum. A comprehensive (but not simple) account of this complex area of development.

Plomin, R. and McClearn, G. E. (eds) (1993) *Nature, Nurture and Psychology.* Washington, DC: American Psychology Association. Useful papers putting this concept into the current psychology framework.

Chapter *Nine*

Cognitive Development

NICOLA LEATHER

Some of the most important ideas from a selection of cognitive theories are described. Key concepts are explained and examples are given which show how children respond in a variety of situations.

Cognitive development is the development of thinking and reasoning. Historically, the most widespread approach to the study of cognitive development or intelligence is focused on observing the way that people differ. It was this that gave rise to the development of intelligence tests. One problem that arose was that this method did not take account of the fact that as children grow their thinking becomes more abstract and they are able to cope with more complex ideas. The fact that thinking changes as we develop led to the next important milestone in the study of thinking and intelligence: the cognitive developmental approach. Over the past 20 years another approach has developed which is seen as integrating the first two approaches, and is known as the information-processing approach.

The cognitive developmental approach was first utilized by Jean Piaget (1896–1980) and has been taken forward by many researchers since. Piaget's focus was on the development of cognitive structures and patterns of development rather than intellectual power and individual differences. His model of development is of a self-regulating interaction between the child and the physical and social environment, which leads to new forms of thinking. Piaget's central assumption was that the child is an active participant in their development of knowledge, in that the child must learn how to adapt to the world around and make sense of it. He described four major stages of development that extend from infancy to adulthood and his ideas on the development of thinking have had a profound influence on developmental psychology and all who work with children.

Where Piaget was most concerned with the biological roots of development, another influential researcher considered cultural influences. Lev Semeonovich Vygotsky (1896–1934) was concerned with the historical and social aspects of human nature and the importance of social and cultural factors in the development of intelligence. He argued that there was a close link between language and thought and that children acquire their culture's values, beliefs and problem-solving strategies through collaborative dialogues with more knowledgeable members of society.

From these two theorists have arisen two possible definitions of how intelligence and thinking function in the human: firstly, intelligence is the ability of the person to adapt to the environment; or secondly, intelligence is the capacity to learn through instruction and interaction.

Concepts of Cognitive Development

Object permanence

This is the understanding that objects have substance, keep their identity when they change location, and usually continue to exist when they are out of sight. Piaget's theory of the sensori-motor stage and the development of object permanence relies heavily on the idea that the child's perception is insufficient to inform them about the properties of the world. Other researchers have argued that Piaget underestimates the ability of the infant, and that the lack of physical searching is not due to a lack of understanding, but to the inability to coordinate the required physical actions. Bower has conducted numerous experiments to look at the infant's understanding of objects and has found that they appear surprised by changes (as evidenced by alteration in heartbeat) that Piagetian theory would not expect them to react to. One source of evidence about object permanence comes from studies looking at infants' reactions to objects when the light was turned off – so in essence the object has disappeared. If visual contact is so important for object permanence, then loss of visual contact should result in the ending of object search by the infant (as it does when the object is covered). A number of researchers have found that this is not so and infants still attempted to reach for the object even if they could not see it. Thus, out of [illegible] may not be out of mind. The concept of object permanence is related to [illegible]nt of attachment by the infant. If the infant has not developed the [illegible] object permanence then they will not understand that the parent still [illegible] when they cannot see or hear them. The infant may cry on being left, but will not attempt to make the parent return by engaging in proximity seeking and maintaining behaviours (CHAPTER 3).

Egocentrism

This means to consider the world entirely from one's own point of view. Piaget described the pre-operational child as one who looks at things from entirely their own perspective and frame of reference. The child is not selfish in the adult sense but thinks that everyone sees things in the way that they do. Experiments to consider egocentrism have been conducted in many ways and it appears that the more the child understands the task and can interact with it, the more likely it is that egocentric behaviour will not be shown.

Scaffolding

This word is commonly used when describing the work of Vygotsky. It is taken to mean a particular learning environment that is provided by an expert (teacher, parent, and more competent person in that area), within which the child can act as though they are competent to solve the problem. By so acting the child can learn how to reach the solution to a problem or task effectively. As the task becomes more familiar and more within the child's competence the expert can leave more and more for the child to do until at last the child can undertake the whole task successfully; the scaffold has been removed.

Hypothesis development

This is usually considered to be a central part of the highest form of cognition. In order to reason effectively and logically it is necessary to be able to develop a hypothesis and to test it, thus coming to a conclusion about the original hypothesis. This enables the individual to rethink many aspects of life but does not guarantee that they will do so.

Appearance and reality

The difference between appearance and reality runs through many areas of cognition. A key point of development is reached when the child is able to understand that appearances can be deceptive. Flavell and his colleagues carried out a number of important studies (Flavell 1986). They showed children a piece of sponge that had been painted to look like a rock. The children were allowed to squeeze the object and found that it was spongy. The child was then asked two questions. The first was a reality question: is it really a rock or is it really a sponge? The second was an appearance question: when you look at it now does it look like a rock or does it look like a sponge? The majority of three-year-olds were unable to distinguish between appearance and reality. They thought it looked like a sponge and was a sponge. But the majority of four-year-olds were able to understand and explain that it looked like a rock but was really a sponge. Once a child has mastered the idea of appearance and reality they are able to attempt a group of tasks that look at false belief.

False belief

The most famous false belief task was devised by Wimmer and Perner (1983) and is called the Smarties task. The child is shown a Smarties tube and asked what they think it contains. The child answers that it contains sweets, Smarties. The tube is then opened by the experimenter and is shown to contain pencils. The child is asked what is in the tube and they correctly answer pencils, but when asked what they thought it contained they state that they thought it contained pencils all the time. The child is then asked what another child will think it contains and they answer pencils. This child has not yet understood that they had a belief (that the tube contained Smarties), which has now been shown to be false (as the tube contained pencils). By about the age of four or five the child is able to recognize their false belief and predict the belief of others.

The evidence gained from the false beliefs tasks has led many researchers to propose that four- to five-year-old children begin to develop an understanding of the behaviour of other people in relation to their beliefs and desires. This understanding has been termed a *theory of mind*. The child develops various ideas about other people's ideas, beliefs and desires, and how they affect behaviour. This allows the child to predict how other people will react in a situation. The child is then able to use this information to understand the behaviour of other people. Once the child has developed a 'theory of mind' they are able to tell jokes and understand sarcasm, whereas before everything is taken to have a literal understanding.

Most theories of cognitive development use a linear, stepwise or stage approach. But it is possible to consider the development of cognition in a different way, which utilizes the concept of a spiral of development. Each stage of our life, be it starting school, moving to secondary school, leaving school, mid-life or retirement, can initially be considered as a time of transition from the old life to a new way of life. A time of transition usually involves significant changes in virtually every aspect of functioning. If we take a neo-Piagetian approach we could describe this as a time of **assimilation**, when we take in a range of new experiences and experience disequilibrium when old ways of functioning are no longer appropriate. Once we settle and get used to the changes we could be considered to be in a phase of consolidation, when we have **accommodated** to the changes and are able to work effectively at what is required. The spiral continues throughout life, with changes in complexity as we develop. An example may help here, so let's consider the preschool phase and adolescence. Two-year-old children are usually characterized by traits such as the constant drive for independence and a struggle to learn a wide range of new tasks, but by the time they are ready to start school (at about four years of age) they have developed a sense of balance, with increased self-esteem and low levels of confrontation. Consider now the stages of adolescence. At a particular point the young person once again pushes to be independent, this time trying to learn how to be an adult in a changing world by asserting their independence. Once they reach the age of about

15 years they are usually more settled and focused, with increased self-esteem and reduced levels of confrontation. Although the experiences of children aged 2 or aged 15 are clearly not identical, you can see that the key concepts that form part of the spiral of development are present for both but operate at different levels.

Activity

Can you think of any examples of egocentrism in your own behaviour?

REFERENCES

Flavell, J. (1986) Really and truly. *Psychology Today*, January 1986: 40–4.

Wimmer, H. and Perner, J. (1983) Beliefs about beliefs: Representations and constraining functions of wrong beliefs in young children's understanding of deception. *Cognition*, Vol. 13: 103–28.

FURTHER READING

British Psychological Society: http://www.bps.org.uk/index.cfm. Includes a publication area where you can access a sample of recent journal articles on a range of psychological topics.

Donaldson, M. (1978) *Children's Minds*. London: Fontana. A classic text which explores Piaget's and others' ideas about the way that children's minds work.

Harris, M. and Butterworth, G. (2002) *Developmental Psychology: A Student's Handbook*. Hove: Psychology Press. This text contains useful chapters on cognitive development at each developmental stage, along with criticisms of classic works.

Schaffer, R. (2004) *Introducing Child Psychology*. Oxford: Blackwell. In order to take forward some of the key concepts that we have introduced in this chapter you will find that this book gives a comprehensive introduction.

Chapter *Ten*

The Development of Language and Literacy

DOMINIC WYSE

Case studies of individual children and other studies are used to explain how children develop their talking, reading and writing. Key developmental milestones are identified.

Many of you will work in jobs where you have a role in supporting children's language and literacy development. In order to do this it is necessary to be aware of the ways in which children learn to talk, read and write. By studying children's development in language and literacy we have been able to identify common milestones that children usually pass as they progress toward being experienced language users.

The skills and understanding that are required in order to become experienced talkers, readers and writers begin at birth. Babies are surrounded by print in their environment. Think of all the kinds of print that bombard us as we walk down the average high street. As soon as babies' eyes are able to focus properly they start the job of making sense of these things. Many of the things that they come into contact with in the home are covered in labels: food packages, cleaning items, texts on television screens, shopping lists, etc. So, it would not be true to say that the language modes of talking, reading and writing should be taught in a particular order. However, progression in talk is quicker and in many ways easier than progression in reading and writing.

The Development of Talk

Birth–six months

In the first few weeks of life the sounds that babies make reflect their biological needs. Hunger and pain or discomfort result in crying noises. Bodily functions such as eating result in a further range of noises. The main way that these link with future speech is through the exercise of the vocal chords. From between six and eight weeks the positive interaction with adults contributes to cooing noises when the baby is happy. Later on these cooing noises are strung together in repetitive patterns such as /ga/ or /gu/. The baby begins to control the tongue, lips and vocal folds in preparation for their use in speech. There are strong similarities between the babbling of babies in different languages, although only /m/ and /b/ occur in all language environments.

Six–twelve months

The sounds of 'babbling' are more deliberate and much less varied than the previous vocal play. For the first time, parents sense that there may be some communicative intention behind the sounds. For example, the repetition of /ma/ma/ or /da/da/ may be referring to mum and dad. The child who is able to use the word 'mama' develops a variety of pronunciations to express different needs. By changing the inflection at the end of the word the child turns it into a question: 'mama?' could mean 'Where is my mother?' For the first time, different languages produce different sounds.

One–two years

Babble and more word-like sounds are both used, but increasingly there are key words and phrases which appear on a regular basis. Speech is less likely to be duplicated and there is a greater variety to the babble that takes place. Two-word and three-word utterances are used for a variety of meanings. Sometimes these two words are able to convey a simple message, such as 'all gone'. But at other times they may take on a variety of meanings; for example, 'mum car' could mean 'mummy is in the car', 'mummy has got a car' or 'mummy, where is the car?'

Two–three years

Gradually, more verbs and adjectives are added to speech. Sentences begin to take on greater length and complexity. Sentence structure may still appear shaky, but typically there are enough words and non-verbal clues to convey meaning. David Crystal describes some of the important grammatical developments that take place:

> At around 2 years of age, many children produce sentences that are three or four words in length, and combine these words in several different ways to produce a variety of grammatical constructions. Typical sentences at this stage include 'Man kick ball; Him got car; Where mummy going?; Put that on there.' . . . The 'telegraphic' character of early sentences has often been noted in many children – an impression derived from the omission of grammatical words (such as 'the' and 'is') and word endings (such as '-ing'). By the end of the third year, this character has largely disappeared, and children's sentences more closely resemble their adult counterparts. (*Crystal 1997: 245*)

The repetition of nursery rhymes and songs is an important feature of language development in the early stages and children use these memorized snippets of meaning to help them understand the language-use taking place all around them. Stories take on extra significance, and children become aware of the ways in which the voice can be controlled, so that a whispered section of a story has quite different meaning to a section which is shouted in a booming tone. These linguistic behaviours are often re-enacted through play with dolls and other toys.

Three years onwards

An interest in questions is evident at this stage. The 'why' question can be used to excess:

Child: Why is the sea blue dad?
Dad: It is to do with the colour of the sky.
Child: Why is the sky blue?
Dad: I'm not sure, that's just the colour of the atmosphere.
Child: What's 'atmosphere'?

Children begin instinctively to recognize that verbs use 'ed' to place them in the past tense, but this knowledge is often overemphasized. In the majority of instances the result is a standard word, but sometimes the child produces examples like 'eated' (for 'ate'), 'goed' (for 'went') and 'throwed' (for 'threw').

The range of development from three years onwards varies greatly, but it is generally accepted that spoken language acquisition is in place by the age of five, leaving more sophisticated features to be acquired by the age of seven. Maggie Maclure constructed a 'Communicative Inventory at Age Five'; she suggested that by the age of five, many children will:

- Draw on a vocabulary of several thousand words.
- Control many of the major grammatical constructions of their language – though some aspects of grammar will not be acquired until later.
- Speak with a regular, adult-like pronunciation, adopting the speech patterns of their community.
- Talk for a range of purposes – including many 'higher-order' ones such as hypothesizing, speculating, predicting.
- Use talk to further their own learning.
- Express their feelings through talk, and understand the feelings of others.
- Disconnect talk from the 'here-and-now' where appropriate.
- Assess other people's background knowledge and adjust their own talk in the light of this.
- Assume joint responsibility for the meanings that are produced through talk.

- Know (or quickly learn) many of the cultural and procedural rules for talking with different kinds of people – peers, parents, teachers, strangers.
- Engage in role play, and experiment with different interactional 'identities'.
- G Deploy a range of **rhetorical and persuasive tactics** for increasing the likelihood of securing their own goals, avoiding blame or trouble, etc.
- Have some metalinguistic knowledge, i.e. be able to reflect on, and talk about, talk itself.
- Get some pleasure out of playing with, and through, language.
- G Have a developing sense of **genres** of talk, e.g. jokes, stories, 'news', etc. (National Oracy Project 1990: 23–4)

The Development of Reading and Writing

Case studies of individual children have been invaluable in providing detailed descriptions of children's development. One particularly notable study was published in 1980. It featured the development of Paul Bissex between the ages of five and ten, which was documented by his mother. By comparing this study with other studies it has been possible to describe some developmental milestones which we outline at the end of this chapter.

Age five

At age five years and one month Paul recognized his first words and was consolidating his understanding of the concept of 'word'. An important understanding at this stage was that of the spaces between words. Word spaces are unique to written text, as when we are speaking the meaning is composed of continuous sounds with pauses mainly for breathing or interruptions.

Signs, labels and captions were of more interest to Paul than continuous text and he tended to concentrate on whole words when he was reading, but on sounds when he was writing. At five years six months for the first time Paul was able to decode words out of context, such as: baby, stop, yes, duck, join. These were on cards for a reading game that he played with his mother.

During a time when mum was reading *Dr Dolittle* Paul stopped her and reread the sentence himself. It seemed that he suddenly became aware that he could follow the text. At five years seven months he read most of his first whole book and three months later he completed his first whole book (apart from one word).

Paul started to experiment with spellings. On one occasion his mother was reading; in order to grab her attention he wrote a sign: RUDF (are you deaf?). At this stage he was still very much dependent on support from his mother, so he would often ask questions about how to write particular sounds.

Age six

Paul was beginning to read silently at five years and eleven months and this coincided with a change in his attitude to reading. Reading was becoming much less hard work and he was enjoying it much more. He was also reading with appropriate expression that Bissex presumed had been supported by the regular story reading that the parents did, and their use of expression during these times. At six years and three months Paul no longer needed to use his finger to point at words. Using the finger to point to the words is something that usually happens when children first start decoding. Unknown texts were read with less expression than known texts at this stage.

By six years and eleven months most of Paul's reading was silent. The school had moved him up the reading scheme, but he wasn't particularly motivated by the literacy experiences at school. He no longer asked his parents to read aloud and he had advanced to short novels. Names were the main source of his reading mistakes and he was getting interested in informational reading.

From five years ten months to six years three months Paul wrote very little. One of the few texts he did compose was a game with letter cards and word cards. At this time he became aware of some words that he could read but not spell. Up to six years and seven months Paul started doing more writing again, but reverted to some of his favourite earlier forms such as signs and labels, a list, a cookbook and notes. He also created four newspapers, which included sections such as 'funnies, weather, news, advertisements'; these were constructed on large sheets of paper with lines and boxes drawn on them. Sometime later when he looked back over them he commented: 'It's got funnies and advertising and news and weather! How did I get all this? Did I have some interpretation of what was in a newspaper?' At this stage there was some evidence that he was moving towards conventional punctuation.

Age seven to nine

The remaining minor difficulties that Paul faced with words were to do with definitions and multiple meaning. He became interested in the derivations of words and would frequently ask questions about unfamiliar words. He could read many difficult words in context but sometimes found it hard to define them out of context. At eight years and three months Paul invented names for new chemicals as a result of playing with a chemistry set. His interest in definitions resulted in much exploration of dictionaries. By nine years he had developed awareness of puns and multiple meanings.

Age nine to ten

Paul was now interested in acquiring information on a wide range of subjects. He enjoyed using encyclopedias and he developed skim-reading skills. At nine years and eight months he read his first adult novel: *Star Wars* (part 4). This sparked his imagination, resulting in the design of *Star Wars* quizzes and the taped recordings of excerpts from the book. One month later he reread *Star Wars* and was amazed at how much he had missed the first time. The range and amount of his reading was now wide and this included literature, non-fiction, comics and the rereading of favourites such as *Danny Champion of the World.*

At age nine Paul was beginning to develop greater sophistication in his style of writing. For example, another attempt at a newspaper resulted in:

> PISTOL PAUL GONE GUNWACKY Pistol Paul just bought a new pistol and is using up ammo like a lawn mower uses of gasoline Scientists say that he must have a terrible earwax problem because anyone else in his position would be deaf by now. (*Bissex 1980: 83*)

Summary of Developmental Milestones

Reading

Beginning reading: Age two–five

- Understands the differences between text and pictures
- Can read words/logos which are part of print in the child's environment
- Understands that text carries meaning and conveys messages
- Understands that text is an aid to memory
- Understands that the meaning of text does not change
- Enjoys playing at reading, including re-enacting known stories
- Uses 'book language' during retelling of stories, such as 'They roared their terrible roars . . .'
- Understands that there are many languages
- Will express preferences for favourite texts

Learning to decode: Age four–seven

- Knowledge of favourite 'real' texts supports decoding of reading scheme texts
- Needs help with concepts of words and spaces
- Uses finger pointing to show level of one-to-one correspondence
- Begins to be able to read words out of context
- Temporarily a strong emphasis on sounding words out
- Independent reading starts for first time
- Beginning to realize the limits of the One Letter Makes One Sound Method (OLMOSM)

Silent reading: Age five–eight

- Silent reading starts for first time
- More reading of unknown texts

- Greater fluency and appropriate expression when reading aloud
- No need for finger pointing
- Choosing to read a greater range of texts
- Temporarily a return to a larger number of reading mistakes because of more demanding texts
- Pronunciation and word-stress problems are main area of difficulty

Wide-range reading: Age seven onwards
- Silent reading is preferred
- Enjoys short novels
- Likes to reread favourite books sometimes
- Finds difficulties with unfamiliar proper nouns
- Enjoys a wider range of reading, including information texts
- Shows interest in word definitions out of context (like dictionaries)
- Shows ability to segment words
- Enjoys word play
- Uses reading to learn
- Occasionally may enjoy adult-level texts
- Interested in foreign languages and translations

Writing

Beginning writing: Age three–five
- Interested in environmental print
- Makes distinctions between text and pictures
- Enjoys playing at writing
- Attempts to communicate messages with writing
- Uses personal experience as influence for writing

Learning to encode: Age four–seven
- Has the confidence to invent spellings
- Will use various written forms as models
- Attempts story writing
- Revisits favourite forms with greater sophistication
- Increasing amount of writing
- Growing awareness of need for standard conventions

Extending written forms: Age five–eight
- Expresses preference for particular forms
- Exploration and increasing knowledge of wider range of forms
- Uses writing to organize and categorize
- Aware of multiple meanings for words

- Uses standard conventions of written English most of the time
- Experiments with presentational features and special effects

Writing to learn: Age seven onwards

- Greater sophistication in narrative (e.g. awareness of audience) and/or other forms
- Will collaborate effectively on appropriate stages of writing process
- Uses impersonal language when appropriate
- Develops particular writing styles: personal and imitative
- Sustained concentration on writing projects
- Growing use of drafting and editing

The ability to communicate effectively through language and literacy is a particularly important attribute in modern societies. There is great pressure in the education system to ensure that the necessary skills are acquired early. Knowledge of these kinds of developmental milestones is important for many people who work with children, but in particular for early years and primary school workers. However, it is not only educators who benefit from greater understanding of developmental milestones. Health workers use this kind of evidence as a way of judging whether children's development is 'normal'. For some children speech problems need extra support and this support comes after recognition that a child is not progressing normally. Parents also need to know if their child has any language problems and greater awareness of language development can help them.

> **Activity**
>
> Listen to a young child talking or observe them doing some reading and writing. See if you can match the child's language with our developmental milestones.

REFERENCES

Bissex, G. (1980) *GNYS AT WORK: A Child Learns to Read and Write*. Cambridge, MA: Harvard University Press.

National Oracy Project (NOP) (1990) *Teaching, Learning and Talking in Key Stage 1*. York: National Curriculum Council.

FURTHER READING

Crystal, D. (1997) *The Cambridge Encyclopaedia of Language*, 2nd edn. Cambridge: Cambridge University Press. An amazingly rich picture of language and linguistics.

Gentry, R. J. (1982) An analysis of developmental spelling in GNYS AT WRK. *The Reading Teacher*, Vol. 36: 192–200. Interesting development of the Bissex work which gives more detail about spelling development.

National Literacy Trust (2002) NLT Homepage: http://www.literacytrust.org.uk/ [retrieved 20 November 2002]. This site includes reference to various initiatives and research relevant to children's language and literacy development.

Wyse, D. and Jones, R. (2001) *Teaching English, Language and Literacy*. London: Routledge Falmer. A comprehensive guide to the teaching of English. Shows how the developmental patterns that we outlined in this chapter relate to the teaching of English.

UNIVERSITY OF WINCHESTER
LIBRARY

Chapter *Eleven*

Mental Health

JOHN HARRISON

Just like physical well-being, the functions of the mind are an important aspect of our daily existence. However, when these functions are affected in one way or another the individual can be said to suffer a mental illness. Children are affected by this in ways that are similar to adults, but they also have their own special considerations. This chapter indicates the levels of mental illness among young people and its impact on their lives. It examines some of the main causes of mental illness and the treatments available.

Before we identify the nature of child mental illness two factors should be taken into consideration. Firstly, unlike adult mental health in which individuals can seek treatment, few children will identify themselves to services. Instead, it is often parents or teachers who feel that some aspect of the child's mental health is affected. Secondly, the developmental age of the child is a factor. For example, temper tantrums are an accepted feature of the interactions of toddlers, yet such behaviour would be viewed as abnormal in a teenager. Thus the extent of mental health problems in children can be difficult to measure. Despite this a number of studies have measured the frequency of mental illness among young people. Rates of illness vary according to age and the difficulties of adolescence result in higher levels of mental ill-health within the population.

The Causes of Child Mental Ill-health

Brain (neurological) injury can have a profound affect on mental well-being. Injuries to the brain are common, particularly in childhood. As a result of these injuries, the child can show inappropriate and impaired behaviour. While some of these problems are caused by head injuries, there are others that have their roots in congenital conditions.

One of the most common of these conditions is Foetal Alcohol Syndrome. This is caused by the consumption of alcohol by the mother while the child is in the womb. As a result the child can be of low birth weight and suffer from hyperactivity and behavioural problems. The condition is suggested as affecting 1 in 300 births.

Fragile X Syndrome is one of the more common inherited conditions. This is seen more commonly in male than female children. As well as physical abnormalities, the child may show poor social functioning, such as gaze avoidance.

It is not just neurological conditions that can lead to child mental illness. Any form of physical illness will have consequences on mental health. Think about a time when you were ill. How did it make you feel? There are a number of conditions that could mean many months away from school and friends. Others may result in a physical change to the child. Such things have a profound influence on a young person's mental well-being and those involved in childcare should be aware of this.

For the majority of children the most important environment is the family. Families provide us with a micro-society in which we learn to interact with others and develop a sense of what makes behaviour right or wrong. However, when problems occur within the family this can have serious consequences. The loss of a stable family environment can leave children with complex emotional problems. They may feel unable to trust and may develop low self-esteem. Indeed, the importance of the family is such that many child mental health services have the word 'family' incorporated into their title.

Throughout childhood there are certain events that could result in mental health problems. The loss of a parent, either through death or divorce, can have lasting effects. The child will have to adjust to a change in family life. This may mean the move to a new home and the need to learn new rules and methods of communication. As the child becomes older, the wider social environment begins to play an increasingly important part in the process of personality development. Peer groups play a vital role, particularly in adolescence.

Worldwide, many children suffer poor mental health as a result of armed conflict. The loss of home, family and in some cases freedom leave children with long-term emotional scars that we are still attempting to understand.

Possible causes of mental illness can be divided into three main groups: environmental factors, home factors and personal factors.

Environmental factors
- War
- Famine
- Poverty
- Poor housing

Home factors
- Parental death
- Parental mental illness

- Divorce
- Abuse
- Separation

Personal factors
- Brain injury
- Genetics
- Cognition

Treatment

Because of the wide-ranging causes of child mental illness, treatments are also multi-faceted.

Behaviour therapy

The main idea of behaviour therapy is that problems are learned and therefore can be unlearned, thus the therapeutic process can alter inappropriate behaviour. One method is the use of positive reinforcement. The child knows that there are rewards for showing appropriate behaviour. These rewards can include playing video games or visits to the cinema. If inappropriate behaviour is shown then these rewards can be removed.

Psychotherapy

This is a long treatment process in which a one-to-one relationship with a therapist is used to change the child's mental health. A relationship is built up in which the young person's feelings are acknowledged. The process is confidential and the child learns that they have an understanding person who will listen to them. The process can involve a number of techniques and some therapists make use of play, drawing and painting. Others may use stories that allow the child to discuss how they feel.

Group therapy

As with individual therapy, group therapy employs a range of techniques. Again, the therapist may make use of play or stories as a means of treating mental health problems. In many cases the children will support each other. Poor mental health can leave children feeling isolated and it can be helpful to know that there are others who feel the same way.

Family treatments

Within the treatment process each family member is seen as part of a unit. When problems within the unit are dealt with it is expected that individual difficulties will be removed. As with individual therapy, the process can be protracted. In some cases, the treatment involves changing parental attitudes. This may be achieved by helping them to understand the nature of their child's illness. It may involve treatment for parents (many parents of children in treatment have their own mental health problems). Others approaches deal with parenting itself and help parents cope with their child's needs.

For the majority of children such treatments take place in the community, so as to allow them to remain at home and in school. For some, however, there is a need for in-patient care.

Treatment example

David is seven years old and lives alone with his mother following the death of his father from cancer. He has found this loss hard to cope with and has convinced himself that he too will develop cancer and die. He was referred to a child mental health team and seen by a psychotherapist. In a process of individual sessions, David and his therapist developed a story about Tom, a little boy who had also lost his father. Through Tom, David was able to express his fears. When the therapist asked about ways of helping Tom, David began to see ways of dealing with his own anxieties.

As with all illnesses, mental ill-health affects the way we live our lives. Factors such as schooling and friendship can be affected by long-term mental health problems. The way that we view ourselves, and our sense of self-worth, are a vital part of our development. Children who are in contact with psychiatric services have been found to have lower levels of self-esteem. A child may feel that they are less worthy than others, feelings that could continue into their adult life.

The child who suffers a mental illness, particularly one that is long term, can have their education greatly affected. This not only means that they are limited in terms of what they learn academically, but also in terms of their social development. There are a number of mental conditions that result in absence from school. Overall, there can be general unhappiness and increased reluctance to go to school. Some children are kept away through parental choice, other because they choose to. There are those whose lack of attendance is caused by their fears and anxieties. Children may even be excluded from school because of disruptive behaviour resulting from illness.

Stigma is another aspect of child mental illness that further handicaps the young person. Mental illness remains a hidden topic within society. Despite its prevalence we are often reluctant to talk about it. For the majority of people, childhood is a period of relative innocence, in which we explore the world around us. When confronted with the child who is mentally ill these images are challenged. Thus we feel uncomfortable and this is transmitted to the young person. If you think about how this prejudice affects adults, consider its impact on children.

Activity

Some people suggest that we all have mental problems at times during our lives. Usually we are able to cope, but for some people this develops into serious mental illness. Think about some of the events in your life and how you dealt with them mentally.

FURTHER READING

Child and Adolescent Mental Health. Oxford: Blackwell Publishing. Designed for anybody with an interest in mental health issues in children.

Journal of Child Psychology and Psychiatry. Oxford: Blackwell Publishing. A well-established journal that covers the whole spectrum of child mental health.

Kazdin, A. (ed.) (2000) *Psychotherapy for Children and Adolescents: Directions for Research and Practice.* Oxford: Oxford University Press. A very useful book that identifies which treatments work best in specific situations.

Sociology

Chapter *Twelve*

The Sociology of Childhood

JOHN CLARKE

Definitions of sociology are offered, followed by several sociological perspectives that have had an important effect on the way that we look at society. The influence of postmodernism and the views of childhood sociologists conclude the chapter.

Sociology is the discipline that studies social life. It is concerned with the ways in which human beings live in groups and relate one to another. As such it offers a particular view of the child as a *social being*, and is interested in the ways in which children relate to others through institutions like the family and the school. It is also preoccupied with the ways in which childhood as a process prepares people for their adult roles.

Socialization

A sociological perspective on human life lays strong emphasis on the ways in which we become adults through a process of learning. Sociologists stress the fact that despite our biological nature it is the process of social learning facilitated by the human capacity for language which determines the vast majority of human choices and responses. Sociologists tend to see human characteristics such as sex roles, educational ability or aggressiveness as being far more determined by social learning than by genetic inheritance.

This emphasis on the human as social draws attention to childhood as a key setting for the process which sociologists describe as **socialization**: the learning of the norms, values and accepted behaviours of the particular society in which a person lives. While most sociologists share this view of the central importance of socialization in determining who we are and how we live, they differ on the processes which underpin social life.

One of the most significant approaches within the history of sociology has been **functionalism**, a perspective developed especially in the United States in the period after the Second World War. Functionalists take a 'holistic' view of the social structure; they stress the ways in which different social institutions like the family and education contribute to the maintenance of the broader social order.

Talcott Parsons was one of the most significant writers in this movement. He stressed the idea of 'consensus': the ways in which society is held together by *shared* values, attitudes and feelings. As an example, he suggests that modern US society is 'held together' by shared attachment to values such as individualism, competition and the ideals of equal opportunity, sometimes described as the 'American Dream'. Parsons did not suggest that these values were universally observed or governed everyday conduct; what he argued was that society maintains its order and stability because people share a commitment to these things as ideals. Therefore, although the United States in the 1950s was characterized by systems built on structured inequality and brutal racism, critics of this state of affairs could refer to the 'shared values' of the American Dream in attacking such abuses. Hence, Martin Luther King in his famous 'I have a dream' speech tried to hold the nation to its own stated values, hoping that the US would 'live out the true meaning of its creed – that all men are created equal'.

Parsons argued that social order is only possible when the population adheres, albeit imperfectly, to a shared set of values of this sort. Where does this shared value system come from? How is it created? Parsons identified the key process here as socialization – the social learning process which mostly takes place in childhood – and the key agencies in creating consensus as being the family and the school (Parsons 1947; Parsons and Bales 1955).

In the family the child first encounters other adults: initially, in the one-to-one relationship with its mother, according to Parsons. This is broadened by the development of a relationship with the father, who 'gives access' to a social world outside the narrow family circle (Parsons saw women as essentially concerned with the sphere of the personal and intimate, what he called the expressive, while men were predominantly concerned with the economic and practical aspects of life, i.e. the instrumental) (Morgan 1975).

In essence, Parsons's model of socialization sees the child moving gradually from a personal intimate relationship with one parent (mother), through the relationship with two distinctively different parents, on to siblings, peers and the wider world. The role of the family and interactions within the family was to begin this process of engaging with the broader society while maintaining a protective setting for the child to return to and feel safe. As one child said when asked to define 'home': 'Home is where they have to let you in whatever you have done.'

The school acts as a bridge between the world of the home and the society of adults. The school begins by reflecting conditions at home, e.g. personal relationships, first names, an atmosphere of affection and play. As time goes on, the child moves gradually into secondary and further education settings, where the style more closely imitates that of the broader society. There are impersonal routines, written rules and formal relationships between teachers and students. Thus the school can be seen as facilitating the transition from family to independent adult life by gradually filtering into the child's experience aspects of the ways in which the broader social structure, for example the world of work, operates.

A good example of this is the idea of opportunity and reward. In a classic essay, Parsons (1954) argues that the competitive nature of the school classroom prepares children for the ideas that some people will be winners and losers in society and offers the rationale that this reflects natural ability or hard work. So, as children come to accept their ranking in class tests and exams and see that those better ranked than them get more praise from teachers and gold stars, etc., they are also learning to accept the unequal distribution of status and reward in the broader society.

Criticisms of the Functionalist View

Of course, much of the functionalist view of childhood and socialization is based on a model of human life which needs to be challenged. Firstly, there are many critics who would challenge the view that social order is essentially based on consensus. Marxists argue that societies are divided into social classes, which are brought inevitably into conflict with one another; that rich and poor and different social classes do *not* have a common interest in maintaining the particular social order. Therefore, it is not consensus which binds society together but a mixture of force and what Marxists call *ideology* – ideas taken from institutions such as the media, religion and schools – which makes people settle for their lot and put up with oppression (Willis 1977; Althusser 1968).

In the Marxist view the role of the family and the school is indeed to prepare the next generation for adult life, but this is not by inducting them into the shared values of society; rather, it is by sifting and sorting them through testing, examinations, etc. into different categories to suit the labour force needs of **capitalism**. This process of dividing people into different social positions is then 'legitimated' by an ideology of equal opportunity, which leads people to believe that their poverty and other groups' wealth are the result of differing abilities or hard work. In fact, Marxists argue that the role of socializing agencies like the family and the school is to serve as 'giant myth-making machines', which disguise the reality of oppression and exploitation in an unequal society (Bowles and Gintis 1976).

However, probably the most significant criticism of the functionalist view of childhood has come from feminists, who reject what they see as the male-focused or 'androcentric' view of the family and sex role offered by Parsons (Morgan 1975; Abbott and Wallace 1996). Freud, who was the founder of **psychoanalysis**, had an approach to childhood and the dynamics of family relationships which had a strong influence on Parsons. This left Parsons, it is argued, with a view of masculinity and femininity which reflected the view that 'biology is destiny' (Mitchell 1971). Parsons assumes that it is possible to identify women with an essentially expressive approach to relationships and life, while men can be seen as instrumental. Parsons seems to see these characteristics as biologically given and therefore inevitable. Hence, the dynamics of the child's relationship with its parents must begin with a warm, nurturing, personalized relationship with a mother and move out towards a practical instrumental relationship with the father. Feminist critics saw Parsons's theory as part of a generalized movement in the aftermath of the Second World War in the US and the UK to return women to their 'natural' domestic roles after what was seen as their 'unnatural' involvement in the labour force during the war (Millett 1970).

As far as childhood is concerned it is clear that functionalism and many of its critics were less interested in children as actual social beings than they were concerned to show how their experiences developed them *automatically* into particular kinds of adult. The emphasis on socialization led sociologists to portray children as passive receivers of social norms, or in the case of Marxism, receivers of ideological messages which shaped them into the kind of citizens that fitted the social order or met the needs of capitalism. This fits what Dennis Wrong (1969: 104) described as 'the over-socialized conception of man': the view that children were essentially like lumps of plasticine to be moulded into fully social beings by the time they 'came of age'. What is missing from this view is a concern with children themselves, with childhood as a set of experiences in its own right rather than as a process of becoming.

G An alternative view is offered by traditions in sociology influenced by **symbolic interactionism**. This view, derived from the work of the American philosopher and social psychologist George Herbert Mead, sees childhood as essentially concerned with the ways in which individuals develop the idea of the self (Mead 1998). How do we come to have an image of who we are and how do we separate this from the different roles we play as student, wife, church member, shop assistant, etc. (CHAPTER 2)?

Mead argues we develop this self-image during childhood in interaction with what he calls 'significant others' such as parents, teachers and peers. These others reflect back to us images of who we are and what we are like (e.g. by saying 'Who's a pretty little girl then?' or 'Look how he kicks – he's going to be a good footballer when he grows up!'). It is through this interaction that we develop our own idea of who we are. This is described by Cooley (1902) in the famous phrase 'the looking-glass image of the self'.

Where this viewpoint differs from functionalism and most Marxist views of childhood is in giving the child an *active* role in creating their own social identity. Socialization is seen as a two-way process of negotiation: the child interprets the actions and statements of 'significant others' and creates his or her own idea of who he or she is.

More recent sociological approaches to childhood (Jenks 1996; James and Prout 1990) have started from this more active model of childhood and developed a view which emphasizes the study of children as social actors who contribute to the making of society in a direct way. Thus, studies of teachers' effects on children's lives cease to view the child as the passive recipient of positive or negative views, but also stress the resistance to social influences and rejection of adult views which underlie many of the social processes which happen in school.

Postmodernism and the Contemporary Child

In the last decade of the twentieth century and the beginning of the twenty-first a variety of perspectives have been developed by sociologists which suggest that in some ways the nature of childhood has changed completely. One approach is the idea of the 'death of childhood' associated with writers such as Neil Postman. This view argues that in the present day the divisions between childhood and adulthood have been undermined, especially by media such as television. Children are no longer protected from the brutality and injustice of the world, as images such as those of 11 September 2001 are beamed directly to their screens. They are the objects of the most sophisticated advertising and merchandising, which dominate leisure, diet and clothing. They are presented with images of adult sexual behaviour at every turn and popular magazines blur the distinctions between pre-adolescence, young teenagers and mature adults (Postman 1983).

G This view is paralleled by the ideas of **postmodernism**, which is a movement within sociology that dismisses the ideas of fixed categories and identities developed by functionalists and Marxists. For postmodernists, childhood is not a settled condition with a clear set of characteristics. Rather, it is an area that people talk about in different ways – it is subject to different discourses. Thus the kind of ideas of childhood innocence and vulnerability which underlie the functionalist view of the child's role in the family are just one form of discourse available to commentators and is not inherently any more valid than the view of all children as manipulating selfish brutes (which is to be found in some of the writing on 'childhood in crisis').

Postmodernism sees the way in which identity develops in childhood as a much more fluid process than most previous models of socialization would suggest. The postmodern world offers a kind of smorgasbord of different identities and self-images to the child and individuals can assemble disparate elements of different cultures into their own individual style.

In its extreme form, postmodernism sees a separate status or condition of childhood as having been a temporary interlude in the history of society between the premodern absence of childhood described by Ariès (CHAPTER 1) and the postmodern 'death of childhood' anticipated by Postman.

Activity

Work with a partner. Relate your own experiences to the functionalist, Marxist and feminist perspectives.

REFERENCES

Althusser, L. (1968) *For Marx*. Harmondsworth: Penguin Books.

Bowles, B. and Gintis, H. (1976) *Schooling in Capitalist America: Educational Reform and the Contradictions of Economic life*. London: Routledge.

Cooley, C. H. (1902) *Human Nature and the Social Order*. New York: Scribner's.

James, A. and Prout, A. (1990) *Constructing and Reconstructing Childhood: Contemporary Issues in the Sociological Study of Childhood*. London: Falmer.

Jenks, C. (1996) *Childhood*. London: Routledge.

Mead, G. H. (1998) The development of self. In I. Marsh (ed.) *Classic and Contemporary Readings in Sociology*. London: Longman.

Millett, K. (1970) *Sexual Politics*. London: Virago.

Mitchell, J. (1971) *Women's Estate*. Harmondsworth: Penguin Books.

Parsons, T. (1947) The social structure of the family. In R. Anshen (ed.) *The Family – its Function and Destiny*. New York: Harper.

Parsons, T. (1954) *Essays in Social Structure*. Glencoe, IL: Free Press.

Parsons, T. and Bales, R. (1955) *Family Socialization and Interaction Process*. Glencoe, IL: Free Press.

Willis, P. (1977) *Learning to Labour: How Working Class Kids get Working Class Jobs*. London: Falmer.

Wrong, D. (1969) The over-socialized conception of man in modern sociology. In L. A. Coser and B. Rosenberg (eds) *Sociological Theory*, 4th edn. London: Collier Macmillan.

FURTHER READING

Abbot, P. and Wallace, C. (1996) *Introducing Sociology: A Feminist Perspective*. London: Routledge. Looks at a range of issues related to childhood from a feminist perspective.

Morgan, D. H. J. (1975) *Social Theory and the Family*. London: Routledge. Morgan's book offers the best summary of functionalist approaches and critiques.

Postman, N. (1983) *The Disappearance of Childhood*. London: W. H. Allen. Postman's bleak view of childhood provides a good setting for postmodern approaches.

Chapter *Thirteen*

Childhood and Juvenile Delinquency

JOHN CLARKE

Juvenile delinquency is a long-established term for criminal behaviour of children. A danger in any discussion of such behaviour is the tendency to assume the worst about children. This chapter tackles some of the misconceptions about children and crime and hints at some of the issues that are taken up in the demonization of childhood (CHAPTER 30).

A major theme of much writing about childhood has been concerned with issues of social control. How does a society maintain social order and prevent rule-breaking? While this is a general concern of sociologists, psychologists and criminologists, it has developed particularly in relation to the study of children and adolescents. There are two central reasons for this. The first is that most approaches to crime and delinquency adopt a 'career' model, whereby they try to show how the offender begins in crime and anti-social behaviour and then moves on to extend or abandon a deviant lifestyle. The second reason is the reality displayed by official criminal statistics that late childhood and adolescence are peak times for offending. The age-distribution of convicted offenders shows that people are more likely to break the law between the ages of fourteen and twenty than at any point in their lives.

Significantly, the kinds of crimes that the mass media emphasize and feature strongly when they express concern about the breakdown of law and order in society are typically carried out by young urban males according to police statistics. Car theft, street robbery, housebreaking and misuse of drugs are largely young persons' crimes. Fraud, tax evasion and embezzlement, which cost fellow citizens dearly, may typically be plotted by middle-aged, middle-class inhabitants of suburbia, but these are not crimes that arouse media concern on a daily basis. Young people seem to commit more crimes and more of the sorts of crimes that 'public opinion' cares about.

This concern about young people and crime is not of course a new phenomenon. Robert Roberts in his autobiographical study *The Classic Slum* (1971) describes relations between the young men who stood on street corners, dressed in the latest fashionable clothes, and the police force, who saw them as a dangerous threat to social order in Salford in the 1900s.

Pearson (1983) points out that the tendency to see 'today's young people' as being particularly out of control and prone to bad behaviour is one that continually recurs throughout recent history. Along with the despairing view of contemporary youth goes a lament for a lost 'golden age' of good behaviour and proper conduct, which is contrasted with current patterns of hooliganism and aggression. In the 1960s mods and rockers were seen as corrupted by a new teenage affluence (Cohen 1987), while a decade earlier teddy boys were thought to have been the product of wartime childhoods blighted by evacuation and absent fathers (Wilkins 1960). Pearson points out that the groups who originally gave rise to the name 'hooligan' were themselves young people in Victorian England, supposedly the classic example of a lost golden age of restrained polite behaviour. Similarly, writers like Dickens despaired of the lost generations of children and youth abandoned in the inner city to the mercies of villains like Fagin, and imagined a more peaceful and orderly rural past before the coming of the cities and industrial life.

While it is right to be sceptical of the alarms raised about children and young people and their tendency to offend, there is nevertheless considerable evidence that the period of adolescence is a time when large numbers of people do get involved in delinquent behaviour, and this is something which has real damaging consequences for the broader society and for them. Sociologists and criminologists have therefore been concerned to try to investigate juvenile delinquency as a way of understanding it better and perhaps identifying causes, using their findings as a basis for policy.

Delinquency and the Urban Child

The starting point of most approaches to understanding delinquency is the way in which it is clearly patterned in its incidence. Not all young people get involved in crime to the same extent (although the number who do is significantly larger than official figures suggest). The figures collected by the police paint a picture of the typical offender as young, male, working class, of low educational achievement, and living in a city. At different times all of these characteristics have been identified as the single key to understanding delinquency. However, much of the classic research and theory has focused on delinquency as a particular issue for the urban poor.

The most influential tradition in the twentieth century was the subcultural theory of delinquency developed by a group of sociologists associated with the University of Chicago in the 1920s and 1930s. This Chicago School model linked delinquency to the nature of urban life and deprivation in cities like Chicago. It attempted to show that high rates of delinquency occurred in certain areas of modern cities because the patterns of living and settlement created social disorganization and the breakdown of community. In these areas young people grew up with two different sets of pressures to conform. On the one hand, the school, the church and aspects of the child's family would constitute pressure to be law abiding and aim at success by legitimate means. On the other hand, the neighbourhood, the street gang and perhaps other family members would constitute a pressure to use illegitimate means such as crime to achieve what they wanted. According to the Chicago School model, it was this balance of 'differential association' that determined whether a particular young person became a model citizen – stayed in school, settled down and fitted in – or took the path of a career progressing through children's gangs into youth gangs and adult organized crime.

The Chicago School model is based on the idea that delinquency arises from a subculture, i.e. a group within society whose values differ from those of the mainstream. This subculture arises in deprived urban areas among people of low income and lacking in educational success. It provides an 'alternative status system' for young people at a time when their identities are being formed and they are anxious and uncertain about their worth. Young people rejected as failures by school and unable to identify routes of opportunity in conventional jobs find in the 'delinquent subculture' of gangs an alternative means of self-assertion (think of the song 'When you're a jet' from *West Side Story* – the lyrics are at http://www.westsidestory.com/site/level2/lyrics/jet.html).

Problems with Subcultural Theories

There are of course criticisms of the Chicago School's model of delinquency. Some of these rest on the difficulties of applying a model based on American urban life to other contexts. David Downes's (1966) study of delinquency in London in the 1960s, for example, found little evidence of the kind of structured gang system described in Chicago and New York. The main problem with all subcultural models of delinquency, however, is that they emphasize how *different* delinquents are from the rest of the population – how their backgrounds, education, jobs, etc. set them apart from those who conform. Criticism of these theories has generally stressed that in fact delinquency is much more normal than statistics would lead us to believe. Self-report studies (where people are asked about crimes they themselves have committed) seem to show that minor law breaking is a relatively normal aspect of the lives of young males. Consequently, it is difficult to argue that the origins of delinquency lie in the particular backgrounds of that minority who come to the attention of the police and law courts.

Labelling

Labelling theorists – following the theories of Edwin Lemert (1972) – suggest that while offending may be relatively evenly spread through the population, being labelled as an offender is likely to happen to only certain groups: those who are already seen as marginal and powerless. So, while we may all offend, it is the poor urban male who fits the label of 'delinquency prone' and therefore comes to be the object of police attention, and have a greater likelihood of court appearance and more severe punishment. People who go through these processes move from what Lemert calls primary deviation, where the offending is a 'fact of life' (the odd bit of shoplifting or vandalism, perhaps), to a situation of secondary deviation, where offending is central to the person's identity – actually a 'way of life'. This new identity, perhaps combined with the effects of custodial sentences alongside other more established offenders and the impact of conviction on the individual's life in the community (loss of job, friends, etc.), is likely to lead to more offending and create the spiral which labelling theorists call **deviancy amplification**.

David Matza (1964) builds on subcultural theory and labelling approaches to develop his theory of drift. He argues that certain social and economic factors like poverty, urban deprivation and unemployment create for young people a kind of limbo state he describes as *drift*. These are not organized criminals, nor even really identifiable gangs, but rather groups of young people with little sense of purpose or sense of a link between their behaviour and the system of rewards presented as normal by the mass media. In this situation minor delinquency is an unremarkable fact of everyday life. For most people this period of drift has a natural life span and they eventually 'drift out', usually into long-term commitments like engagement, marriage, children, etc. Such commitments make even minor offending too risky and they give it up. For others – those subject to the labelling process identified above – the period of drift changes into a clear, settled, deviant identity and these people tend to be those who go on to have criminal careers as adults.

Matza argues that delinquency can be made worse by two separate aspects of policy: (1) policies that create drift (e.g. increasing poverty, the lessening of educational opportunity, or the creation of youth unemployment, which put more youngsters into this uncertain position); (2) criminal justice policies that reinforce the young person's identity as a 'delinquent' (perhaps by turning to custodial solutions too quickly) prevent the natural growth away from drift.

Delinquency and Childhood in Crisis

The end of the twentieth century saw a growth in popular concern about crime and young people, largely as described by Pearson's model of a contrast between an imagined golden age of respect and good behaviour and a present reality of childhood insolence, rule-breaking and apparent loss of control. In the UK, there were a number of high-profile cases like that of the Rat Boy, a child criminal in the northeast of the country whose diminutive size enabled him to avoid arrest by hiding in small spaces. He was accused of crimes which ranged across a large housing estate and was alleged to be immune from capture or punishment. It was suggested that this showed a society whose children were 'out of control'.

This concern was most painfully dramatized in the early 1990s by the murder of Jamie Bulger (CHAPTER 30), a small child who was led away under the gaze of security cameras and passers-by and then murdered. His murderers were themselves children, who were truanting from school. The case dramatized many of the social anxieties of the time (Sereny 1995). The fact that no adults intervened seemed to symbolize the decline in a sense of community, as compared with a time when people would have felt it right and proper to question two boys leading a crying toddler along the road. Mostly though, the case provided the mass media with a focus for thinking about contemporary childhood, both in emphasizing the innocence of the victim and the apparently incomprehensible behaviour of the two primary age children who committed the murder. Media reactions tended to ignore the fact that the killing of children by other children is an incredibly rare event, and instead saw the case as a symptom of the decline of authority in society, whether from teachers or parents. This led to demands for swifter, faster punishments and a return to stronger discipline in schools and families (Davis and Bourhill 1997).

G This **moral panic** about criminal children dominated discussions of policy in the UK throughout the 1990s and lay behind the policies of New Labour (Scraton 1997). Initiatives to deal with child crime included the introduction of curfews to prevent children from being out late and new tougher responses to truancy and repeat offending. Thus Tony Blair's promise to be 'tough on crime – tough on the causes of crime' was partly applied to young people. Crimes committed by young people fell during the 1990s according to police figures, but this did little to lessen the public alarm reflected in media headlines and opinion poll data on fear of crime. Consequently, policy often seemed to be driven by reactions to the most recent 'scare' (e.g. street thefts of mobile phones) rather than a systematic approach to dealing with the economic and social sources of offending.

Activity

Look at some of the data from the British Crime Survey (see address below). What kind of picture do you get of the 'typical young criminal'? What problems might there be in relying on data based on crimes reported to the police?

REFERENCES

Cohen, S. (1987) *Folk Devils and Moral Panics: The Creation of the Mods and Rockers*, 3rd edn. London: Paladin.

Davis, H. and Bourhill, M. (1997) The demonization of children and young people. In P. Scraton (ed.) *Childhood in Crisis*. London: UCL Press.

Downes, D. (1966) *The Delinquent Solution*. London: Routledge.

Lemert, E. (1972) *Human Deviance, Social Problems and Social Control*, 2nd edn. Englewood Cliffs, NJ: Prentice-Hall.

Matza, D. (1964) *Delinquency and Drift.* New York: John Wiley.
Pearson, G. (1983) *Hooligan: A History of Respectable Fears.* London: Macmillan.
Roberts, R. (1971) *The Classic Slum.* Harmondsworth: Penguin Books.
Sereny, G. (1995) *The Case of Mary Bell* [with an essay on the Bulger case]. London: Pimlico.
Wilkins (1960) *Delinquent Generations.* London: HMSO. Quoted in J. Davis (1990) *Youth and the Condition of Britain.* London: Athlone Press.

FURTHER READING

British Crime Survey: http://www.homeoffice.gov.uk/rds/cjschap8.html. Official figures for crime produced by the Home Office.
Davis, J. (1990) *Youth and the Condition of Britain.* London: Athlone Press. Provides an excellent summary of past alarms and present debates.
Scraton, P. (ed.) (1997) *Childhood in Crisis.* London: UCL Press. Takes a critical look at recent moral panics about children and youth.

Chapter *Fourteen*

Sexuality

JOHN CLARKE

Sexuality is a subject that is often neglected in books about childhood. The chapter starts by describing the important different meanings of the word 'sex'. The influence of history on our views about sex is examined. The chapter concludes with a reminder about the ways that sex and social control are linked.

Sex and sexuality are topics that excite embarrassment and controversy in relation to most human beings in most societies. Linking sexuality and childhood adds dramatically to the potential difficulty. Talking about sex highlights key issues of power and morality, the links between the personal and the social, gender differences, and images of sin, guilt and innocence. It is unsurprising that this has been an area fraught with difficulty and anxiety.

In discussing sexuality it can be useful to distinguish different aspects of what sex means to human beings. Firstly, sex is a *biological fact about human bodies.* We have specialized organs and body parts (genitals, breasts, etc.) directly linked to the process of reproduction. There are other secondary sexual characteristics, such as body shape and body hair, which biologists argue arise out of our reproductive role and play a role in sexual attraction. Secondly, sex describes a *range of activities* (sexual intercourse, oral sex, masturbation) which use these sexual characteristics, sometimes to bring about reproduction, sometimes solely for pleasure. Thirdly, sex is a range of *social and personal meanings* given by people to what they are doing. Is this activity right or wrong? Is it sinful or holy? Is it consensual or forced? How does it make me feel? Does it give me pleasure? This leads on to a fourth element of sexuality – that of *sexual orientation.* Are the objects of sexual desire the same sex as me or different?

These four different aspects of sexuality need to be separated because they have different implications for thinking about sex in people's lives. For example, it is clear that societies need to find methods to control and schedule reproduction (Malinowski 1927). If a social group fails to reproduce it can die out. This fate threatened the Ik, an East African tribe evicted from their ancestral lands who simply refused to reproduce in their new government-allocated homeland (Turnbull 1975).

It is obvious though that not all sex is directed towards reproduction. People engage in sexual activity for enormously varied reasons and it is not always clear what the real meaning of a particular act is to the participants, let alone to an objective outsider. As Ken Plummer (1975) points out, the same set of actions (e.g. conventional intercourse between a male and female adult) can have totally different significance depending on the different meanings the participants attribute to them. Are they both full, enthusiastic partners? Do they both feel that what is happening has the approval of their religion or personal morality? Has money (or some other favour) changed hands previously? Is one partner fantasizing about having sex with another person altogether?

All societies have rules about acceptable and unacceptable sexual behaviour. These include rules about appropriate partners as well as appropriate activities (**taboos** on incest and homosexuality, for example). According to Steven Box (1981), in different US states there have been laws against fornication, adultery, oral sex, masturbation, sodomy, and even sex with the light on! Societies see sex as a threat to social stability and frequently identify a need to repress sexual activity as a way of re-channelling energy towards other purposes, such as survival or fighting.

Social rules vary from time to time and culture to culture. For example, while it seems that all known societies have had taboos on incest, the precise application of this rule varies enormously from society to society – both the kinds of relatives who are forbidden partners and those who are allowed or even required. Of all the rules about sexual behaviour the ones referring to sex and children have tended to be the most powerfully enforced.

Children and Sexuality

Sexuality plays a vital role in popular thinking about childhood largely because it is absent from definitions of childhood's 'true' nature. Part of the ideal of childhood innocence is the idea of the asexual child. Associating children with sexuality breaks significant social taboos. An advertising campaign against child prostitution by the NSPCC pressed home the horror of this abuse by showing montages of children's bodies with old people's faces, thus referring back to the Victorian idea of 'children without childhood'. The childhood of which these children are deprived is characterized by sexual innocence.

For the Victorians the idealized view of childhood excluded sex. Children were seen as pure and asexual. In many ways this reflected the Victorian view of 'respectable' women, who were seen as having no sexual desire and were encouraged to see sex as a necessary submission to their husband's animal desires ('lie back and think of England!'). Active sexuality was seen as the prerogative of adult males and 'fallen women' (Marcus 1966). The idealization of childhood did not of course prevent the recruitment of such fallen women at a very young age:

> A Royal Commission in 1871 found that in three London hospitals there were 2,700 cases of venereal disease among girls between the ages of 11 and 16 years. The sexual use of young girls was indirectly sanctioned as 12 was the age of consent. Girls of this age could be procured for the (substantial) price of £20, a valuation which gave some clue to the social class of the purchasers. (*Hawkes 1996: 47*)

Children's lack of sexuality was assumed at one level, but at another it was something which needed to be enforced by social rules. The classic example of this was the nineteenth-century campaign against masturbation. This was a long-term campaign that brought together religious writers who saw pleasure not linked to procreation as inherently sinful, with doctors and psychologists who identified dire personal and social consequences resulting from the practice. Masturbation was seen as leading to imbecility, mental illness and infertility, as well as a general lack of moral strength (Weeks 1989). As Comfort (1968) points out, this led to a range of painful techniques to restrain children identified as in danger of engaging in 'self-abuse', including physical implements fitted to the body and brutal punishments for transgression (Porter and Hall 1995).

In this atmosphere of Victorian repression it is not surprising that the ideas of Freud (1986) about childhood sexuality met with horror and incredulity. Writing in Vienna at the turn of the twentieth century, Freud put forward the view that sexuality was not something which came suddenly to children after puberty along with body hair and acne. Freud argued that children are born with the capacity for sexual pleasure, but that this is a capacity dispersed throughout the body – children can take sexual pleasure from all kinds of touch, stimulation, tickling, etc. and from all parts of the body (mouth, anus, nipples, toes). Freud's model of 'normal' sexual development saw this generalized capacity for pleasure ('polymorphous perversity') gradually channelled into reproduction. So, for boys, the key site of sexual pleasure becomes the penis, while for girls it centres on the womb. Freud's theory was truly revolutionary in that it undermined the Victorian image of asexual childhood. It suggested that adult sexuality was a creation of the ways in which we bring up children, as an outcome of the dynamics of family life, which some writers perceived might result in other possible sexualities.

During the twentieth century much of the thinking of Freudians and other writers about sexuality became gradually incorporated into 'common sense' views about sexual life. Ideas about the key influence of early experience, the negative consequences of repression and the links between sexual behaviour and good mental and physical health became part of everyday language. They were powerful influences on theorists of childcare such as John Bowlby (1953) and writers of advisory books like Benjamin Spock (1979). Their broader impact was felt in what was described as the 'permissive' era of the 1960s. As the poet Philip Larkin put it: 'Sexual intercourse began in 1963 . . . between the end of the [*Lady*] *Chatterley* ban and the Beatles' first LP'.

The 1960s were perhaps not as permissive in sexual terms as some people suggest. Nevertheless the decade was identified by numerous writers of the 1980s as the source of many of those social problems that could only be solved by a return to traditional rules or, in the words of Margaret Thatcher, 'Victorian values' (these Victorian values never seemed to include the nineteenth century's vast industry of prostitution and child sexual slavery, incidentally). Rolling back the 1960s tide of sexual liberalism was at the forefront of this movement, and the sexual behaviour of the young was the key target. A first goal was to combat what was identified as a movement to 'promote' homosexuality among children.

Freudians and other psychoanalysts have emphasized this idea of sexuality as socially constructed rather than as something determined completely by the logic of biological necessity. Such a view sees the ways in which children are treated and the patterns of relationships they engage in as critical for how they develop a sexual identity. This gives particular significance to debates about choice of sexual orientation. If people realize that they are predominantly attracted to people of the same sex, then psychoanalytic theories would suggest that this arises from processes which take place very early in life. Therefore, it could be argued that much of the alarm about 'vulnerable' adolescents being seduced into homosexuality by predatory adults is misplaced. The problem with Section 28 – the clause in the 1988 Local Government Act which outlaws the *promotion* of homosexuality in schools – can then be seen as stopping teachers responding appropriately to adolescents' emerging awareness of their own sexual preferences. It is not about protecting impressionable youth from being 'led astray' (Durham 1991).

Sexual Behaviour and Social Control

According to Michel Foucault, the development of a society which is increasingly rationally administered was based on control of people's bodies, especially the medicalization of aspects of our bodily life which had previously been seen as private. Foucault (1979: 26) says of the seventeenth century: 'Sex became an issue, and a public issue no less; a whole web of discourses, special knowledges, analyses and injunctions settled upon it'.

This need to scrutinize and control people's bodies becomes a key element of developing forms of social control and focuses on children through debates about masturbation and the return of Victorian values, through to current concerns about the sexualization of media for pre-teens. Most recently the sexual content of magazines for young people has been described as too explicit by some, but as a genuine reflection of what young people know and need to know by others.

Thus it is impossible to separate arguments about sexuality from broader debates about the rights of children and the role of adult power in controlling their lives. Controversies about Section 28, the age of consent, contraceptive advice to under 16s and sex education in schools all centre on competing images of childhood as vulnerable and dependent, characterized by an innocence requiring protection, as against a perspective which stresses children's rights as citizens able to decide for themselves and take greater responsibility for their own choices and their consequences (Corteen and Scraton 1997).

In the era of HIV/AIDS this is a major issue for those working with the young. It is important to place initiatives on sexual behaviour and sexual health within a context of the experience of contemporary childhood and adolescence. As Moore and Rosenthal (1993: 4) put it, 'Education about sexual values and sexual health is likely to be most effective if educators take into account the current beliefs and practices of their target audience'. Thus the need to accord children a right to be heard and a recognition of their own preferences and orientations are likely to underpin the most effective strategies to protect their health and well-being.

Activity

One of the aims of this chapter is to inform you about issues to do with sexuality. This is one example of a teaching and learning experience. As far as children are concerned, they have the right to appropriate sex education. Discuss the way that you think children should be informed about sex in school.

REFERENCES

Bowlby, J. (1953) *Child Care and the Growth of Love*. Harmondsworth: Penguin Books.

Box, S. (1981) *Deviance, Reality and Society*. London: Holt Rinehart Winston.

Comfort, A. (1968) *The Anxiety Makers*. London: Pantheon.

Durham, M. (1991) *Sex and Politics: The Family and Morality in the Thatcher Years*. London: Macmillan.

Foucault, M. (1979) *The History of Sexuality: Vol. 1: An Introduction*. Harmondsworth: Penguin Books.

Freud, S. (1986) [1905] *On Sexuality: Three Essays on the Theory of Sexuality and Other Works*. Harmondsworth: Penguin Books.

Hawkes, G. (1996) *A Sociology of Sex and Sexuality*. Buckingham: Open University Press.

Malinowski, B. (1927) *Sex and Repression in Savage Society*. London: Routledge.

Marcus, S. (1966) *The Other Victorians: A Study of Sexuality and Pornography in Mid-Nineteenth Century England*. London: Book Club Associates.

Moore, S. and Rosenthal, D. (1993) *Sexuality in Adolescence*. London: Routledge.

Plummer, K. (1975) *Sexual Stigma: An Interactionist Account*. London: Routledge.

Porter, R. and Hall, L. (1995) *The Facts of Life: The Creation of Sexual Knowledge in Britain 1650–1950*. New Haven, CT: Yale University Press.

Spock, B. (1979) *Baby and Child-Care*, 4th edn. Oxford: Bodley.

Turnbull, C. (1975) *The Mountain People*. London: Picador.

Weeks, J. (1989) *Sex, Politics and Society: The Regulation of Sexuality since 1800*, 2nd edn. London: Longman.

FURTHER READING

Corteen, K. and Scraton, P. (1997) Prolonging childhood, manufacturing 'innocence' and regulating sexuality. In P. Scraton (ed.) *Childhood in Crisis*. London: UCL Press. Provides a good overview of recent debates.

Gittins, D. (1998) *The Child in Question*. London: Macmillan. The final chapter is a very personal account of the fears and anxieties which surround sexuality and childhood, relating some aspects of the above discussion to concerns about child protection.

Nye, R. A. (1999) *Sexuality*. Oxford: Oxford University Press. A good collection of readings on the history of thinking about sexuality.

Part *Two*

Children and Services

Chapter *Fifteen*

Interdisciplinary Perspective: Children's Rights

DOMINIC WYSE

The idea that children have rights of their own is one that can challenge many adults' thinking, but for the last 12 years children have had strong international legal backing for their rights. The chapter examines the UK's progress in implementing these rights. It reveals the complacency and inaction that have characterized UK governments' response to the Convention on the Rights of the Child.

Childhood in twenty-first-century Britain is characterized by uncertainty. However, an important possibility for beginning to address some of this uncertainty is reflected in the powerful international legislation which defines children's rights. On 2 September 1990 the United Nations Convention on the Rights of the Child (CRC) became part of international law. According to the Vienna Convention on the Law of Treaties, if a treaty has been ratified by a country (countries are known as nation-states) this means that the nation-state is under an *obligation* to comply with it and give it full effect in domestic legal order. It is instructive to examine the UK's progress with what was a radical and internationally popular treaty.

The CRC: First Report by the UK

The UK, like other countries, was required to submit a report to the UN Committee on the Rights of the Child about the progress of implementation of the CRC after the first two years. It is interesting to examine some of the recommendations of the UN committee following their scrutiny of the UK's report. The committee had 15 areas of concern in relation to the report submitted by the UK. First on this list was their worry that the UK registered six reservations about the convention. The committee considered that the most serious of these was the reservation that the UK may not apply the convention in the case of refugees. The committee felt that this breached **articles** 2, 3, 9 and 10 on non-discrimination, the best interests of the child, separation from parents, and family reunification. The second concern registered by the committee was the lack of an independent means to coordinate and monitor the implementation of children's rights. It was in the light of this problem that the Children's Rights Development Unit (CRDU) produced their *UK Agenda for Children* (CRDU 1994), which was an analysis of the extent to which law, policy and practice in the UK complied with the principles and standards contained in the convention. The CRDU consulted more than 180 voluntary, statutory and/or professional organizations that worked with children and held 40 consultation sessions with children and young people throughout the UK.

The introduction to *UK Agenda for Children* provided a stark contrast to the rosy picture portrayed by the UK report to the UN Committee on the Rights of the Child.

> The UK's initial report to the UN Committee illustrates not progress but complacency. It is dishonest by omission, highlighting particular laws and statistics that indicate compliance, without adequate recognition of gaps, inconsistencies and blatant breaches. (*CRDU 1994: xi*)

This situation underlines the importance of pushing for meaningful involvement of children in political processes. The UK government felt a political necessity to present a report that showed the UK progress in a positive light. However, if British society was structured to give children greater political rights this should include a contribution to such reports, which would have resulted in a less biased picture.

UK Agenda for Children was divided into 14 reports covering: personal freedoms; care of children; physical and personal integrity; an adequate standard of living; health and healthcare services; environment; education; play and leisure; youth justice; child labour; immigration and nationality; children and violent conflict; Northern Ireland; abduction; and international obligations to promote children's rights.

The first question asked in the report called *An Adequate Standard of Living* was: 'Does poverty exist?' The answer to the question is not so obviously self-evident, as most governments tend to downplay the existence of poverty. Questions of finance get to the nub of the political agenda and as such are fought strongly by governments. For example, whereas for much of the population the payment of very high wages to significant segments of society is obscene and represents an indication of inequality, governments tend to argue that a lack of incentive to earn large sums of money would have a number of negative consequences. In the context of strong resistance by government it is difficult to argue that (a) poverty does exist and (b) children are suffering. Statistical claims and counter-claims are often used to frustrate positive action. CRDU suggested that the two best definitions of poverty include the level of income support, or to define the poverty line as 50 per cent of average full-time income after housing costs, which is widely used in many European countries. In the European Community between 1957 and 1985 the UK had the largest increase in the incidence of poverty, where the percentage of children living in poverty had increased from 9 per cent in 1980 to 18 per cent in 1985. Government figures published in July 1993 revealed that there were 13.5 million people – including 3.9 million children – living in poverty; 1 in 3 of all children. In recent years small gains have been made in reducing poverty, but the picture is still bleak.

Article 31 of the CRC safeguards children's rights to play and leisure. However, *An Adequate Standard of Living* indicates that poverty interferes with that basic right. In modern British society the expectations of parents go far beyond the basics necessary for survival (although this is not to minimize the importance of the fact that thousands of children do not have these basics): parents are expected to provide a range of toys, outings, holidays, etc. Poverty restricts parents' ability to provide the increasing range of experiences that are deemed necessary.

The following quote from the report gives some idea of the seriousness of poverty and its implication for children's rights:

> A survey of poor families in the North East of England concludes: 'The picture that emerges . . . is one of constant restriction in almost every aspect of people's activities . . . The lives of these families and perhaps most seriously the lives of children within them, are marked by the unrelieved struggle to manage with dreary diets and drab clothing. They also suffer what amounts to cultural imprisonment in their homes in our society in which getting out with money to spend on recreation and leisure is normal at every other income level. (*CRDU 1994: 87*)

The CRC: The Second Report by the UK

You will remember that one of the biggest concerns of the UN Committee on the Rights of the Child (following the first report) was that the UK lacked an independent means to coordinate and monitor the implementation of children's rights. At the time of the first report it was necessary for a non-government organization to coordinate a meaningful response. You would expect that this problem would have been tackled soon after the first report came out in the early 1990s. Unbelievably, the appointment of a minister for children and the establishment of the Children and Young People's Unit only came about in 2000. In late 2002 the unit was still attempting to build a strategy for children and young people by waiting for responses from a consultation.

It is this kind of lack of direction that contributed to the hostile and scathing response from the UN Committee to the UK's second report:

> The report itself was very disappointing . . . confusing, complicated and chaotic in its presentation. It was to be hoped that the new Children and Young People's Unit would follow the guidelines more carefully in drafting the next report. The report contained much information on various Green Papers, White Papers and studies, but did not present their results. It gave no account of how compliance with the provisions of the Convention was assessed, or any information on jurisprudence related to the rights of the child. (*Committee on the Rights of the Child 2000a: 3*)

It is shameful that a country with the wealth of the UK has been so roundly condemned for its record on children's rights. The tone of the first paragraph of the UN report set the scene for what is a damning indictment of government inaction. The UK is criticized for doing little to adopt a rights-based approach because of a dependency on the philosophies of service, welfare and interest. The word 'rights' hardly appears in UK legislation. Further serious problems include:

- No change to the age of criminal responsibility.
- Best interests of the child not addressed in the juvenile justice system.
- Children expelled from school have no right of appeal and there are no mandatory hearings prior to expulsion.
- Considerable shortcomings in the attitude and practice of the government with regard to coordination at the national level.
- Lack of reliable statistics concerning child poverty.
- Lack of strategic planning to ensure that rights would be upheld when the private sector became involved with children's services.
- The age of 13 is too young for children to begin work.
- Poor knowledge of the convention by children.
- Racial discrimination evident in the high numbers of black children who are expelled.

Most worrying of all is the blatant disregard of the committee's recommendation in the first report that corporal punishment (smacking children) should be made illegal.

> The State Party's acceptance of the principle of reasonable chastisement was clearly a violation of its obligations under the Convention, and by leaving open the threshold of physical violence as a legally acceptable means of punishment it put the lives of many children at risk. A large number of children died from such violence in the United Kingdom, often because of the accidental use by their parents of excessive force. (*Committee on the Rights of the Child 2000a: 4*)

The defence from government that a ban on smacking would be unpopular and unenforceable and would violate parents' rights to raise children as they see fit is simply unacceptable. The committee rightly pointed out that perhaps more children should have been asked about their views on corporal punishment. One of the final comments that was made by the committee was to emphasize how important education should be in addressing all of the problems outlined during the meeting: 'Education should be compatible with the environment of the child' (Committee on the Rights of the Child 2000a: 12). In the itemization of major issues developed in preparation for the meeting, education had the longest list:

> 3. Policies and programmes promoting the participation of children.
> 6. The use of corporal punishment in families, schools, care and other institutions.
> 12. Education: educational opportunities and outcomes for children in care; school

> privatization; *participation of children in schools*; *quality of education*; *school curricula including children's rights*; bullying; violence and abuse by teachers; exclusion procedures and alternative education for excluded children; psychological support in schools; national database on students; right to play and leisure, etc. (*Committee on the Rights of the Child 2002b: 4; emphasis added*)

In view of the fact that the UN placed this emphasis on the importance of education in securing children's rights it is useful to look in more detail at this part of UK society.

Education in Britain

English educational legislation does not give rights to children. Rights are given to parents, who have to ensure that their children attend school, and rights are given to local education authorities (LEAs), which have to provide schooling. This means that there is no practical way for children to enforce their rights to education, although the courts have been used to try to argue that children with special educational needs have not been given an adequate education by LEAs. However, recent legislation in Scotland offers an important step forward in the battle for children's rights. For the first time, children have a right in national law to be consulted on their education:

> Of greater significance arguably is section 2 (2), which provides that:
>
> In carrying out their duty under this section, an education authority shall have due regard, so far as is reasonably practicable, to the views (if there is a wish to express them) of the child or young person in decisions that significantly affect that child or young person, taking account of the child or young person's age and maturity.
>
> Although this section is open to widely divergent interpretations and is highly qualified in its terms, it remains true that the imposition of a duty on education authorities to consult children and young persons over educational decisions of any sort – with its correlative right in the child or young person to be consulted – is unique in education legislation within the UK. (*Meredith 2001: 5*)

It is not only Scotland that has made changes to educational provision that will have a positive effect on children. The devolved powers for the countries of the United Kingdom have increasingly led to the education systems developing in different ways. Northern Ireland has proposed a National Curriculum that is radically different to the **curriculum** in England; the inspection system has undergone reform in Wales; statutory testing processes in Scotland do not include league tables and the system allows children to be tested when they are ready, not at a set time in the year. Regrettably, the UK government used the issue of devolution as an excuse for its poor record on children's rights. This was not accepted by the UN committee, who reminded government that they have the absolute responsibility to ensure that the CRC is upheld in all countries of the UK.

Further afield, Norway has led the world in its record on rights. In 1981 it was the first to establish an ombudsman for children. Flekkoy (1995: 182) argues that the ombudsman achieved some notable gains for children and their rights:

- Legislation prohibiting physical punishment and physical and psychological treatment threatening the physical or psychological development of children. *A prohibition which includes parents* [emphasis added].
- Raising the age at which young people can be tried and sentenced by adult courts and imprisoned in adult prisons.
- The establishment of national governmental guidelines to incorporate the needs of children into all urban and rural planning considerations.

Hague's (1998) analysis of the role suggests that the ombudsman has also had considerable impact on the process of school reform. Equality, participation, appropriate environment and the need to take account of children's interests have all been enhanced by the work of the ombudsman.

Participation rights, including the necessity to be informed about the CRC, are key to future improvement of children's rights. Evaluating the extent and nature of children's participation is a difficult job. Ochaíta and Espinosa (1997: 294) did some work in this area and concluded that 'New studies are needed which would analyse, quantitatively and qualitatively, the actual participation of European children and adolescents in their families and schools'. Internationally, there have been a significant number of quantitative studies which have attempted to address children's participation. In England the work of Alderson (1999) has been carried out in this way. My own research was the first published qualitative work to examine children's participation in English schools. It focused on two primary schools and two secondary schools. Greater detail about this work can be found in Wyse (2001), but for this book I wish to focus on the roles that school councils played in the lives of the secondary pupils.

School Councils

The use of school councils is fairly well established in secondary schools in England, but less so in primary schools. Alderson (2000) claimed that the numbers of school councils in the UK may be higher than the previous literature suggested, but she recognized that her survey may have included unusually 'enthusiastic' schools as the result of a low response rate. Alderson also makes the important point that 'only councils provide a formal, democratic, transparent, accountable, whole school policy forum' (p. 124). The two primary schools in my research did not have school councils; the two secondary schools did.

At Graysham secondary (all school and pupil names are fictionalized) the children agreed that a school council was a good idea 'if it worked, but it wouldn't always work'. The use of future tense here was interesting in view of the fact that I had been told that the council was still operational. It was also explained that the process of gathering information from the form representatives was inadequate: 'we're put on the spot, we don't get time to think about what we're going to say or make notes, we just get told.'

The head girl at Graysham articulated with clarity some of the reasons for the school council not being effective. She felt that although it had not been deliberately disbanded, it had been neglected. One of the main obstacles to effective working was that 'they [the teachers] need to listen to what people say. They have our views but they don't listen to them.' It was agreed that the fact that the council secured some lockers was a good thing, but the locker issue was relatively unimportant. There was a perception that most issues raised by the school council members resulted in a lack of action combined with a lack of communication over the reasons for this lack of action.

In addition to the school councils, both secondary schools also had a prefect system with a head boy and girl. As it became clear that the children thought that the school councils were not working I wondered if the head boy and girl might offer a useful means of communicating the children's wishes.

R: Do you think the head boy and girl, because they're pupils the same as you, do you think they could be useful for you in helping to express your views, is that how it might work?

C: We used to . . . when we used to go to him every week, he used to write everything down and give it to Mr Norden and Mr Norden passed it on to Mr Coole, but he never does anything like that, the only thing he's done is lockers, which everyone knew we were getting anyway.

R: So if you don't feel that the head boy and girl can help you, what's the answer then, because they're like the head boy and girl aren't they, if they can't be advocates for you – do you know what an advocate is? Someone who speaks on your behalf, somebody that takes your side of the argument and puts it forward to someone else.

C: I don't think it's really their fault, I think it's Mr Norden, he doesn't do anything about it.

C: We were asking about our class . . . we wanted to change it but he hasn't got back to us.

The children's difficulties with the participation systems could in part be attributed to the theories of the headteachers. At Graysham any notion that the boundaries between child and adult might be problematic were clinically dispatched: 'Children are children: adults are adults. Children are different . . . We love the children in a way but we are in control. As they get older they get more responsibility. They have rights and responsibilities.' The head at Railton also conceptualized rights with their corresponding responsibilities and like the head at Graysham emphasized the responsibilities. He felt that rights on their own could cause confrontation and felt that in the recent past the pendulum had swung too far in favour of rights:

> A right is an idea which has to be balanced; counterweights – I am in the middle ground . . . Ideally there should be an audit of what happens but schools have been asked to do colossal amounts – almost like everything the church used to do schools now have to do. We are not as cohesive as we used to be. This rights thing does not bring about citizenship. Nobody should use the term 'right' until the next [this] millennium. (*Headteacher of Railton Secondary School*)

Meaningful participation is clearly difficult if you are not sufficiently aware of your rights. The requirement to inform children and adults about the CRC itself (article 42) was not being adopted in the schools that participated in the research. On completion of the data collection the headteacher from one of the primary schools was the only person from all the children and teachers that we met who was aware of the convention. However, when asked to define what rights were, most of the children articulated significant principles: 'What children think they should do; What children want; People should ask children what they want; Adults should ask instead of adults getting their own way; Have the responsibility to go where the mums don't want them to go; Save children on their own.' Issues such as the potential conflict between children's rights and adults' responsibilities, differentiating between mothers' and children's rights, and an undue educational emphasis on protection rights, came through in the children's statements. An assembly at one of the primary schools illustrated how discussion of rights could emphasize protection of children. During the assembly the headteacher reminded the children that they had talked about rights in the past by referring to the 'stranger danger' work that they had done.

Karen Williams extended an aspect of the work described above by investigating the work of two school councils in more depth as part of her dissertation for an undergraduate childhood studies degree. St Matthew's Primary School is based in the middle of a small semi-rural village, with 155 children in the school and 30 in the preschool nursery. It is in a predominantly white, working-class area. Woodland High School also has predominantly white working-class pupils and is located in a semi-rural traditional farming area where over half the children use school buses. It has around 600 pupils. The participants were all school council members who had been voted for by their peers. There were eight St Matthew's pupils taken from years 3 to 6 and ten pupils from years 7 and 8 from Woodland High School.

Williams attended two school council meetings in each school and during this time she wrote field notes to record the conversations that took place. A semi-structured interview schedule was used to record the meetings that Williams held with the pupils after the school councils. Another schedule was used to record interviews with the head of the primary school and the senior teacher from the high school who coordinated the school council meetings.

Although this was a small-scale study some significant issues arose which need to be investigated further. The pupils welcomed the opportunity for greater involvement in the running of their schools. There was considerable optimism that things could be changed. For example, in one of the schools a water fountain was requested and this was duly installed. However, both councils were in the early stages of development and the optimism may partly have been a product of the novelty of the experience.

Both councils suffered from a lack of systematic organization. The meetings did not appear to be as high a priority as other school meetings, so they tended to be postponed at short notice. The reasons for this included impending OfSTED inspections or even simply that staff were too busy. Systems were not in place to encourage council members formally to gather the opinions of their peers, which resulted in them tending to rely on their own opinions. For example, they did not have any documentation with them at the time of the meetings.

Issues of power and control are always interesting as part of democratic processes. The headteacher at St Matthew's Primary School chaired the meetings and also set part of the agenda. At this school the council members had some responsibility for behaviour management during lunch breaks.

Arran: We have some problems controlling some boys' behaviour at lunchtime. The behaviour has improved slightly over the last few weeks because one of the teachers has intervened.

Brian: Some children are still running around the classroom, and it's not safe.

Head teacher: It's not safe for children to run around. They need to be aware of health and safety, and others. As school council members you need to push on other children to control behaviour. Any problems the school council must report to the teachers.

Rebecca and Terry: When the teacher asks the class to put away the equipment there is some people who don't help.

Gemima and Terry: The same in our class, some people don't help putting the items away at the end of class.

Brian: The turn-taking of the Playstation could cause problems.

Head teacher: In the warmer weather we need playground patrol by pupils, as there is more area with the field being used.

Brian: Yes, we tell the teacher and the dinner ladies if we see something that's not allowed.

Head teacher: I'll be meeting the dinner ladies tomorrow to see if the system of patrolling is working. Do you think it's working?

Rebecca: Mostly working.

Brian: Not many people know about the patrol.

Milly: Need to remind every one (all the children) about the playtime rules, they don't listen to the patrol by year sixes.

Brian: We need to stop children and make children aware of the patrol duties and remind them of the rules.

One of the key questions is whether the use of council members for these duties supported their rights or not. The headteacher saw this as a positive initiative because the children were 'taking responsibility for their own lunchtime'. However, it is necessary to ask what the real benefits are for the children. It is possible to argue that a structure which is designed to be democratic has been subverted in order to use the children as unpaid helpers. There is a tradition in primary schools of year 6 children being given various practical tasks to support the running of the school, but this is quite different from the behaviour management roles that the children are being asked to take on. Another question is to what extent were the children properly informed about the initiative and genuinely consulted on whether they would like to take part? Will there be an evaluation by the children which is not just about the effectiveness of the scheme from the teachers' point of view, but about its benefit to the school council members and the children in the school generally? The difficulties of power and status can be seen in the following exchange, which came after the head had been trying to improve 'door duty':

Milly and Arran: We've had enough of the school council.
Headteacher: Can you stick with it till after Easter? What is the reason that you don't want to continue?
Milly: I'm missing my friends at lunchtime.
Arran looks disheartened, but decides to stay, possibly because of the headteacher's comment and the fact that all the other children are looking at him.

Both the school councils were in the early stages of development and sometimes this leads children to make fairly 'safe' requests for school resources, such as equipment at playtime. Unless the adults who are supporting the children encourage them to combine straightforward issues with more complex ones then children may lose interest. There are already schools that have had extensive periods with school councils in place. In contrast to Williams's findings, the school council website gives examples where children have had significantly more responsibility, but these schools are very much in the minority:

> *In Colby County Primary, Norwich, the children:*
> - Have been asked by the local education authority to help train pupils from other schools on an INSET day.
> - Run their own school bank. They have set up a tuck shop and are responsible for dealing with suppliers.
> - Have been involved in evaluating lessons.
>
> *In Grove Junior School, Essex, the children:*
> - Have been involved in selecting teachers.
> - Will be involved in making the new school development plan.
> - Are responsible for the organization of fundraising. In particular, they support a child in Nepal and are responsible for making sure that enough money is raised. (*School Councils UK 2002*)

School councils represent a vital opportunity for enhancing children's participation rights. We have seen that the picture across the UK is patchy. In a minority of schools there is some excellent practice, but *all* children have the right to this level of participation.

As far as both the study of childhood and the practice of working with children are concerned, children's rights represent the next significant shift in our understanding of childhood. The shameful way that the UK denies rights to the largest group of vulnerable citizens is completely unacceptable. For all those who work with children and who study childhood there is a responsibility to fight for the rights of all children.

Activity

Discuss with groups of children their knowledge about the UN Convention on the Rights of the Child. If they are unaware, offer them information and discuss their response.

REFERENCES

Alderson, P. (1999) Children's rights in schools: The implications for youth policy. *Youth and Policy*, Vol. 64: 56–73.

Alderson, P. (2000) School students' views on school councils and daily life at school. *Children and Society*, Vol. 14: 121–34.

Children's Rights Development Unit (CRDU)/Lansdown, G. (ed.) (1994) *UK Agenda for Children*. London: CRDU.

Committee on the Rights of the Child (2000a) Summary of the 811th meeting. Consideration of reports of states parties: Second periodic report of the United Kingdom of Great Britain and Northern Ireland, 19 September 2002. Retrieved 18 November 2002, from: http://www.unhchr.ch/data.htm.

Committee on the Rights of the Child (2000b) Implementation of the Convention on the Rights of the Child. List of issues to be taken up in connection with the consideration of the second periodic report of the United Kingdom of Great Britain and Northern Ireland (CRC/C/83Add.3). 10–14 June 2002. Retrieved 18 November 2002, from: http://www.unhchr.ch/data.htm.

Flekkoy, M. G. (1995) The Scandinavian experience of children's rights. In B. Franklin (ed.) *The Handbook of Children's Rights*. London: Routledge.

Hague, T. (1998) Promoting children's interests and rights in education: The contribution of the Ombudsman for Children to the Compulsory School Reform. *International Journal of Early Childhood*, Vol. 30 (1): 52–5.

Meredith, P. (2001) Editorial comment: the child's right to education. *Education and the Law*, Vol. 14 (1): 5–8.

School Councils UK (2002) *School Councils in Primary Schools*. Retrieved 18 November 2002 from http://www.schoolcouncils.org/NewFiles/Primary%20Schools.html.

Wolff, S. and McCall Smith, A. (2001) Children who kill: They can and should be reclaimed. *British Medical Journal*, Vol. 322: 61–2.

Wyse, D. (2001) Felt-tip pens and student councils: Children's participation rights in four English schools. *Children and Society*, Vol. 15: 209–18.

FURTHER READING

Children and Young People's Unit (CYPU) (2002) *Young People and Politics: A Report on the YVote/YNot? Project by the Children and Young People's Unit.* London: CYPU. The full report which enables you to check the methodology of the survey which is reported on the CYPU website. Does not include reference to children under 14.

Ochaíta, E. and Espinosa, A. (1997) Children's participation in family and school life: A psychological and developmental approach. *International Journal of Children's Rights*, Vol. 5: 279–97. Persuasively argues that proper use of child development research to inform practice can lead to better participation from children.

United Nations Human Rights Documents: http://www.unhchr.ch/data.htm. This database holds all relevant documents including the CRC itself and the minutes of meetings of the Committee on the Rights of the Child.

Social Welfare

Chapter Sixteen

Overview of Social Welfare

ALI MEKKI

An examination of the history of social welfare reveals a number of themes that continue to exercise government. The chapter stresses the significance of a number of key reports such as the Beveridge Report. It concludes by showing you that the governmental prescription that is a feature of other services is present in the social welfare system.

The Elizabethan Poor Laws represented the earliest form of social welfare. Under this system local parishes were responsible for providing a minimal or subsistence level of assistance to parishioners who had no means to support themselves and no relatives who could assist them. The assistance was provided through *outdoor relief* (the provision of money or goods to people in their own homes) or *indoor relief* (which meant providing accommodation in workhouses where the poor, elderly and disabled were required to work in return for food and shelter). The nature and level of relief varied from area to area and relief was available only to applicants who could prove they had settlement in the parish, i.e. that they were local parishioners. Disputes about settlement led to the passing of the Law of Settlement in 1662. This meant that to qualify, applicants had to prove that they had lived in the parish for more than a year and that they qualified by marriage or by being apprenticed in the parish. False claimants were called vagrants and were subjected to corporal punishment for a first offence and capital punishment for a third offence.

This system of support was widely criticized as too expensive for ratepayers and too generous to the poor. A Royal Commission resulted in the passing of the Poor Law Amendment Act 1834. The Act was designed to introduce a system of less eligibility. This meant that conditions for recipients of relief should be so unattractive that only the truly desperate would ask for help. At the same time the 15,000 parishes were required to amalgamate. These new units were administered by guardians elected by local ratepayers. A national body, the Poor Law Commissioners, was responsible for establishing regulations designed to encourage consistency. Relief was generally provided in large segregated workhouses where families would be separated. Although some outdoor relief was still provided this was discouraged and some groups such as unmarried mothers were completely ineligible for any assistance except entry into the workhouse. The poor were divided into the **deserving poor**, such as the elderly and disabled, and the undeserving poor, such as unmarried mothers and the unemployed able-bodied. By the end of the nineteenth century infirmaries were also being built for the treatment of the impoverished poor. At the same time the children of the poor were subjected to policies designed to rescue them from poverty by placing them in charitable or board schools and by placing them for adoption or boarding.

Social Insurance

In 1890s Prussia an alternative approach to social welfare was being developed. The Chancellor, Bismarck, had introduced a scheme of social insurance to provide pensions and sickness benefits. In 1911 the government of Lloyd George introduced a similar scheme in the United Kingdom. The scheme was funded with contributions from the employee, the employer and the government. Benefits included an entitlement to unemployment benefit for a limited period and access to the services of a doctor (general practitioner) from a panel. However, only workers who contributed to the scheme were eligible for benefits. Those who were not eligible were still dependent on the local authority relief, until its replacement by the National Assistance Act in 1948.

Serious expansion of the unemployment insurance scheme and a large-scale programme of social housing took place in the period after the First World War. However, the country's economy, especially its share of foreign markets, had been adversely affected by the war. Between 1920 and 1922 there was a recession. Unemployment remained consistently high between 1920 and 1940 and the insurance fund could not honour the demand. The result was that the Treasury agreed to accept responsibility for unemployment benefit and, by default, the principle of state-funded social security had been established. In 1929 the government transferred responsibility for long-term unemployment benefit to public assistance committees run by local authorities. The benefits available from this source were strictly means-tested, a process which was operated crudely and insensitively and which caused widespread resentment. In 1934 public assistance committees were replaced by the National Unemployment Assistance Board. Local authorities retained responsibility, as in the Poor Law system, for children, the elderly and disabled. Because they were no longer responsible for unemployed potential wage earners, some local authorities began to develop services similar to those which would later evolve into modern social services

The Health of the Nation

One of the effects of poverty and deprivation was that the health of a large part of the nation was so poor that it compromised the state's ability to raise an army in times of war. This was first seen in the medical examinations which took place as part of the recruitment process. In the Boer War (1899–1902) almost half of those volunteering for service did not pass the basic medical examination. The physical health of a large proportion of the population was clearly being adversely affected by poverty and deprivation. This was consistent with the findings of contemporary social reformers such as Rowntree and Booth. Seebohm Rowntree in his studies in 1899 and again in 1936 had demonstrated that low pay and large families were the main causes of poverty. By the time of the First World War the number of conscripts unfit to serve was found to be a third of all those examined. Another third had some physical or medical condition which meant that they were not considered grade one in terms of their fitness to serve. This was improved by the time of the Second World War: despite the effects of the depression of the 1930s, 7 out of 10 conscripts were found to be fully fit.

The Beveridge Report (Social Insurance and Allied Services 1942) is traditionally identified as the starting point of the modern welfare state. The report set out to address the 'Five Giants' on the road to postwar reconstruction: Want, Disease, Ignorance, Squalor and Idleness. These demanded reforms in social security, health, education, housing and employment policy. The report in its full and abridged forms sold 600,000 copies – unprecedented for a government report. It was very popular and was supported by politicians in all the major parties. Beveridge described a view of social justice which saw the state as responsible for providing citizens with the resources and services necessary for a reasonable standard of life. In return the citizen would take advantage of education and employment opportunities (also provided or stimulated by the government) and contribute to the social insurance fund through national insurance and income tax, which would pay for the provision.

Child benefit, formerly known as family allowance, was introduced as a universal benefit payable to all families with more than one child however much they received from any other source. This was designed to avoid discouraging those on low incomes from working. The basis of the idea of social security was that all citizens should be entitled to certain minimum resources and services. Minimum subsistence-level income, child benefit, free education and healthcare were to be considered the basic right of all citizens. This definition of a minimum level of service provision was known as the postwar welfare settlement and lasted well into the 1970s. The postwar settlement has since been replaced by a new welfare consensus which places much greater emphasis on the duties and responsibilities owed by citizens to society as a condition of their eligibility for rights and benefits.

Social Exclusion and the Modern Welfare State

More recently the concept of social exclusion has replaced the use by the government of terms such as poverty and deprivation to describe those groups to whom welfare provision is directed. More responsibility has been shifted to individuals, families and communities. This is reflected in the robust system of outcomes which welfare agencies are required to demonstrate as a precondition for government funding. The funding arrangements seek to influence the design of services at a local level to a far greater extent than was previously the case. Another development has been the explicit requirement for agencies to collaborate with each other in delivering improved outcomes in terms of health, child protection, educational attainment and crime and disorder. Included in this shift is the acknowledgement that childcare is an important factor which affects the opportunity for all parents, but particularly lone parents and women, to take advantage of employment and training opportunities.

Demographic, economic, health and education data have been used to identify the areas of greatest social exclusion. These areas have been designated Health Action Zones, Education Action Zones, etc. and have become eligible for specific funding to improve outcomes. This means that resources are being allocated to neighbourhoods rather than populations. While this approach recognizes the effects of deprivation on an area, the danger is that deprived families living outside the specific neighbourhood are discriminated against because of where they live.

The postwar welfare reforms led to the creation of large and powerful government departments. In recent years these have been subject to criticism, especially in relation to the extent to which they compete with each other and therefore work at cross-purposes. In the light of this problem the present government introduced the concept of *cross-cutting*. This refers to an approach which concentrates on a specific social problem and then generates a solution which ignores the boundaries between different government departments and partner agencies. Sure Start, the Children's Fund and the various community safety initiatives are examples which have illustrated this approach. All of them require cooperation between different government and local authority departments, local communities, and independent and voluntary agencies. Another feature of these initiatives is that they are required to quantify the effects of their activity in order to qualify for continued funding.

Accountability

In 1995 it became evident that public care was failing the children it was set up to look after. In response, the Department of Health introduced detailed practice guidance which set out new minimum standards of parenting for local authorities. The guidance formed part of a system for recording and managing the cases of looked-after children. It introduced seven core areas which must be addressed in all looked-after children's cases:

- Health
- Education
- Emotional and behavioural development
- Identity
- Family and social relationships
- Social presentation
- Self-care skills

As with assessment, child protection and family support, the social worker's responsibilities in respect of looked-after children have become much more defined and detailed. This has encouraged the development of specialist teams. These teams can concentrate on ensuring that looked-after children receive the highest possible standards of parenting and planning for the future.

In response to dissatisfaction with a lack of clarity about standards, central government has introduced a variety of performance indicators for social services. These include performance in the following areas:

- Number of assessments completed on time
- Health outcomes for looked-after children
- Educational outcomes for looked-after children
- Number of looked-after children's reviews held on time
- Number of child protection conferences and reviews held on time
- The length of time that children's names stay on the child protection register
- The proportion of children's budget spent on family support

One immediate effect of these was that local authorities were required to introduce information systems and changes in practice in order to provide this information. This has had the additional effect of generating much better information to inform the planning of services generally. The information is published nationally, rather like the school league tables, and authorities deemed to have failed can be subject to corrective action by central government. This can range from replacing the management of the organization with outside consultants, to imposing a strict set of conditions on the provision of future funding. It has made social work more accountable to the people who receive and pay for it and has allowed for a more disciplined approach to evaluating the effectiveness of the service.

Activity

Look through newspaper articles that feature social welfare issues (many newspapers are now archived on the Internet). Think about the emphasis that is given to health, education and social work.

FURTHER READING

Lund, B. (2002) *Understanding State Welfare: Social Justice or Social Exclusion.* London: Sage. A description of the models used to analyse social welfare policy.

Timmins, N. (1996) *The Five Giants: A Biography of the Welfare State.* London: Fontana. A standard text on the development of the modern welfare state.

Chapter *Seventeen*

The Role of the Child and Family Social Worker

ALI MEKKI

The Children Act 1985 had a major impact on the work of social service departments. This chapter reviews some of the key concepts that were strengthened by the Act and considers the role of the field child and family social worker. The chapter is concluded with some issues for looked-after children.

Social services departments were created by the Local Authority Social Services Act 1971, which followed the publication of the Seebohm Report in 1968. The report was commissioned by the government and recommended the amalgamation of a number of different central government and local authority departments into a single, family social work service. This new service was intended to provide a single point of referral and service provision in place of the former Children's Department, Mental Health Department and Welfare Department. A generic post of social worker was introduced for the first time. Social workers would be trained to work with a number of different client groups, such as disabled people, children who were abused, young offenders, the mentally ill and vulnerable older people.

The new service typically provided the field social work service from area offices with teams split into short-term or intake teams and long-term teams. Social work with children and families was both long term and short term. Work with children in care or with complex needs in the community was held in the longer-term teams. Work which involved vulnerable adults was generally short term and held in the intake teams.

A significant proportion of the social work staff was unqualified, especially in the short-term teams where a large part of the caseload was made up of elderly people and disabled adults requiring the provision of specific services such as home help, day care and placements in residential homes. The short-term teams also managed new child protection investigations. These cases were a priority for allocation to a social worker and were subject to strict time limits. If necessary other work would be postponed or not allocated if the service was under pressure.

The Children Act 1989

The next major change in social work came in 1991 with the implementation of the Children Act 1989 and the NHS and Community Care Act 1990. For children and vulnerable adults respectively, the two pieces of legislation required substantial changes in social work practice and management. It was not possible to manage all of the new responsibilities for the different client groups within the same teams and most local authorities quickly began the process of reintroducing specialist teams. The Children Act introduced a number of key principles which have had a major impact on social work practice.

Children in need are defined as those who are prevented from developing to their full potential because of a specific need, either for services or for protection. The local authority must identify and assess children in need in its area; it is then obliged to provide services to meet those needs. Because the obligation to provide services costs money, local authorities have exercised caution in their interpretation of the concept of a child in need. Significantly, disabled children were defined as children in need on the same basis as children eligible for family support services, children who are abused or at risk, and children who are involved in offending behaviour. Local authorities have been required to keep a register of disabled children in their area in order to plan and develop appropriate services for those children and their families.

Local authorities are required to involve parents, relatives and friends in assessments and service provision for children in need. For example, children should not normally be accommodated with unfamiliar carers if it is possible to find a placement with a relative or someone known to the child who is also an appropriate carer. Parents retain responsibility for their children, even in those cases where the courts grant a Care Order to the local authority. There had been widespread dissatisfaction with the previous practice of replacing the child's parents and excluding them completely from any role in decision making and planning for the child once a Care Order had been granted. Social workers are now required to involve parents in planning for the child and to encourage regular contact between the parent and child unless there are reasons (and evidence) to suggest that this would not be in the child's best interests.

The *no order principle* addresses the former practice of court orders being granted wherever the grounds could be proved. Courts now have a responsibility to look carefully at the local authority's plans in every case, and the likely consequences of a change in status for the child, before granting an order. For an application to be successful, the local authority social worker and legal advisers must convince the court that it will be better for this individual child to be made subject to an order. This has had the effect of encouraging social workers to consider alternatives carefully before applying to the courts in the first place. Children are entitled to separate representation in court proceedings and to access to a specific complaints procedure. Many local authorities created Children's Rights Officer posts within the social services department to enable and encourage children to pursue their rights.

The Field Social Work Service Today

Currently, local authority children and families social workers work in a variety of specialist teams, which may include:

- Assessment
- Family Support
- Looked-after Children (formerly called children in care)
- Youth Offending
- Disability
- Child and Adolescent Mental Health
- Family Placement and Adoption
- Residential
- Day Care

The nature and extent of specialization varies in different local authorities, but all areas have teams dedicated to the three main functions of the field social work service: assessment, family support (including child protection) and looked-after children. The three main functions involve the largest proportion of field social workers who work with children. They are the people in the profession who are subject to the closest scrutiny and severest criticism whenever there is a tragedy reported in the press. For some time there has been a recruitment and retention crisis in this area of social work. Many social services departments are heavily dependent on agency staff or carry large numbers of vacant posts.

Assessment

Social workers are responsible for completing assessments. This involves gathering and analysing a large amount of information from a variety of sources in a short space of time. The Department of Health has issued guidance which is called the *Framework for the Assessment of Children in Need and their Families* (the Assessment Framework). This stipulates the form that assessments should take, the content and the timescales for initial assessments and more detailed core assessments. The guidance was informed by substantial research into the effectiveness of social work practice in this area of work. Previously, the standard of assessments was extremely variable, especially outside the formal child protection system. Children and families were receiving a very inconsistent service, determined to a large extent by the area they lived in. There are criticisms of the framework (for example, that it is too detailed, too prescriptive and intrusive), but it has introduced a common national standard for assessments and consistency across geographical areas. The areas which must be covered in a social work assessment are set out in figure 17.1.

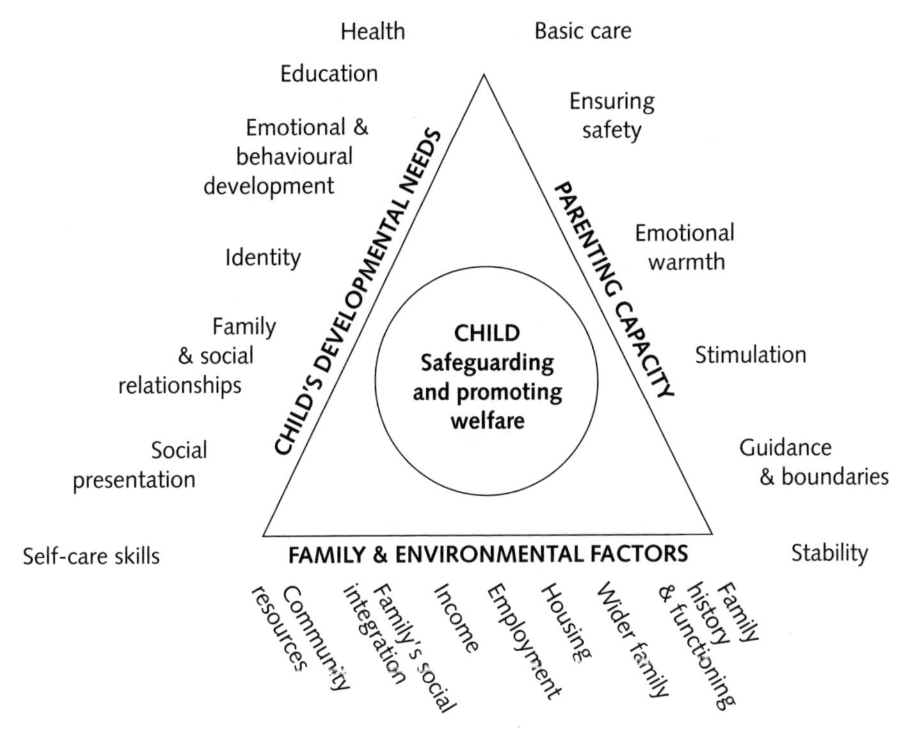

Figure 17.1 Framework for the assessment of children in need and their families (Department of Health 2000: 89)

An initial assessment must be completed within seven days of referral and a core assessment within 35 days of the initial assessment. The Assessment Framework contains detailed guidance for social workers as to the minimum standard of information which should be covered in both. The guidance also stresses the importance of effective multi-agency cooperation in this process. Local authorities and partner agencies such as the police, health trusts and local education authorities are required to develop individual local protocols to reflect the needs of their particular area. These should make clear that each individual agency has a specific commitment to cooperation with the other agencies, and with social services as the lead agency, in delivering assessments in line with the guidance. Examples of how this works in practice might include a requirement for social workers to include health visitors whenever an assessment is undertaken in respect of a preschool child, or for schools to make a specific contribution in the education section of all assessments. The framework also encourages social workers to involve families in all stages of the assessment process. The circumstances and needs of each individual family member must be addressed as part of the assessment. It is also important that the views of the children are recorded and taken into account throughout the assessment and during any subsequent work with the family.

Family Support

Historically, the main area of work for child and family social workers has been 'preventive work'. This is work designed to prevent the need for the family to become involved in court proceedings or the child protection system by providing them with timely, targeted help. In reality, time and resources for preventive work will depend on competition for the social worker's attention from child protection cases and children in the looked-after system. This means that work will often only be allocated resources when there is spare capacity. Paradoxically, it is this form of social work which is most likely to succeed in helping families to care for their children to a reasonable standard and stay together.

In some local authorities there are specific teams that deal with children on the child protection register and with the investigation leading up to registration. The advantage of this way of organizing the service is that these teams are able to build up expertise in the specific area of work. They will also be able to form close working relationships with other agencies such as the police and healthcare workers who are also involved in child protection. However, research demonstrates that the *needs* of children at risk have been overlooked because social services departments have tended to concentrate on *protection.*

> At the time the research was undertaken, the balance between services was unsatisfactory. The stress upon child protection investigations and not enquiries, and the failure to follow through interventions with much needed family support, prevented professionals from meeting the needs of children and families. (*Department of Health 1995*)

One response to this problem is to combine the two areas of work in the same team. Using this model, family support social workers are involved with the families of children whose names have been placed on the child protection register after initial or core assessments have been completed. Their role in these cases is to ensure that the risk to the child has been reduced or removed by the implementation of a child protection plan which has been agreed by the agencies involved in the child protection conference. However, because this work is allocated in the team responsible for preventive work, it is more likely that families in the child protection system will receive services and support as well as monitoring and scrutiny.

These teams may also work with children who are looked after, where there are plans to return the children to their parents' care. This will normally depend on the successful completion of work with the family or the provision of services to improve the standard of parenting and care the child will receive. In these cases the local authority may or may not have parental responsibility for the child, but there is a clear indication that the problems which have led to the child being looked after are temporary. The parents' circumstances may be about to change (for example, they may have agreed to undergo a drug rehabilitation programme or to separate from a partner who is violent or abusive). The social worker has a duty to consider the long-term interests of the child. In some cases this will mean making a decision to return a child to parents who still have significant problems. Children can be worse off in the care system if there are no placements which can meet their needs or if the effects of being separated from their parents outweigh the advantages of placing them with alternative carers.

Looked-After Children

A consistent message from social work research is that children who grow up in public care are disadvantaged. They will often be placed with a number of different carers and, if they spend any length of time in the care system, will lose information about their past. In the general population a large part of a child's personal, family and medical history is kept by their parents and other interested adults who are a consistent feature in their lives. For looked-after children, especially if they have been moved several times during their childhood, the knowledge of their past depends significantly on the quality of recording in their files. Looked-after children suffer worse outcomes than their peers. They are more likely to leave school with no formal qualifications, to suffer from physical and mental ill-health, to be homeless as young adults and to go to prison.

Unless the carer takes steps to assume parental responsibility, the allocated social worker is responsible for ensuring that the local authority's responsibilities as a parent are carried out. Arrangements for the child's care should be clear and comprehensive. Each looked-after child should have a care plan drawn up with the child (if of an appropriate age) and with the child's parents and carers. The child's plan should be reviewed formally by an independent reviewing officer at least once every six months and refined if necessary. Nationally, the standard of performance in all of these practice areas has been poor.

Activity

Talk to a social worker about their work with children.

FURTHER READING

Department of Health (1995) *Child Protection: Messages From Research.* London: HMSO. A powerful collection of findings from a range of research projects. One of the striking things about this is how difficult it is to research child abuse.

Jackson, S. and Kilroe, S. (eds) (1996) *Looking After Children: Good Parenting, Good Outcomes.* London: HMSO. This is one of the documents that social workers must use as the basis of their practice. It includes an extensive reference list.

Chapter *Eighteen*

Child Abuse

ROBERT BANTON

Two contrasting definitions are used to reflect on recent examples of child abuse. The official definitions are contrasted with the work of David Gill. The smacking of children and the extent to which society should be held responsible for abuse is also examined.

Some of the worst cases of child abuse are reported in the national media. Here are some recent examples:

- Victoria Climbié was murdered by her aunt and her partner in 1999. The inquest recorded how she was often tied up in a black bin bag and kept in the bath. At the time of her death Victoria had 128 marks on her body. She was just eight years old.
- In July 2002 six British members of a sophisticated Internet paedophile ring were arrested as part of a series of worldwide raids. The Shadowz Brotherhood offered images of babies and children being raped and tortured, plus advice on how paedophiles could lure children through Internet chat rooms (Dodd 2002).
- The American Catholic Church is having to respond to the conviction of a Boston priest for multiple abuse. Many priests have been accused with varying degrees of certainty, 250 have been forced out, two have committed suicide and one has been shot.

These stories point to the contemporary nature and scope of child abuse. The statistics for child abuse in the UK continue to be very worrying. The National Society for the Prevention of Cruelty to Children (NSPCC 2002) cites the following facts:

- Each week at least one child will die as the result of an adult's cruelty.
- Up to 170 babies may be injured by being shaken violently each year in this country.

- A quarter of all rape victims are children. Most abuse is committed by someone the child knows and trusts.
- The abuse is often known about or suspected by an another adult who could have done something to prevent it.
- Three-quarters of sexually abused children do not tell anyone at the time. Around a third are not able to tell anyone about the experience later.
- More than 30,000 children are on child protection registers because they are at risk of abuse. Each week over 600 children are added to the child protection registers.
- Recent NSPCC research involving 2,869 young adults revealed that 1 in 10 of them had suffered serious abuse or neglect during childhood.
- Each week at least 450,000 children are bullied at school.
- The current cost of child abuse to statutory and voluntary organizations is £1 billion a year. Most of this is spent dealing with the aftermath of abuse rather than its prevention.

At the end of March 2001 there were 26,800 children on local authority child protection registers. This means that for every 10,000 children under 18 years old in the UK, 24 are on the child protection register (Department of Health 2002). ChildLine reported that in 2000/2001, 9,857 children and young people (7,154 girls and 2,703 boys) called ChildLine about sexual abuse and 13,285 about physical abuse (8,639 girls and 4,646 boys). Most of these children who called were between 10 and 15 years old.

These figures make depressing reading. Typically, reported cases are much lower than the true amount of abuse. Many cases of abuse will go unnoticed by professionals and are therefore not dealt with. Because these cases do not end up on the official lists they are not recorded. Additionally, children may not report the abuse because they have been threatened into keeping silent or made to feel ashamed and guilty. Unfortunately, the abuse of children is not only a recent problem. Lloyd De Mause (1976) states that the further one goes back in time the more likely it is that children were being beaten, terrorized and abused.

What is Child Abuse?

If you were asked to think about what child abuse is, pictures of the cases mentioned above might well spring to mind. You may also have seen the NSPCC's recent and somewhat controversial television advertisements showing miserable unkempt children who are subject to beatings and neglect at the hands of their parents. These too seem to capture just what child abuse is all about. But do they? Is there more to child abuse than physical violence and neglect?

The Department of Health (1999: 14) defines child abuse under four headings: physical abuse, emotional abuse, sexual abuse and neglect. These definitions of types of abuse are widely accepted and used by professionals working with children and families.

> Physical abuse may involve hitting, shaking, throwing, poisoning, burning or scalding, drowning, suffocating, or otherwise causing physical harm to a child. Physical harm may also be caused when a parent or carer feigns the symptoms of, or deliberately causes ill-health to a child whom they are looking after. This situation is commonly described using terms such as fictitious illness by proxy or Munchausen syndrome by proxy.
>
> Emotional abuse is the persistent emotional ill-treatment of a child such as to cause severe and persistent adverse effects on the child's emotional development. It may involve conveying to children that they are worthless or unloved, inadequate, or valued only insofar as they meet the needs of another person. It may feature age- or developmentally inappropriate expectations being imposed on children. It may involve causing children frequently to feel frightened or in danger, or the exploitation or corruption of children. Some level of emotional abuse is involved in all types of ill-treatment of a child, though it may occur alone.
>
> Sexual abuse involves forcing or enticing a child or young person to take part in sexual activities, whether or not the child is aware of what is happening. The activities may involve physical contact, including penetrative (e.g. rape or buggery) or non-penetrative acts. They may include non-contact activities, such as involving children in looking at, or in the production of, pornographic material or watching sexual activities, or encouraging children to behave in sexually inappropriate ways.
>
> Neglect is the persistent failure to meet a child's basic physical and/or psychological needs, likely to result in the serious impairment of the child's health or development. It may involve a parent or carer failing to provide adequate food, shelter and clothing, failing to protect a child from physical harm or danger, or the failure to ensure access to appropriate medical care or treatment. It may also include neglect of, or unresponsiveness to, a child's basic emotional needs.

What do these definitions tell us of the abuse, the victim and the abuser? Child abuse is defined as those acts which harm the child in some way, or behaviour that fails to provide basic care for the child. The victim is a child or may be a group of children. The abuser is usually an adult individual who is caring for the child in some capacity.

Although we have described events and situations that are clearly abusive according to the definitions above, there are some actions which are open to debate. Would you define *any* hitting or smacking a child as abusive, because some people would? Organizations such as Ending the Physical Punishment of Children (EPOC), the Young People's Organization Article 12, and the NSPCC would argue that it is always wrong to smack a child. If you were to smack an adult it would be a criminal offence, so why is it acceptable to smack children?

This brings us to an interesting point in trying to define abuse. In trying to define what abuse is we are also discussing the nature of childhood and parenting. Children, it is argued, need to be disciplined. Parents may argue that very young children do not understand reasoning, so a 'short sharp smack is the only way to help them learn'; after all, 'it does them no harm'. Some parents argue that for some children a smack is 'all they really understand'. The argument is that light smacking does the child no harm and is an effective means of discipline when used as a last resort. The UK government, eager to support parents in bringing up children, has consistently refused to ban smacking and has allowed parents to use 'reasonable chastisement'.

The argument from ministers is that most parents actually want the freedom to smack their child if they deem it necessary, and would resist any ban on what might be seen as government interference in family life.

However, recent research carried out by the NSPCC in 2002 suggests that parents might back a call to ban smacking. The research reported that 96 per cent of parents support the banning of hitting toddlers with implements such as belts, wooden spoons or coins. More than 75 per cent would support a ban on hitting children over the age of three. If parents could be confident that 'trivial smacks' would not lead to prosecution, 58 per cent of people would want an end to the physical punishment of children of any age – rising to 62 per cent among those with at least one child under 16 and 68 per cent of those with at least two. Legislation is imminent in Scotland which will ban hitting children over the age of three and limit parents' defence of reasonable chastisement. Similar moves are planned for Northern Ireland.

Abuse is not only something done by individual adults to individual children. David Gill takes a very different approach to defining child abuse. Gill makes explicit what he believes about the nature of a child and this is the rationale for his definition:

> Every child, despite his/her individual differences and uniqueness, is to be considered of equal intrinsic worth, and hence should be entitled to equal social, economic, civil and political rights, so that he/she may fully realize his/her inherent potential and share equally in life, liberty and happiness . . . therefore any act of commission or omission by individuals, institutions or society as a whole . . . which deprives children of equal rights or liberties and/or interferes with their optimal development constitutes by definition, abusive or neglectful acts or conditions. (*Gill 1975: 348*)

Gill points to the fact that abuse is not only perpetrated by individuals, but also by institutions and society as a whole. Gill would cite the failure of social service departments to ensure the safety of children in care as an example. There have been a number of high-profile investigations into allegations of the abuse of young people in local authority children's homes. Stories have emerged that describe horrific beatings, harsh discipline regimes, and sexual abuse at the hands of individuals charged with the care of these vulnerable young people.

Gill sees abuse not just in terms of physical, emotional or sexual harm as a result of neglectful acts of carers. For Gill, child abuse is anything that deprives children of their rights and hinders their optimal development. Types of abuse mentioned at the start of this section would certainly count, but so too would any action that violates the rights of children such as those set out in the United Nations Convention on the Rights of the Child (CHAPTER 15). For Gill, poverty is just as abusive as any physical assault. Poverty stops children achieving their optimal developmental potential, as does poor education, healthcare and housing. These factors affect many more children than the 24 per 10,000 recorded on child protection records. Gill's ideas are not given wide recognition and are often labelled idealistic. But the strength of his ideas is that they encourage us to think about children's rights and the social factors that harm children in a way that the Department of Health's definitions do not.

Activity

Before you read this chapter what did you think child abuse was? How have your ideas changed as a result of reading the chapter?

REFERENCES

ChildLine (2002) *What is Child Abuse?* Retrieved 10 November 2002 from http://www.childline.org.uk/Childabuse.asp.

De Mause, L. (1976) *The History of Childhood.* London: Souvenir Press.

Department of Health (1999) *Working Together to Safeguard Children and Families.* London: HMSO.

Department of Health (2002) *Numbers of Children on Child Protection Registers in England and Wales: Year Ending March 2002.* London: HMSO.

Dodd, V. (2002) 'Britons arrested as worldwide child porn ring smashed.' The *Guardian* (electronic version), Wednesday 3 July 2002. Retrieved 10 November 10 2002 from http://www.guardian.co.uk/child/story/0,7369,748257,00.html.

Gill, D. (1975) Unravelling child abuse. *American Journal of Orthopsychiatry,* Vol. 45: 346–56.

NSPCC (2002) *Child Abuse – The Facts.* Retrieved 11 November 2002 from http://www.nspcc.org.uk/html/home/home.htm.

FURTHER READING

Corby B. (2000) *Child Abuse: Towards a Knowledge Base.* Buckingham: Open University Press. This excellent and easily readable book provides a good general introduction to the research on child abuse and the child protection system.

Lord Laming (2003) *The Victoria Climbié Inquiry: Summary and Recommendations.* Norwich: HMSO. In spite of the legal obligation for multi-agency cooperation, which is part of the Children Act 1988, this report reveals a catalogue of failures by services who have a responsibility to protect children. Needs to be read by all who work with children.

National Society for the Prevention of Cruelty to Children website: www.nspcc.org.uk. The NSPCC is a charity with a long history in both raising awareness and working with the victims of child abuse. The website is a useful source of up-to-date information and links to research and campaigns run by the NSPCC.

Wattam, C. (2000) The prevention of child abuse. *Children and Society,* Vol. 13: 317–29. This article deals with a number of issues to be considered in attempting to prevent child abuse.

Education

Chapter

Nineteen

Overview of Children's Education and Care

NELL NAPIER

The distinctive features of most of the wide range of childcare settings are described. Several important government initiatives that link the settings are explained. The chapter concludes with some reflections on the quality of learning that different settings achieve.

The care and education of children have changed dramatically in recent years. In the early postwar period it was common for mothers to remain at home and care for their own children until they reached statutory school age at five years. Women were no longer needed in the workplace when men returned from the war, so they were encouraged to see their role as homemakers. Work by researchers such as Bowlby (1969), who talked of the dangers of separation and maternal deprivation, added to the argument that women should care for their own children at home (CHAPTER 3). More recently, for a number of reasons, it is more common for women to work outside the home and the need for childcare has increased. The UK government has supported the view that women should work outside the home and its childcare strategy recognizes the need for quality childcare. One of the major reasons for the government to support women working is the desire to encourage people who are claiming welfare to support themselves.

The Green Paper *Meeting the Childcare Challenge* was published in May 1998. It set out proposals for a National Childcare Strategy in England. One of the major goals has been to ensure that every four-year-old has the entitlement to free part-time early education for three terms before they reach compulsory school age. Funding has also been provided to raise the proportion of three-year-olds with a free early education place to 66 per cent from 2002 onwards. Places are currently being phased in and targeted on areas where there is the greatest social need.

Settings and Services

At present, children in the UK of preschool age can spend their time in a variety of settings. They may be cared for at home, but they may (and increasingly do) spend at least some of the time being cared for by someone other than their parents. They may be with a childminder, but they also may be in one of the wide variety of other settings that exist.

Day nurseries

Day nurseries look after children under the age of five for the length of the adult working day. They may be run by social services departments, voluntary organizations, private companies or individuals as a business, community groups as a cooperative enterprise, and employers in the public or private sectors, including local authorities, health authorities and government departments for their workforce. Children will attend part-time or full-time depending on their needs and those of their parents. Social service day nurseries usually admit children who are considered to be at risk. It is increasingly common for these nurseries to combine with local authority education nurseries, as it is thought that children's all-round experience is delivered more effectively where care and education are provided in a balanced way. Family centres offer special help to families in need. They provide care for children and also run classes in such things as parenting skills.

Playgroups

Playgroups provide sessional care for children aged between three and five, though some may take children as young as two. They aim to provide learning experiences through structured play opportunities in groups, and with involvement of the parents in all aspects of the operation of the group. Most playgroups are run on a self-help basis by groups of parents, with one or two paid staff. A few are run by local authorities. Some are called opportunity groups and cater specifically for children with special needs. Playgroup sessions last for no longer than 4 hours. The parents usually receive training provided by the Preschool Learning Alliance and they must be registered with a social service department under the Children Act 1985. Extended day playgroups provide care for children for more than 4 hours a day and many will be used by working parents on the same basis as a day nursery.

Crèches

This term is commonly used to describe two different facilities: a day nursery managed by or on behalf of an employer for the children of employees; or a facility attached to a shop, shopping centre or leisure centre where children are left by their parents for short spells of time. Both types are like day nurseries.

Private nursery schools

As more families opt for both parents to work outside the home there has been an increase in private nurseries. They vary considerably in character, but all offer educational and day-care facilities. They remain open for the length of the school day during term time. In order to qualify for government funding they have to be OfSTED-inspected and meet high standards. Their practice should be informed by the curriculum guidance for the foundation stage (CHAPTER 21). Nursery units in independent schools are integral parts of an independent school and provide for early access to the school. Children usually attend part-time.

Maintained nursery schools and classes

Nursery schools are establishments with their own legal identity. Nursery classes or units are integral parts of primary schools. Both kinds of provision are open during the normal school day, but the great majority of children attend part time – commonly five mornings or five afternoons a week. They provide care and education and are staffed by qualified teachers and people with NNEB qualifications. Children are not required to attend nursery before the age of five. However, the curriculum at foundation stage has clear expectations of children's achievements before they reach the age of five. Where classes are attached to schools there is more opportunity for schools to make demands on the staff to prepare children for school. This can be good, but it also has drawbacks if, for example, an inappropriately formal education is followed for very young children.

Reception classes in primary schools

A large number of primary schools admit children to reception classes before they are five. Most are four-year-olds admitted at the start of the school year or the term in which they reach five. The great majority attend full-time. There is a concern that the curriculum provided may not be appropriate if the reception class curriculum is driven by level 1 targets, but it is hoped that with the implementation of the foundation stage guidance this will not be so prevalent.

Combined nursery centres

These centres combine educational and day care facilities and are managed jointly by education and social services departments. They take children from 18 months (and sometimes younger) to the age of five. They may offer a range of support services to parents.

Childminders

Childminders look after children aged under five and school age children outside school hours, including during the holidays. They work in domestic premises, usually the childminder's own home. They offer this service all the year round for the full adult working day. Parents and childminders negotiate the terms and conditions, although childminders still have to be registered and monitored by local authorities. Some parents employ a nanny or mother's help or au pair to look after the child or children in the home. This is a private arrangement, like childminding, with both parties agreeing about terms and conditions.

Out of school clubs

These offer to care for the school age child in the absence of the parents or carers from the end of the school day until the parent can collect the child and also sometimes before school starts. They are not open access. They may be run by the local authority, a voluntary or community group, or a private company. Children will be escorted to the club by a responsible person and not allowed to leave until collected by the parent or person who has parental responsibility, or the person looking after the child. Holiday schemes involve looking after children of school age during the school holidays and operate like out of school clubs.

Supervised activities

This term covers specific activities provided for school age children out of school hours and in the holidays. Leisure centres may offer supervised activities for children, who will be instructed in a particular skill, sport or pastime. The arrangements for bringing and collecting the children will vary and there will usually be a limit on numbers.

Other opportunities arise on an ad hoc basis depending on local resources; they include play sessions in playgrounds, local parks or community centres. Some libraries organize play sessions on an irregular basis, and voluntary bodies or community or special interest groups will put on organized events during the school holidays. District councils, police departments and other bodies also organize activities for school age children. Many will be open access, but some will place a limit on numbers.

Government Initiatives for Early Years

The UK government claims to have a strong desire to tackle poverty and some of its initiatives have this aim in mind. The initiatives can be helpful in ensuring that very young children who are vulnerable, including those who are looked after by the state, receive high-quality educational provision which matches their needs. This should include the early identification and assessment of children's needs and active monitoring of young children's attainments. There are several important initiatives which you should know about: Sure Start, Early Years Development and Childcare Partnerships, Early Excellence Centres, and Home Start.

The Sure Start programme was instigated by the government to provide early years intervention with the aim of preventing later exclusion. Resources are targeted at those with greatest social need to help children who for various reasons are at risk of failure. Sure Start aims to improve the health and well-being of families and children before and after birth. Local Sure Start programmes are designed to improve services for families with children under four. Good practice learned from local programmes is spread to everyone involved in providing services for young children. Sure Start programmes aim to improve children's life chances by giving parents and parents-to-be better access to:

- family support;
- advice on nurturing;
- health services;
- early learning.

The aim of Sure Start is to work with parents-to-be, parents and children to promote the physical, intellectual and social development of babies and young children – particularly those who are disadvantaged. It is hoped that by supporting early bonding between parents and their children, helping families to function and by enabling the early identification and support of children with emotional and behavioural difficulties, later problems can be avoided. It is also hoped that there will be a consequent reduction in the proportion of children aged 0–3 who are re-registered within the space of 12 months on the child protection register: it is hoped that in the 500 Sure Start areas there will be a 20 per cent reduction by 2004. A target for health is that there will be a reduction in mothers who smoke during pregnancy.

Parenting support and information are available for all parents in Sure Start areas. All local programmes give guidance on breastfeeding, hygiene and safety, and it is hoped that there will be a reduction in children in the Sure Start area aged 0–3 admitted to hospital as an emergency with gastro-enteritis, a respiratory infection or a severe injury.

Sure Start also aims to encourage high-quality environments and childcare that promote early learning, provide stimulating and enjoyable play, improve language skills and ensure early identification and support of children with special needs. A target has been set to reduce by five percentage points the number of children with speech and language problems requiring specialist intervention by the age of four.

The design and content of local Sure Start programmes vary according to local needs, but all programmes are expected to include a number of core services:

- Outreach and home visiting.
- Support for families and parents.
- Support for good-quality play, learning and childcare experiences for children.
- Primary and community healthcare, including advice about family health and child health and development.
- Support for children and parents with special needs, including help getting access to specialized services.

The activities of Sure Start programmes link with the work of the Early Years Development and Childcare Partnerships (EYDCPs), which exist in all authorities across England. EYDCPs were established by the Labour government in 1998 to bring together all parties with an interest in **early years education and care**. Planning and delivery of early education until compulsory school age is carried out through the partnerships. They bring together all the local partners with an interest in childcare to plan early education and childcare provision. The partners include local education and social service departments, voluntary and private providers, employers, parents and other interested parties. They make decisions about the development of services in their geographical areas and are responsible for drawing up annual plans that describe how the local authority will meet its statutory duty to provide early years education and promote equality of access and opportunity for all children receiving early years education and childcare provision. They have to meet local and government targets, reporting on an annual basis, and make decisions about how finance is to be allocated to services in their area. Other initiatives in the remit of EYDCPs include Early Excellence Centres and Home Start.

The Early Excellence Centre programme is a government strategy for raising standards and integrating services. It plans to have 100 centres established by March 2004. There are currently 49 centres. These centres not only provide nursery care and education, but also parent education, training and other services required by families. It is anticipated that the centres will identify and disseminate successful and innovatory professional practice in integrated service delivery, act as exemplars of a range of models and organizational types of integrated service delivery, and provide an increasing range of education, care and family support services.

Home Start is an organization supported by the Department for Education and Skills and the Department of Health and is committed to promoting the welfare of families with at least one child under five years of age. Trained and committed volunteers from the local community offer regular support, friendship and practical help to young families under stress in their own homes, helping to prevent crisis and breakdown. The variety of difficulties faced by parents include loneliness, isolation, children's behavioural problems, depression, ill-health, multiple births, poverty, lone parenthood and bereavement. By supporting families at an early stage it is hoped that Home Start can prevent child abuse in all its forms. By means of the support provided, it is often possible to prevent the breakdown of relationships, as difficulties can be discussed and addressed.

The Home Start organization reports that families value the service provided, as they form firm friendships with their volunteers and know that they have someone who will listen and be there for them. Home Start volunteers, whose chief qualification is that they have parenting experience, are trained to provide a 'negotiated friendship' with families. It is valuable for families to have someone who will listen and offer support while being neutral – someone who does not judge. It is good to have someone who shows concern about the well-being of the family and provides a close and confiding relationship. Unlike many charities in the field of childcare, Home Start does not employ professional visitors.

You can see that there is a huge range of early years settings and government initiatives. Recently, researchers have started to try to identify which settings best support children's learning. The Effective Provision of Pre-School Education (EPPE: Institute of Education 2003) project is the first major study in the United Kingdom to focus specifically on the effectiveness of early years education. The EPPE project is a large-scale longitudinal study of the progress and development of 3,000 children in various types of preschool education. The study is exploring the characteristics of different kinds of early years provision and is examining children's development in preschool education, influences on their later adjustment and progress in infant school up to the National Assessment at age seven (end of Key Stage 1). It will help to identify the aspects of preschool provision that have a positive impact on children's attainment, progress and development and so provide guidance on good practice.

So far the project has reported on several aspects of provision. As part of the study, all preschools were assessed using observational assessment scales to examine provision in terms of factors such as space and furnishings, personal care routines, language and reasoning, activities (e.g. fine motor, art, blocks, dramatic play, etc.), staff–child and child–child interactions, programme structure (schedule, free play, group time, provision for children with disabilities) and provision for parents. It was found that nursery schools with a main focus on education, nursery schools combining care and education, and nursery classes were rated consistently good-to-excellent on these assessment scales. Local authority day care (social services) centres were rated as adequate-to-good provision. Private day nurseries were rated as minimal/adequate provision. Preschools/playgroups were consistently lower than all the other types of provision, although on the 'social interaction' dimension they approached the good range.

The EPPE project has shown that we are a long way from achieving universally good provision for all early years children. While government attention to the early years is welcome, it may be that there is a need for better coordination and fewer initiatives. The monitoring of the various settings is certainly problematic. OfSTED is perhaps not the most appropriate organization to carry this out in view of the ever growing range of commitments that it has, and the questions that have been raised about its objectivity and independence.

Activity

Carry out a survey of some parents. Find out what they prefer in terms of childcare and why.

REFERENCES

Bowlby, J. (1969) *Attachment and Loss: Vol. 1*. Harmondsworth: Penguin Books.

Institute of Education London University/Department for Education and Skills (DfES) (2003) *The Effective Provision of Pre-School Education (EPPE) Project.* Welcome [online]. Available at http://www.ioe.ac.uk/cdl/eppe/index.htm [accessed March 2003].

FURTHER READING

Abbott, L. and Moylett, H. (1997) *Training to Work in the Early Years – Developing the Climbing Frame*. Buckingham: Open University Press.

Drury, R., Millar, L. and Campbell, R. (eds) (2000) *Looking at Early Years Education and Care.* London: David Fulton Publishers.

Pugh, G. (2001) *Contemporary Issues in the Early Years: Working Collaboratively for Children.* London: Paul Chapman Publishing. These three books provide a deeper understanding of the issues surrounding the complexity of provision for early years care and education.

Department for Education and Skills website: http://www.dfes.gov.uk. Information provided by the government on provision of services for young children.

Chapter *Twenty*

The Role of the Early Years Practitioner

ÁINE SHARKEY

Simplistic ideas about the role of the early years worker are challenged. Four key features are used to describe this complex and demanding role: relationships, the learning environment, play and assessment.

When people in other occupations hear that you work with very young children they usually comment on your unending patience. To some extent this response gives us an indication of the public's perceptions of children and the professionals who work with them. Constant reference to patience could suggest that children are difficult to tolerate and that the professionals who work with them are placid. This is far from the case and part of your role as practitioner is to challenge this unhelpful attitude.

So how can we challenge these long-held views? Firstly, at an individual level, we must be more vocal and take the opportunity to explain the delights, demands and dilemmas that we face when working with young children. At a wider level we must also be more vocal in our fight for children's rights to high-quality early years education and care. This high quality is not only found in the buildings and resources provided, it is shown through the practitioner's knowledge, skills and understanding.

The *Curriculum Guidance for the Foundation Stage* (Qualifications and Curriculum Authority 2000: 1) defines early years practitioners as 'the adults who work with children . . . whatever their qualifications'. It recognizes the complexity of this role and identifies four key areas:

- Establishing relationships with children and their parents.
- Planning the learning environment and the curriculum.
- Supporting and extending children's play, learning and development.
- Assessing children's achievements and planning the next steps.

Establishing Relationships with Children and Their Parents

Think back to your favourite teacher at school. What is it about this teacher that you can remember? Whenever we ask this question, students usually comment on the teacher's manner and the way in which they as pupils were valued. What then can we take from this observation? One key point is the importance of good communication and interpersonal skills, so that positive relationships can be built with children, parents and colleagues. Working in an early years setting makes great demands on these skills.

All relationships are based on trust and the belief that we will be treated fairly and with respect. Our youngest children are entitled to this basic human right and it is our responsibility to make sure that we create a climate based on trust and security. Many early years settings have developed a system whereby each practitioner in the team works closely with a group of children and their families. This allows for better communication between setting and home and between practitioner and child. Gone are the days when parents were seen as having little or no role in their child's education and it has long been recognized that parents are children's first educators and that they have knowledge about their child that is unknown by anybody else. Therefore, to help us get to know each child's interests, needs and worries, we need to work in close partnership with parents. This means much more than communicating with parents on a formal basis once or twice a year. It means regular contact and a two-way sharing of information about the child. This will ease the transition from home to school and make the settling-in process much easier for all concerned. It will also ensure that we develop a better understanding of the child so that we can offer appropriate support and experiences.

Having built trust between home and setting we must then consider our practice within the setting, as this is crucial in creating a sense of security. It is important that the early years team should develop a consistent approach to early years education and care. For example, if one practitioner in the team encourages children's independence in art work while another encourages the use of templates, the children will get very mixed messages about what is expected and accepted. This might result in confusion and anxiety for the children. A consistent approach can only be brought about through discussion and the sharing of ideas about what is considered to be appropriate practice for young children. Once the team is in agreement about the teaching and learning process, then children will begin to feel more secure.

In this section you will have noted the constant reference to effective communication with children, parents and colleagues. The success of all our relationships lies in our ability to communicate with a diverse range of adults and children.

Planning the Learning Environment and the Curriculum

What do we mean by the term 'learning environment'? This is best defined as the way in which the resources, experiences and routines of the setting contribute to children's learning. For example, creating a Post Office in the role-play area give children the opportunity to work together to sort and deliver mail, sell s and give receipts. This in turn would enhance the development of children's so skills, as well as support learning in the areas of language, literacy and maths. addition to these specific resources and experiences the day-to-day routines also have a particular learning focus. For example, many settings have created a system of self-registration and this involves children finding their name card and locating it in a specified place in the nursery. At face value this may appear a mere ritual, but when we examine this further we see that children are learning to distinguish the features of print in order to recognize their name.

What then is the practitioner's role in planning the environment and the curriculum? The key aim for the practitioner is to provide the highest quality environment for every child. This means that activities and experiences need to be relevant to the needs and interests of the children. Learning at this stage is active and therefore we must provide opportunities for children to use all their senses to explore and learn. Play is a central part of the young child's world and as early years practitioners we need to exploit all opportunities to teach and learn through play. This should not suggest an ad hoc approach or an 'easy way out'. Planning for play requires as much rigour – if not more – as a more formal subject-based approach.

In the early years the child's self-image is shaped through their interaction with the environment and the responses they get from adults and other children. Therefore, in order to develop confidence and self-esteem, it is important that our planning builds on children's prior experiences. If we ignore children's needs and interests we cannot provide an appropriate curriculum; ultimately, this will damage children's confidence and self-esteem. If one of the aims of early years education is to foster in children a positive disposition to learning, then our emphasis must be on what children can do independently and what they can do with our support. This means that we need to have a good understanding of child development and a thorough knowledge of the individual children in the setting, as this will enable us to plan activities that are developmentally appropriate.

The *Curriculum Guidance for the Foundation Stage* identifies the six areas of learning and the stepping-stones which lead to the early learning goals. This is a key source of information for all early years practitioners and it is from this that teams develop their planning and their practice. One of the key roles of the early years team is to develop planning which meets the needs of the children, the needs of the setting and the requirements outlined in foundation stage documentation.

Supporting and Extending Children's Play, Learning and Development

Earlier in this chapter we talked about the importance of providing a stimulating environment to encourage children's learning. While this remains central to the

there is more to supporting learning than simply providing
ck!

rs or so, there has been a growing recognition of the
raction. If we consider that children learn to communicate
parents and carers then we can begin to appreciate the
and the role that the adult plays. When interacting
ult praises and reinforces the child's attempts at com-
bles the child to make links between words and ideas and to
use of language. The adult has an active role in interacting with
hape the communication and clarify the intended meaning. This import-
e continues beyond the home and into the early years phase. It is through
ensitive and timely interaction that children's play, learning and development can be supported and extended.

Many studies have revealed that the quality of children's play improved when there was some degree of adult participation. This was particularly noted in the role-play area; here, the interaction brought about greater involvement from the children: they became more engrossed in the play and 'soaked up' the new vocabulary that the adult had used in a meaningful context. Additional benefits were also evident in the children's developing social skills, with increasing use of verbal and non-verbal communication to negotiate and settle conflict. More recent work in this area has highlighted the power of adults 'thinking aloud' and encouraging children to offer suggestions and solve problems. The use of phrases such as 'I wonder what would happen if . . . ?' and 'How can we?' invites children to make links between cause and effect and generally encourages them to explain their thinking and extend their talk.

Interacting with children demands considerable skill and knowledge. To do this effectively we need to monitor ourselves and our own language use: we need to know when to listen, when to interact and how to interact. It is easy to fall into the trap of mainly asking closed questions (e.g. 'What colour is it?'). Such questions usually require a one or two word response and generally have a right or wrong answer. While the answer may tell us that the child can recognize a particular colour, there are other ways of finding this information and better ways of assessing it. For example, children's requests for specific toys or resources often reveal the extent of their knowledge about colours, shapes, sizes and numbers. Therefore, to extend children's play, learning and development we must make sure that the activities and experiences provided genuinely spark their curiosity and imagination. As children demonstrate their interest and their learning through action and commentary we must look and listen closely to their responses and then use the information to shape our planning and interaction.

Assessing Children's Achievements and Planning Their Next Steps

It is natural for people to reflect on their experiences and plan changes accordingly. We might glance at the weather before we leave for work and decide to wear different clothes, or after a holiday we may reflect on our diet and lifestyle and decide to change our habits and routines. From these general examples you can see that having made an assessment we often make some change to our future planning and action.

In all phases of education the principles of assessment are the same. The purpose of assessment is to help us support children's learning and to do this we need to have a good knowledge of the child. Many settings operate a home-visit scheme, where the practitioner visits the child and parents in their own home. Such arrangements are usually scheduled before the child attends the nursery setting and it is through this initial contact that we begin to develop our knowledge of the child. From this starting point and through working together we can begin to develop a profile of the child. This may include some of the child's drawings, their comments, or information about the child's likes, dislikes or fears. This shared information helps to ease the transition between home and school and allows us to plan appropriate experiences to support the child.

If we keep in mind that the key aim of all assessment is to help us support children's learning, we realize that this is an ongoing process and not something that is left until the end of a particular year or phase in the child's life. Observation is one of the most useful forms of assessment in the early years and it enables us to build a picture of the child's development across the different areas of learning and in different social contexts (e.g. playing in groups, playing alone, etc.). Observation allows us to focus on the 'how' as well as the 'what'. That is, 'how' the child approached the task (their interest, confidence, independence) and 'what' they achieved or found difficult. When this assessment information is shared with other practitioners in the team, future plans can be developed so that children's interests, strengths and needs are provided for. Remember, assessment is not used to label children. Its purpose is to help us provide appropriate experiences and learning activities to support each and every child.

By now you will have a better understanding of the complexity of the early years practitioner's role. You will have noticed in this chapter that the term 'patience' did not feature in any of the discussions. Many people in 'high-powered' jobs could benefit from the early years practitioner's understanding of human development, their organizational talents, communication and interpersonal skills, and ability to adapt to constant change.

Activity

Visit an early years setting and find out about the roles and responsibilities of different practitioners. Think about how these are shared by members of the team.

REFERENCES

Qualifications and Curriculum Authority (2000) *Curriculum Guidance for the Foundation Stage*. London: QCA/DfEE.

FURTHER READING

Early Years Educator. London: Mark Allen. A monthly publication for all those working with children from 0 to 5. It can be accessed via the following website: http://www.earlyyearseducator.co.uk.

Edgington, M. (1998) *The Nursery Teacher in Action: Teaching 3, 4 and 5 Year Olds.* London: Paul Chapman Publishing. Further discussion on the role of the early years practitioner.

Chapter *Twenty-one* National Curricula

NELL NAPIER AND ÁINE SHARKEY

The recent history of curriculum reform in England reflects the way that successive governments have taken more and more control of the education system. We describe the current national curricula and reflect on the different influences that have affected their development.

In 1987 the secretary of state for education published the 'consultation' papers for the original national curriculum. However, he chose not to publish the responses. In spite of the timing of the consultation – during the summer holidays – 20,000 responses were received. Julian Haviland collected some of these responses and highlighted that of the Campaign for the Advancement of State Education, which he says was representative:

> None of the documents makes any mention of the effects the proposed changes will have on present pupils of our schools, their teachers or on the role and responsibilities of headteachers. None draws on either experience or research to inform the ideas contained in them. There is a fundamental inconsistency in the proposals which is so blatant that we must look to the political philosophy which has generated them to find an explanation. (*Haviland 1988: 5*)

Until 1988 schools controlled the content of what was taught and the teaching methods, but the Education Reform Act 1988 introduced a national curriculum for the first time. Although adults were consulted on this first curriculum, children were not. In the light of many complaints about the national curriculum a review was ordered with the task of making the national curriculum smaller. In 1993, following a review, a second document was produced which seemed to do little to improve matters.

The national curriculum for 2000 (published in 1999) was written with a similarly inadequate consultation process. Although adults were consulted fairly widely, we could only find one document that made any mention of children's views on the changes.

The Qualifications and Curriculum Authority, the quango that was leading the national curriculum developments, invited the MORI organization to survey the opinions of five interested parties in relation to their views of the proposed national curriculum (MORI 1998). Twenty children were interviewed as part of one of five focus groups. Apart from the inadequate methods used in this survey, the final document also missed the opportunity to elicit children's views on some fundamental questions, such as: Do you want a national curriculum? Should the curriculum be dominated by maths, English, science and information technology? Is the literacy hour the best way to support learning needs? Do you think you should have statutory tests? Do you think it is right that you are expected to do more homework?

The National Curriculum

The national curriculum for England is underpinned by a series of aims. These are important because they are part of the bigger picture that policy makers sometimes lose sight of in their rush to create new initiatives and prescribe teaching methods. The first aim is as follows:

> The school curriculum should aim to provide opportunities for all pupils to learn and to achieve.

Following this there is a range of statements which outline what the curriculum should do for pupils – an example being to give them the opportunity to become 'creative and innovative' and contribute 'to the development of their sense of identity through knowledge and understanding of spiritual, moral, social and cultural heritages of Britain's diverse society and of the national, European, Commonwealth and global dimensions of their lives.'

The second aim:

> The school curriculum should aim to promote pupils' spiritual, moral, social and cultural development and prepare all pupils for the opportunities, responsibilities and experiences of life.

One of the more contentious ideas in relation to this aim is that of pupils as *consumers*: 'It should also equip pupils as consumers to make informed judgements and independent decisions and to understand their responsibilities and rights.'

There are four key stages in the English national curriculum:

- Key Stage 1 (Years R (Reception), 1 and 2: Age 5–7)
- Key Stage 2 (Years 3–6: Age 7–11)
- Key Stage 3 (Years 7–9: Age 11–14)
- Key Stage 4 (Years 10 and 11: Age 14–16)

The national curriculum is hierarchical in its emphasis on different subjects. There are three core subjects which are deemed to be the most important: English, maths and science. There are eight foundation subjects: design and technology, information and communication technology, history, geography, art and design, music, physical education, and a modern language (from 11 years old). From August 2002 citizenship became a statutory national curriculum foundation subject at Key Stages 3 and 4. Other areas which have a different status include religious education, sex education, and spiritual, moral, social and cultural development. Programmes of study set out what pupils should be taught in each subject at each key stage, and provide the basis for planning schemes of work.

The introduction of the national curriculum brought with it some new concepts which we will explain. The attainment targets set out the knowledge, skills and understanding which pupils of different abilities and maturities are expected to have by the end of each key stage. Attainment targets consist of eight level descriptions of increasing difficulty, plus a description for exceptional performance above level 8.

Each level description describes the types and range of performance that pupils working at that level should characteristically demonstrate. The level descriptions provide the basis for making judgements about pupils' performance at the end of Key Stages 1, 2 and 3. At Key Stage 4, national qualifications (such as GCSEs) are the main means of assessing attainment in national curriculum subjects.

Children are formally assessed (given specific tests and tasks which all children in state schools across the country must undertake) at the end of each key stage. The level descriptions are also used for teacher assessments, which are both informal during the year and statutory at the end of a key stage. There are also optional tests and tasks for teachers to use at the end of the school year if they wish.

If we go further than a basic description of the national curriculum we see that specifying the content of any curriculum is a highly complex and contentious issue. Golby (1989) suggested that notions of children's needs, views of teaching and learning, and the assessment process all influence the content of the curriculum. Difficult questions such as what aspects to include and what to leave out are not easily answered – nor are they always answered with widespread agreement.

Why should the content of the curriculum be such a complex and contentious issue? The answer lies in the fact that the school curriculum reflects a large number of interests: those of children, teachers, parents, employers and the wider community, and national government. All these groups would generally agree that the aim of education is to develop confident, happy, well-rounded children who are achieving their potential in all areas, but they differ on the way that this can be achieved.

Greater political control over the curriculum has resulted in some unwelcome developments. For example, certain areas of the curriculum are emphasized at the expense of others. In English primary schools this imbalance is evident in the increased attention given to the three Rs and the 'squeezing' of time for the arts, humanities and physical education. While we recognize the importance of literacy and numeracy, we would argue that children need a broad, balanced and stimulating curriculum.

Curriculum Guidance for the Foundation Stage

Some years after the implementation of the national curriculum there was a call for a further stage which would apply to preschool children. There were several reasons for this:

- Early years practitioners came under pressure to emphasize formal learning in order to prepare children for the national curriculum. This was of great concern to early years specialists who felt that a play-based and child-centred curriculum was very important.
- Government saw a greater need for more women to work in order to address poverty. This required more and better early years education and care.
- It was felt that good-quality preschool education would lead to better performance later in life.

A nationwide debate concluded that a foundation stage with curriculum guidance which clearly set out what preschool children (aged 3–5 years) should experience was necessary. The *Curriculum Guidance for the Foundation Stage* (FSG) is not a legal requirement, unlike the national curriculum; however, if preschool establishments want to receive government funding they must offer high-quality educational provision as measured by OfSTED inspections.

The FSG was published in May 2000. It superseded the previous *Desirable Outcomes* document but retained the notion of 'Early Learning Goals'. The FSG sets out principles for early years education and suggests goals that young children can be expected to have reached by the end of the foundation stage. The Early Learning Goals establish expectations that most children should have met by the end of the foundation stage, but they are not a curriculum in themselves. The FSG is organized into six areas of learning:

- Personal, social and emotional development
- Communication, language and literacy
- Mathematical development
- Knowledge and understanding of the world
- Physical development
- Creative development

Here the emphasis is on a more 'natural' curriculum, developed from the interests and needs of the children and largely play-based. However, there is little evidence of such a view of the child in today's primary curriculum, where the content and teaching approaches are heavily prescribed and children are expected to fit into a one-size-fits-all curriculum. The move towards more whole-class teaching in literacy and numeracy leaves very little time or 'space' for the individual child.

Assessing the Curriculum

You will remember that the national curriculum specifies the content of the school curriculum and the expected levels of children's attainment: it is against these levels that the children are formally assessed at age 7, 11 and 14. The issue of national testing is in itself fraught with difficulties over what is assessed, how it is assessed and what happens to the results of the assessments. It is the last of these questions that has had the most significant impact upon the educational climate in England. At ages 11 and 14 individual statutory assessment results are reported to parents and the school's overall results are published in league tables in the national press. This has put enormous pressure on children, teachers and schools. In an attempt to maintain or improve their position in the league tables many schools have (understandably) narrowed the curriculum and increased attention on those areas that are tested. Although national testing only takes place at age 7, 11 and 14, many schools also use optional tests for other year groups. So what we see is increased testing and concern with the measurement of children's performance. This has further restricted the breadth of the curriculum and brought enormous pressure on children and teachers.

The impact of assessment and the publication of school results has not only influenced the breadth of the curriculum. It has also brought a more formal model of practice throughout the primary school years. Early years practitioners have fought hard against this downward pressure. They campaigned that our youngest children had very distinct needs and that these needs would not be met through an over-formal approach. Thankfully, the early years voice was heard and in the year 2000 we saw the creation of the Foundation Stage for children aged 3–5. This gave recognition to the very distinct needs of our youngest children and protected them from some of the external or top-down pressures that permeated the primary school curriculum.

Perhaps the success of the early years campaign should act as a wake-up call for those of us in all phases of education. It is now time for us to refocus on what is important: the child and the learning process. Formal assessment has dominated the curriculum for too long; it is now time that it returned to its role as the servant rather than the master of the curriculum.

Activity

Discuss your experience at nursery or primary school with a partner. Think about the subjects that you enjoyed; the subjects that were neglected; the amount of choice that you had; the organization of the classroom; the styles of the different teachers.

UNIVERSITY OF WINCHESTER
LIBRARY

REFERENCES

Golby, M. (1989) Curriculum traditions. In B. Moon, P. Murphy and J. Raynor (eds) *Policies for the Curriculum*. London: Hodder and Stoughton.

Haviland, J. (1988) *Take Care, Mr Baker!* London: Fourth Estate.

MORI (1998) *Attitudes Towards the Aims and Purpose of the National Curriculum*. London: QCA.

FURTHER READING

Anning, A. (1995) *A National Curriculum for the Early Years*. Buckingham: Open University Press.

Anning, A. (1998) Appropriateness or effectiveness in the early childhood curriculum in the UK: Some research evidence. *Journal of Early Years Education*, Vol. 6 (3): 299–314. Includes a child-centred view of what is an appropriate curriculum for young children.

Bleinkin, G. M. and Kelly, A. V. (eds) (1996) *Early Childhood Education: A Developmental Curriculum*. London: Paul Chapman. This and Anning (1995) put forward views on an appropriate curriculum for young children.

Curriculum Guidance for the Foundation Stage website: http://www.qca.org.uk/ca/foundation/guidance/curr_guidance.asp.

National Curriculum website: http://www.nc.uk.net/home.html.

Pollard, A., Broadfoot, P., Croll, P., Osborn, M. and Abbot, D. (1994) *Changing English Primary Schools? The Impact of the Education Reform Act at Key Stage One*. London: Cassell. This book reviews the changes in the curriculum following the Act and looks at its impact five years after implementation. It will help you to adopt a critical attitude to what you read about and see in schools.

Chapter *Twenty-two*

Play

NELL NAPIER AND ÁINE SHARKEY

The importance of play is recognized in the United Nations Convention on the Rights of the Child. The Convention acknowledges 'the rights of the child to rest and to leisure, and to engage in play and recreational activities'. This chapter examines the important contribution that play offers all children and considers how we can improve the quality of play in the early years.

What are your memories of play in childhood? What images come to mind? Generally, regardless of the type of play, you will find that there are some common features. Much of the play will have been child-initiated, which means that you created play themes independently by choosing available resources or toys. You may also have found that play was influenced by stories, television, real life experiences and your interaction with siblings. Perhaps your play involved re-enacting some theme or idea you had experienced or imagined.

What can we take from our childhood memories of play to build into our work with children? The key things are that play can be engaged in without fear of failure and has its own purpose and pleasure. It does not necessarily involve expensive toys or equipment, but children do need access to resources that can be used flexibly and imaginatively (CHAPTER 31).

Children's play follows a general developmental pattern and progresses through the following stages: solitary, parallel and cooperative. In solitary play the child is fully engaged with the object or action and is almost unaware of the presence of other adults or children. In parallel play the child plays alongside others; they may observe other children and imitate their actions, but there is limited involvement with other children. As children's language develops and they become more able to express themselves their play becomes more social and more cooperative. This in turn provides even greater opportunities for children to interact and learn from each other.

The power of play has long been recognized. It is through play that children explore materials, objects and their uses. Jean Piaget noted that children's development is evident in their play and in the ways in which they use objects. For example, a toddler may investigate their reflection in a metal spoon, or they may explore the sound the spoon makes when hit against different surfaces. Once the object has been explored the child may then go on to 'feed' a doll and later the spoon may be used as a 'microphone' for the child to sing into. Piaget describes this playful use of objects as being important in laying the groundwork for children to use the more abstract symbols of letters and numbers. Piaget's work has been developed further by Hutt et al. (1989), who suggested that before children can 'play' with objects they need first to have had opportunities to explore the toy or object. Hutt's play model is highly influential today and it has an important message: children need opportunities to explore materials and objects before they can be expected to use these creatively or conventionally. Without opportunities to explore, the child has a limited knowledge of the materials, their properties and the possibilities of use. Exploration allows children to develop their knowledge, skills and understanding. When these are in place children can then progress to more creative or conventional responses. Practitioners who work with young children need to be mindful of this important process and avoid the tendency to 'hurry' children into more formal activities.

Social Interaction in Children's Play

You will have noted the similarities between Piaget and Hutt's views of exploratory play. It was in the area of social interaction that their views differed. Piaget tended to see the child as a lone agent in the environment, whereas Hutt recognized that the child is a social being and is part of the culture of the family, community and educational setting. Hutt identified with the earlier work of Vygotsky and Bruner and valued the importance of social interaction in shaping children's learning. Through interacting with an adult or a more experienced peer, the younger child's learning is supported and scaffolded. This supported interaction aids the child's learning.

More recent research into adult involvement in children's play has shown that it enhances the complexity of the play and contributes to children's linguistic, social and intellectual development. This has been particularly noted in the area of socio-dramatic play, where adult interaction is seen to develop children's play by adding an extra dimension or situation that needed their cooperation and action. For example, in the role-play area this may involve dealing with an incident in the 'café' or responding to an emergency situation in the 'hospital'. In any context that involves socio-dramatic play, children have to negotiate roles, responsibilities and possible courses of action. This demands considerable social and linguistic skills. If conflict occurs the adult can also help children to listen to the views of others and articulate their own feelings. This form of play tutoring introduces children to the language of compromise, which helps in the development of social skills.

Despite the well-documented benefits of adult involvement in children's play, sensitive interaction is a difficult skill to develop. Some people resort to an inappropriate amount of knowledge teaching (for example, a heavy emphasis on teaching colours, or the time, or counting to five). These things can be taught and certainly need to be learned, but there is a need to find the right balance between different styles of interaction. As far as colours are concerned, provided that the activities of the early years setting encourage the exploration of a range of colours in a range of activities, and the adults use the names of colours where necessary, then children will naturally learn them. Sometimes it is helpful to keep in mind the SOUL acronym: 'silence and observation' can enable us to 'understand' more about children's 'learning'.

Improving the Quality of Play

From the early 1980s onwards a number of important studies have examined the quality of children's play in early years settings [CHAPTER 19] (Sylva, Roy and Painter 1980; Bennett, Wood and Rogers 1997). Three of the key recommendations were as follows. Firstly, practitioners were urged to raise the status of play by abandoning the unhelpful terminology of 'play versus work'. Such a distinction was felt to trivialize the importance of play and only appeared to value more formal written tasks. From this research we learned about the need to seize opportunities to teach through play: if we value learning through play, then surely we need to teach through play. The second point raised by the research was the importance of planning carefully for play and having clear objectives about the learning intentions of each activity. This planning should not be seen as a straitjacket, but should identify the learning potential of the routines, resources, equipment and opportunities available in the early years environment. The *Curriculum Guidance for the Foundation Stage* (FSG) (QCA 2000; CHAPTER 21), issued to support teaching and learning in the early years, adds that planning should identify opportunities for both child-initiated and adult-directed play. The third recommendation urged practitioners to consider a number of strategies to promote more extended interactions with children. In some settings this has resulted in significant reorganization of work patterns and organizational routines. You will often find that a key worker is assigned to liaise closely with particular children and their families. This organizational feature enables the practitioner to interact more fully with children and their families and it assists in the identification of needs, which supports planning.

The FSG stresses the importance of providing stimulating indoor and outdoor play environments. While the indoor area has been well resourced and organized for play, the potential offered by the outdoor environment has, until recently, been largely ignored. Often this was because of the limitations of school sites, but geographical and physical constraints were not the only factors restricting the outdoor environment. Practitioners also failed to capitalize on this valuable resource; despite the wonderful work of Susan Isaacs in the 1930s, it is only recently that we have begun to appreciate the wider contribution that the outdoors can offer children. Previously there was a general assumption that the outdoors was a place for children to 'let off steam' and be physically active, whereas now we realize that outdoor play greatly contributes to children's development in all areas. For example, children can make first-hand observations about the changes in nature that they see all around them and this encourages them to ask questions and develop explanations. With space to play outdoors children develop the language of mathematics; for example, counting as they ascend the steps on the climbing frame; comparing heights, distance, shape, speed, etc. These examples show that in addition to developing children's physical skills, outdoor play also contributes to language, maths, science and many other areas of the curriculum.

Play makes a vital contribution to children's learning and development. The quality of adults' interaction with children and the organizational features of early years settings are part of this contribution. Play helps with the development of children's minds, but it must also be valued for the contribution it makes to promoting children's physical and emotional health.

Activity

Observe children playing in the outdoor area of your school or early years setting. Identify how the environment is organized and resourced to provide opportunities for a variety of play activities. Consider what type of play seems to occur most frequently and how the resources available promote or restrict children's play.

REFERENCES

Bennett, N., Wood, L. and Rogers, S. (1997) *Teaching Through Play – Teachers' Thinking and Classroom Practice*. Buckingham: Open University Press.

Hutt, S. J., Tyler, C., Hutt, C. and Christopherson, H. (1989) *Play Exploration and Learning*. London: Routledge.

Qualifications and Curriculum Authority (QCA) (2000) *Curriculum Guidance for the Foundation Stage*. London: QCA.

Sylva, K., Roy, C. and Painter, M. (1980) *Childwatching at Playgroup and Nursery School*. London: Grant McIntyre.

FURTHER READING

Bilton, H. (1998) *Outdoor Play in the Early Years*. London: David Fulton.

Bruce, T. (1996) *Helping Young Children To Play*. London: Hodder and Stoughton.

Hall, N. and Abbott, L. (1996) *Play in the Primary Curriculum*. London: Hodder and Stoughton.

Moyles, J. (ed.) (1994) *The Excellence of Play*. Buckingham: Open University Press.

These writers have a long track record in thinking about the value of play in education. Reading these books will offer you further insight into the issues of play and indications of good practice. National Children's Bureau website: http://www.ncb.org.uk.

Chapter *Twenty-three* International Perspectives in Early Years Education and Care

ÁINE SHARKEY

The rationale for high-quality provision is considered by examining aspects of early childhood services in Denmark, the US and Italy. In a chapter of this size it is impossible to do justice to each country, so we can only scratch the surface and identify some of their unique features. In focusing on Denmark we consider its wealth of social policies for families and the extensive provision of state-funded childcare. In looking at the US we refer to significant research carried out in a number of states which illustrates the benefits of early childhood provision. Finally, we introduce you to Reggio Emilia in Italy, which is world famous for its innovative approach to **early childhood education and care**. We conclude by outlining what we have learned from these international comparisons and the contribution this has made to our own developing services.

Early years provision in the UK has been described as resembling a patchwork quilt, with each patch representing a different category of provision: nursery schools, nursery classes, early years centres, day nurseries, work-based crèches, playgroups and childminders. Our youngest children are educated and cared for in a variety of settings and each of these settings has its own unique features (CHAPTER 19). Such variety of provision means that in most cases parents have to rely on a combination of nursery, childminders and the extended family in the day-to-day care of their youngest children. Clearly, this puts considerable strain on both parents and children. Therefore, the image of a patchwork quilt is particularly apt: it is only when the patches are 'sewn together' that the needs of children and parents can be met.

However, not all families in the UK have the opportunity to participate in this range of early years provision. The lack of state funding for children aged 0–3 means that parents have to meet the majority of the costs for the education and care of their young children. Access is influenced more by economic factors and personal finance than by the needs of children and families. In the past this situation meant that parents on low incomes or who were unemployed were unable to access preschool provision for their youngest children. This discriminatory situation has been publicized for over twenty years and it is only in the last few years that the government has funded initiatives to bring about wider participation in early years services. Initiatives such as the Childcare Tax Credit and the National Childcare Strategy aim to widen access and reduce the financial burden of childcare for low-income families. DES statistics show that during 2000–1 approximately one and a half million families were helped by these schemes. Further initiatives such as the Sure Start programme have been set up in disadvantaged communities. These programmes offer support to parents and children and aim to break the cycle of generational underachievement. Although welcome, many of these initiatives are of a short-term nature and the difficulty with such measures is that they tend to patch together a mix of projects. They do not provide a systematic, long-term plan for children and families in the twenty-first century.

The UK is out of step with most of its European neighbours. It differs not only in terms of the lack of state funding for preschool provision, but also one of the most significant differences is the comparatively young age at which children begin primary education. In most of Europe children begin full-time schooling when they are six or seven years old, but here children start primary school in the year of their fifth birthday. This means that children who have just turned four may be in full-time primary education. If we investigate how this situation has arisen, we find that the reasons are economic rather than educational. The falling birth rate from the 1960s onwards brought about a surplus in school places. In order to 'balance the books', four-year-old children were actively encouraged into full-time primary education. For many cash-strapped local educational authorities, having four-year-olds in mainstream schools was considered 'better value' than providing nursery education with specialist facilities and high adult–child ratios. If we go back as far as the 1940s, which was a time of significant nursery expansion, we see that political and economic factors were key influences in shaping this development. During this period the war effort demanded that women join the workforce and play their part. Therefore, to accommodate this change in employment patterns, there was considerable development in state-funded nursery education. So, once again, we see the needs of the economy dictating the opportunities offered to our youngest children. It was only in the last decades of the twentieth century that serious questions were asked about what was appropriate for children and their families.

For many years national and international reports have been critical of the patchy and fragmented early years provision in the UK. It has only been in the last few years that attempts were made to develop more child- and family-friendly policies. Comparative reports from the Organization for Economic Development (OECD) and the wealth of international research in the field has forced us to examine the status we give to early years education and care. This examination has not been a happy experience. We have belatedly realized that although improvements have been made in the last few years, there is still considerable scope for developing all aspects of our policy and practice.

Denmark: Policy and Provision of Early Childhood Services

Denmark has a long-established and well-respected tradition for providing high-quality **early childhood services**. This has been built up over a considerable period and is based on the view that it is the government's responsibility to create the best social frameworks to allow families to provide the best possible conditions for their children. This has led to the creation of a National Committee for Children, which oversees the integration of legislation and services across the fields of health, social services, education and employment. At grassroots level we see how this approach supports parents in their entitlement to subsidized maternity and parental leave (26–30 weeks). This protected time for parents and children helps to balance the demands of family life, while also leading to a greater sense of security in terms of employment. In contrast, it is worth noting that although improvements have been made to leave arrangements in the UK, they are still a far cry from that provided in Denmark. In fact, the changes only bring us in line with the lowest standards recommended by the European Union.

The most striking thing that we learn from Denmark is the extent of state-funded preschool provision. Statistics from the European Union and the OECD reveal that in Denmark 45 per cent of children aged 0–3 are in funded day care services, whereas in the UK the figure is only 2 per cent. When we look at children aged 3–6 the figures are 82 per cent and 60 per cent, respectively (though the UK figure is inflated by the inclusion of children in primary school). The Danish provision forms part of an integrated approach to improving the living conditions of children and their families. It is recognized that if parents are to play an active part in the economic and social fabric of the country, then the government needs to provide appropriate childcare. The success of the Danish policy is evident in that approximately 90 per cent of women with children are in employment – these are some of the highest figures in Europe. So, in contrast to the situation in the UK, we see a greater understanding of the needs of children and parents and a commitment to investment in publicly funded childcare services. This model of integrated services makes Denmark a truly inclusive society.

Beyond the levels of policy and their impact on preschool provision, we have learned much from the early years research carried out in the United States.

USA: The Impact of Early Years Education and Care

The United States differs from Denmark in that there is no universal early years provision across all states. Nevertheless, it is here that we must look to find the main body of longitudinal research on early years education and care. It is as a result of this research that we now have a greater understanding of the impact of high-quality preschool provision on the lives of children, their families and the wider society. In the short term, links have been identified with high-quality provision and children's participation in school and their subsequent educational attainment, though this has varied across studies and in some cases early intellectual gains were not sustained throughout the later years of schooling. However, all studies are agreed that the most positive effect of early years provision is the contribution it makes to the development of children's self-esteem and confidence. A further benefit that is universally acknowledged is the opportunity preschool provision provides for the early identification and support of children with special needs. This early intervention has been shown to be highly effective in preventing later educational failure.

The benefits of high-quality preschool provision are not only limited to the years of schooling, as the research has identified longer-lasting benefits such as links with long-term employment and social inclusion. So, if we look beyond the child, not only are there advantages to the educational and social welfare systems, but also there are significant benefits to the economy. In terms of cost-effectiveness, it is estimated that for every dollar invested in preschool education, at least seven dollars is returned to society. This has been calculated on the basis of the reduced need for special education, income support and unemployment benefit. It seems a shame that we should have to justify the case for early years education and care mainly on the basis of finance but, as you will have seen throughout this chapter, lack of state funding has limited the provision in the UK. Clearly, we cannot 'afford' to neglect investment in early years education and care.

Moving on from the global benefits of high-quality early years provision, we now turn our attention to the region of Italy renowned for its innovative approach to early years education and care.

Italy: Reggio Emilia

Italy, like the US, does not have a nationwide approach to early years education and care. Childhood services vary according to the region and it is Reggio Emilia, an area in the north of the country, that is recognized on the world stage for its high-quality nursery provision.

The Reggio Emilia philosophy and approach have their roots in Italian history and culture; they cannot simply be copied or transplanted to any context. For example, if we conjure up an image of Italian life, we generally have a picture of an extended family gathered around a table enjoying food and conversation. This sense of community is at the heart of the Reggio approach. Children's interactions with each other and with adults are highly valued. In a culture where food and family are celebrated, these cultural practices are promoted through nursery routines in which staff and children prepare and share meals together. This helps children to see familiarity in new or 'strange' environments. Such an approach shows real understanding of the learning potential of everyday events. As key players in the nursery community, parents make a vital contribution to their children's education. They provide nursery staff with information about their children: without this, practitioners would be unable to 'teach to the rhythm of the child'. This wonderful phrase shows that it is the children, rather than the curriculum or the timetable, that is truly at the heart of the Reggio Emilia experience.

In Reggio Emilia children are seen as having huge potential for expressing themselves in many different 'languages'. This does not only refer to oral language, but also to children's ability to express themselves through the languages of drawing, painting, sculpture, music and movement. One of the founders of the Reggio nurseries argues that children naturally have a hundred languages, but that society 'steals' ninety-nine of them by only valuing and promoting the more conventional and formal modes of expression (e.g. literacy). Therefore, to give children 'full voice', the arts have a high status in Reggio Emilia. Each nursery has a resident artist who works with the children, designing and creating beautiful artefacts. This provides a tremendous opportunity for long-term projects and in-depth responses.

The influence of the arts and architecture can also be seen in the design of the region's nurseries. Here the environment is seen as vital in stimulating children's learning and development. The buildings are aesthetically pleasing and the child's-eye view has been considered in the design, with the use of glass and light allowing the outside environment to come into the nursery. It is interesting to note that the term 'aesthetic' usually refers to beauty, but here it also refers to a sense of well-being. An attractive, well-organized environment designed specifically for children will undoubtedly influence children's comfort, confidence and self-esteem. Such purpose-built facilities are a far cry from some of the inappropriate buildings that serve as playgroups and nurseries in many parts of the UK. Thankfully, the UK government has learned from this poor comparison and is now committed to greater investment in designing and building appropriate indoor and outdoor environments for young children.

International research has sown the seeds for significant change in the way we think about early education and care. It has forced us to look at policy and practice in other countries and in turn to question our own practice and demand improvements. One of the key developments in the last couple of years has been greater coordination between health, education and social services at both practical and policy levels. The concept of 'educare' is now firmly established and there is a greater recognition that education cannot be separated from care, nor can care be separated from education. Both are vital for children and their families. Across the country the number of integrated centres is rapidly expanding and in these settings staff from a variety of disciplines work together with children and their parents. This 'one-stop' service aims to widen participation by making access to services more family friendly.

In the UK over the last few years there has been considerable expansion and development in early years provision for children aged 3–5. Alongside this there has been increased training and professional development opportunities for all early years practitioners, regardless of their status or setting. The result has been that there is now greater agreement about the developmental needs of young children and a greater willingness to fight for the rights of our youngest children. Plans are afoot to expand provision for the under-3s: while this is a positive step, we know that it will be a very long journey.

Activity

Talk to some parents and explore the range of childcare services that they use. Consider what factors influenced their choices.

FURTHER READING

Anning, A. (1991) *The First Years at School: Education 4–8*. Buckingham: Open University Press. Gives further information on the background to early years education and care in the UK.

OECD website: http://www.oecd.org. More information comparing international provision.

Penn, H. (1997) *Comparing Nurseries: Staff and Children in Italy, Spain and the UK*. London: Paul Chapman Publishing. An analysis of early years educare in other countries.

Health

Chapter *Twenty-four* Overview of Health

ROBERT BANTON

The complexities of defining health and illness are addressed. Current improvements are shown by reflecting on changes to health throughout history. The main causes of death in children and the factors which can influence health are described and the chapter concludes with a brief summary of the main features of the Sure Start initiative.

Most health professionals now agree that being healthy is not just about the absence of illness, but it is virtually impossible to find a satisfactory definition that we all agree on. As for the question of how we measure health, the short answer is that we don't. What we do is measure the rate of ill-health and death in a population. The assumption is that where mortality (death) and morbidity (illness) rates are low, the population is generally healthy, and vice versa.

Mortality data are routinely collected with reasonable accuracy, usually from death certificates. However, mortality data measure only the most extreme form of ill-health; in childhood, other than the newborn period, death is uncommon. Furthermore, mortality statistics do not measure pain, discomfort or handicap and consequent loss of potential for health. In essence, mortality data only measure the total breakdown of health and do not capture the quality of a person's experience of health. Less than 0.1 per cent of the child population dies each year, whereas it has been estimated that up to 3 per cent of children have a significant disability, i.e. a condition that limits normal activity.

The child health services are geared towards preventing illness, but the difficulty is that data about this are not routinely collected; when they are collected, they may be difficult to interpret because of variations in the use of criteria. Death is easy to count, illness less so. Illness is usually counted by the number of patients who consult their general practitioner, or go to a hospital for treatment. More recently the government has used data from the number of calls to the telephone health service, NHS Direct. However, there are problems with this. For instance, not all parents will consult a doctor when their child is ill. They may care for the child at home, or get advice from friends and relatives, or use complementary therapies, none of which are counted. If they do go to the doctor, the illness may be misdiagnosed or missed altogether and so not counted. There may be errors in reporting the number of consultations or data may be entered incorrectly. All of this means that morbidity data are always a little suspect. However, given all of the problems mentioned above, when you examine the mortality and morbidity data for children and young people, there are some positive developments.

If you were to ask most people whether children are healthier today than in the past, probably nearly all would agree that they are. Think about the very small number of children who die in childbirth or during infancy. Look at the range of treatments that are available and the professionals who keep children alive and well. There can be no doubt that children's health has improved dramatically. A look at the past shows some of the reasons for this.

Health in the Past

During the early part of the nineteenth century 1 in 10 infants did not reach their first birthday. Among the poorest members of society the death rate was higher still, with as many as 1 in 5 children dying in their first year. Causes of death were mainly due to infectious diseases. Epidemics of childhood diseases such as measles, scarlet fever and whooping cough ravaged the young and claimed many lives. Figures given to the Royal Commission in 1844 show that only 45 per cent of children born into poorer families would reach their fifth birthday. This is in comparison to children born to the gentry, where 82 per cent of children reached their fifth birthday (Waddington 1989).

The physical environment affects health in a variety of ways. For example, poor air quality can cause respiratory disease; the environment at home or work can be the cause of injury; poor road and vehicle design has a substantial impact on road traffic accidents; poor housing conditions, with overcrowding, increase the likelihood of infectious disease, violence and mental health problems; poor food can cause a wide range of short-term and long-term illnesses. Poverty and poor housing with limited sanitation and overcrowding were major factors in children's poor health. The many cases of cholera and the problems with providing a good water supply to the growing cities acted as a spur to wide-ranging environmental reform through the Public Health Act 1848. The **public health** movement last century concentrated on environmental change to reduce epidemics of disease.

At the end of the nineteenth century politicians began to realize the full extent of the problem when 60 per cent of army recruits for the Boer War (1899–1902) were rejected due to physical defects and general poor health. The period between 1904 and 1910 saw a plethora of government reports into the health of the population, especially children. During this time many important pieces of legislation were enacted that had positive effects upon the health of children. There was legislation to provide free school meals to deprived children, local authorities were compelled to carry out school medical examinations, and the school leaving age was raised to 14 years from 13. Health professionals were also beginning to be better regulated. The 1902 Midwives Act required midwives to be properly trained and registered: by 1910, those who were not registered were no longer allowed to attend women in labour. In 1907 the Notification of Births Act made it the responsibility of parents to register the birth of a new baby; in 1915 this was made compulsory. Registration gave the local authority the information needed so that health visitors could identify whom they had to work with in order to provide information and advice concerning childrearing, general health and hygiene.

Between 1900 and 1935 advances in medical treatments also contributed to reductions in death rates from infection. These included **antitoxin** in diphtheria, surgery in appendicitis, peritonitis and ear infections, immunization against tetanus and improved obstetric care. One of the main areas of debate has been whether environmental improvements or medical improvements were the main reason for improved health. According to Thomas McKeown:

> in order of importance the major contributions to improvements in health in England and Wales were from limitation of family size, increase in food supplies and a healthier physical environment and specific preventive and therapeutic measures. (*McKeown 1976: 36*)

McKeown concluded that the high death rates of the past were due to infectious diseases and nutritional and other environmental factors. Between 80 and 90 per cent of the reductions in all the early deaths were the results of beating infections. From the second half of the nineteenth century the reduction in the exposure to infections was a result of their reduced prevalence and improved hygiene, i.e. higher standards of food, water and sanitation (Ashton and Seymour 1988). With the exception of vaccination against smallpox, which was associated with less than 2 per cent of the decline in the death rate from 1848 to 1871, it is unlikely that immunization or medical treatment had a significant effect on mortality from infectious diseases before the twentieth century. In particular, most of the reduction in mortality from TB, bronchitis and influenza, whooping cough and food- and water-borne diseases had already occurred before effective immunizations or treatment were available. The largest factors in the reduction of conditions relating to premature and immature birth were better maternal nutrition (thereby reducing the incidence of premature birth), better birth control and the legalization of abortion. Better planning of pregnancy enabled mothers to recover from one birth before becoming pregnant again, which meant that babies could be breastfed for longer, which increased protection against infections.

Death rates for children fell dramatically during the twentieth century. Today, mortality rates for children are comparatively low. The infant mortality rate in the United Kingdom in 2001 was 5.5. This means that 5.5 infants died for every 1,000 live births. There were 3,159 stillbirths in England and Wales in 2001 and 1,600 deaths at ages under seven days. The perinatal mortality rate (deaths between

24 weeks of gestation and 7 days following birth) was 8.0 per thousand live and stillbirths. Fewer babies are dying during those vulnerable early days and weeks. Males born during the year 2000 on average could expect to live to age 75 and females could expect even better by living up to 80 years.

Main Causes of Death in Young Children

When we look at the causes of death in childhood we also see marked changes. As we explained above, the majority of deaths in the last century were due to infectious diseases. Today, the pattern has changed. In England and Wales in 1998–2000, cancers were the most common cause of death among girls aged 5–15, and accounted for 23 per cent of the total deaths in this group. Accidents were the second most common cause of death, representing 17 per cent of the total.

For boys of the same age, accidents were the most common cause of death, accounting for 27 per cent of the total. Most of the deaths were caused by transport accidents, accounting for 61 per cent of accidental deaths among boys and 73 per cent among girls. It was the second most common cause among 5–15-year-old boys: 24 per cent of the total (National Statistics Office 2002).

The Department of Health's statistics show that the number of children killed on Britain's roads fell in the 20 years to 2000. In 2000, 191 children were killed, 30 fewer than in the previous year. In the early 1980s the average was around 560 deaths a year. Most children killed or seriously injured are pedestrians rather than car passengers or cyclists. A child's risk of being involved in a traffic accident increases as they grow older, with a marked increase in accident rates among 10–13-year-olds. Young people aged under 16 are less likely to be involved in traffic accidents than older people, with a casualty rate of 45 per 100,000 population, compared with 78 per 100,000 for those aged 16 and over in 2000. In 1999 the UK's record on road safety was good in comparison with other countries: the death rate for children aged under 15 was 1.9 per 100,000 population, compared with an EU rate of 2.6.

Factors Influencing Health

Despite the improving health data, much remains to be accomplished if we are to continue the reductions in child death and illness. In order to do this we need to investigate the causes of ill-health and, more specifically, ask the question: what factors influence our health?

The national infrastructure that contributes to better health includes systems for the distribution of safe drinking water, safe food, shelter and the absence of war. In countries where this is not the case the population's health suffers drastically and very quickly. Local factors in the environment in which people live are also important determinants of their health. These include housing, quality of air, road safety and less directly, knowledge about the kind of lifestyles that contribute to good health.

At the level of the individual there are certain well-known genetic disorders such as cystic fibrosis, haemophilia and **Huntington's chorea**, which are caused by a single gene disorder. But in general, genetic factors are seen as contributing to an individual's *risk* of disease, rather than resulting in that disease with certainty. Genetic factors interact with social and environmental factors to influence health and disease. A particular area of current research interest is the relationship between genes and behaviour. Studies of twins separated at birth show that schizophrenia occurs in twins much more than one would expect from chance. The same is true for alcohol problems and depression. There are even suggestions that smoking and eating habits have a genetic predisposition.

Changing behaviour is the area where most of the current attempts to improve health are aimed. If we look at the health behaviour of young people in three areas – smoking, alcohol and drugs – we see the following:

- In England in 2001 a quarter of young people aged between 11and 15 had reported drinking alcohol in the past week. The number of units drunk has doubled in the past decade, with boys drinking more than girls.
- When we look at smoking in 2001, the figures are more encouraging. Smoking seems to have dropped from 13 per cent to 10 per cent of young people aged between 11 and 15 years old. However, girls are more likely to smoke than boys of the same age. The prevalence of smoking increases with age, with 22 per cent of 15-year-olds smoking. Figures for 2000 showed that children were more likely to smoke if their parents or siblings smoked.
- A fifth of 11–15-year-olds had taken illegal drugs in the previous year. Cannabis was the most commonly used drug, taken by 13 per cent of those surveyed.

As well as these individual factors, a person's health is strongly affected by factors such as income, social class, employment, family background, education and social networks. The particularly damaging effect of poverty is something that government has attempted to tackle in a recent initiative called Sure Start.

An Example of a Current Health Initiative

Sure Start aims to improve the health and well-being of families and children before and from birth, so that children are ready to flourish when they go to school. It does this by setting up local Sure Start programmes to improve services for families with children under four.

Sure Start aims to work with parents-to-be, parents and children to promote the physical, intellectual and social development of babies and young children – particularly those who are disadvantaged – so that they can flourish at home and when they get to school, and thereby break the cycle of disadvantage for the current generation of young children. Local programmes will work with parents and parents-to-be to improve children's life chances through better access to family support, advice on nurturing, health services and early learning.

Sure Start is hailed as the cornerstone of the government's drive to tackle child poverty and social exclusion. By 2004 there will be at least 500 Sure Start local programmes. They will be concentrated in neighbourhoods where a high proportion of children are living in poverty and where Sure Start can help them succeed by pioneering new ways of working to improve services. As with nearly all government strategies nowadays, Sure Start has a set of objectives and targets to meet in attempting to achieve its aim. One of these specifically relates to health:

> *Objective 2: Improving health*
> In particular, by supporting parents in caring for their children to promote healthy development before and after birth.
>
> *Target*
> To achieve by 2004 in the 500 Sure Start areas, a 10 per cent reduction in mothers who smoke in pregnancy.
>
> *Delivery targets*
> Parenting support and information to be available for all parents in Sure Start areas. All local programmes to give guidance on breast feeding, hygiene and safety. A 10 per cent reduction in children in the Sure Start area aged 0–3 admitted to hospital as an emergency with gastro-enteritis, a respiratory infection or a severe injury.
>
> *Core services and key principles*
> The design and content of local Sure Start programmes will vary according to local needs. But we expect all programmes to include a number of core services: outreach and home visiting support for families and parents, support for good-quality play, learning and childcare experiences for children, primary and community healthcare, including advice about family health and child health, and development support for children and parents with special needs, including help getting access to specialized services.
>
> *Key principles*
> To ensure a consistent approach, it is expected that every programme will work from a shared set of key principles. Sure Start services must coordinate, streamline and add value to existing services in the Sure Start area. Key to improving health is the involvement of parents, grandparents and other carers in ways that build on their existing strengths. Thus it is important to promote the participation of all local families in the design and working of the programme. Services should be provided so as to avoid stigma by ensuring that all local families are able to use Sure Start services. Sure Start is aimed at young children but must also ensure lasting support by linking to services for older children. Services must be culturally appropriate and sensitive to particular needs. (*Sure Start 2002*)

According to Glass (1999) Sure Start represents a new approach to both policy and delivery of services. The programme represents 'joined up' thinking. It is accepted that the influences upon health are wider than just those acted upon by the medical profession. Therefore organizations, government departments and professions must work together to act on the determinants of health. Additionally, professionals must work together with families in partnership to achieve health gains. Since Sure Start programmes have only been in existence since the late 1990s, it is too early to judge their effectiveness.

The Sure Start initiative includes the recognition that health can be improved by positive social circumstances. Being part of a 'social network' of family, friends and/or people within a community helps people to feel valued and cared for; evidence suggests that close contacts, some which include confiding relationships, are another important factor in healthier lives. Poor social and economic circumstances, combined with difficult family relationships, can adversely affect children's health and the impact will continue into adulthood.

> *Activity*
>
> Think about two children that you know quite well; if possible, children who have different levels of health. Use the factors that we have identified in this chapter to make a list for each child which shows things that might contribute to their health.

REFERENCES

Ashton, J. and Seymour, H. (1988) *The New Public Health*. Buckingham: Open University Press.

McKeown, T. (1976) *The Role of Medicine – Dream, Mirage or Nemesis*. London: Nuffield Provincial Hospitals Trust.

National Statistics Office (2002) *Special Focus in Brief: Children*. Retrieved 6 November 2002 from http://www.statistics.gov.uk/.

Sure Start (2002) *What is Sure Start?* Retrieved 6 November 2002 from http://www.surestart.gov.uk/.

Waddington, I. (1989) Inequalities in Health. *Social Studies Review*, Vol. 6: 116–20.

FURTHER READING

Sure Start website: http://www.surestart.gov.uk/. This is the official Sure Start website. It gives background to the scheme and regular updates about new programmes and is used to disseminate good practice.

Glass, N. (1999) Sure Start: The development of an early intervention programme for young children in the United Kingdom. *Children and Society*, Vol. 13: 257–64. This article describes the development of the Sure Start programme in the United Kingdom, which marks an important new departure in the provision of services for the early years. Announced in July 1998 as part of the Labour government's comprehensive spending review.

Naidoo, J. and Wills, J. (2001) *Health Studies: An Introduction*. London: Palgrave. This book provides a good introduction to the study of health and health promotion, including comprehensive coverage of all the main disciplines, perspectives and methods of health studies.

Chapter *Twenty-five* The Role of the Health Visitor

ROBERT BANTON

The role of the health visitor is described. The important concept of the family-centred public health role is discussed and examples are given of the way that health visitors work with families, groups and communities.

The role of the health visitor is one of the most misunderstood and least easily defined roles within the National Health Service (NHS). Public perceptions of the role of the health visitor range from a 'nosy woman who tells you how to look after the baby and clean the house' to 'the lady from the social (security)'. Some of the confusions are understandable given the past history of the profession.

Health visiting started in response to the concerns of the Victorian public health movement. In 1862 the Manchester and Salford Ladies Health Society appointed the first health visitors. They were working-class women whose job was to visit the 'poorer' people and teach them the rules of health and childcare.

> The health visitor is a working woman who lives in the district and knows the life of the poor from experience. She visits all the cottages, makes friends with the people, and gives them hints and advice on all sorts of subjects, and has her eyes open for defects of drainage, overcrowding, sickness. (*CETHV 1977: 45*)

These first health visitors were often called health missionaries, as they took the gospel of hygiene into the dark and unhygienic back streets of northern industrial cities!

Until the 1970s health visitors were not employed by the health service, but by local authorities, and were often confused with social workers. Today, health visitors are part of the NHS and work alongside other community-based healthcare staff, such as general practitioners (GPs), midwives and district nurses. In 2000–1 there were

3.3 million 'first contacts' between health visitors and clients. First contacts data are a measure of the number of different people who receive care during the year. Of these, 61 per cent were with children under the age of five.

The aim of the health visiting service is to promote the health of the whole community and to help promote healthy lifestyles, as well as address concerns about physical and mental well-being. Like few other professional groups, health visitors provide a universal service. The Department of Health said in 1992 that the role of the health visitor was

> unique, in the main, because she [*sic*] offers an unsolicited service. Her work is largely with the well population, with visits to families being made over a long period of time, and is concerned with the family as a whole as well as each individual within it. She is trained to recognize deviation from the normal in both health and relationships and is well placed to recognize the need for, and initiate, action at an early stage. (*Department of Health 1992: 4*)

This means that health visitors are concerned with all members of the community, from the very young all the way through to the elderly. Unlike their GPs, individuals may see the health visitor when there are no health problems. Health visitors are the most accessible health professionals in the community. Getting in touch with a health visitor is usually as easy as going to the local surgery or health centre. Health visitors may also visit individuals at their home.

Health visitors are an integral part of the NHS's community health services. All health visitors are qualified nurses, with special training and experience in child health, health promotion and education. The health visitor training covers identification of mental and physical deviation from normal child development and behaviour. Additionally, training in social policy and social aspects of ill-health means that the assessment of the child's well-being extends beyond the parameters of physiological and mental symptoms and includes the wider social and environmental factors.

Family-Centred Public Health Focus

Although as a nation we are living longer, and fewer children die before reaching adulthood, there are still many pressing health challenges facing people in this country. The general improvements in health mentioned above hide the fact that there are still wide inequalities in health. We have increasing amounts of chronic or longstanding health problems. In terms of our mental health, increasing numbers of individuals are either taking medication for stress or depression, or being referred to psychiatrists.

Health visitors have an important part to play in dealing with these problems. *Saving Lives: Our Healthier Nation* (Department of Health 1999a) set out a family-centred public health role for health visitors, working with individuals, families and communities to improve health and tackle inequality. This role aims to strengthen the community-based, whole-population approach of public health and integrate this with individual and family work.

Health visiting has always been based on public health principles with a strong preventive emphasis. In 1977 the Council for the Education and Training of Health Visitors stated that the principles underpinning the role were as follows:

> Planned activities aimed at the promotion of health and the prevention of ill-health. . . . Underlying this preventative work are four key principles of practice. These are the search for health needs, stimulating an awareness of health needs, influencing policies affecting health, and facilitating health-enhancing activities. (*CETHV 1977: 8–9*)

However, services have not always been organized to enable professionals to work flexibly to tackle local health problems, or work with others in teams to address the causes of ill-health. A family-centred public health approach enables health visitors to reclaim their public health roots while providing a framework in which to maximize the impact of their family-based work.

Health visitors have always played a vital role in promoting family health and supporting parents. The health visiting service is offered universally to all families, especially those with children under the age of five. Normally contact will commence following the birth of a new baby. At 28 days following the birth of the baby, the health visitor takes over the care of the family from the midwife. The health visitor is responsible for monitoring the health and well-being of the child and family, alongside other members of the primary healthcare team, such as GPs. This is carried out using national child health assessment tools: developmental screening and monitoring of child health in relation to physical, emotional and social development.

The health visitor also has a key preventive role. *Working Together to Safeguard Children* (Department of Health, 1999b) outlines the role of the health visitor alongside the school nurse and midwife as being uniquely placed to identify risk factors to a child during pregnancy, birth and the child's early care. The regular contact that health visitors have with families gives them an important role to play in the protection of children from significant harm.

Traditionally, the health visitor offered support and advice on everyday childcare difficulties such as teething, sleeping and feeding. Parents may have many questions about procedures such as immunization programmes, or want information about parenting classes or managing difficult behaviour and any special needs that a child may have. This traditional approach is being reviewed and health visitors are now being encouraged to assess each family's health needs individually and plan ways of meeting them. This is in contrast to a 'one-service-fits-all-families approach' that has been used by many professionals who work with families. The implications of family-centred work mean that the traditional role has been expanded to include work with men, older people, carers and others who may have been excluded by the service's emphasis on young children.

The family health plan

Health visitors may use a number of tools to assess the family's needs. The family health plan is just such a tool and enables the health visitor to plan services to meet these needs. This plan, according to the Department of Health (2001: 21), is

> A tool for enabling a family to think about their health and parenting needs. The plan should identify:
> - The family's needs as they see them.
> - How they wish to address these needs.
> - An action plan for the family, including support to be provided by the health visitor and others.
> - What has been achieved.

You can see that the health visitor should work in partnership with family members to assess their needs. This approach is consistent with the public health concept of working with individuals to identify their needs, i.e. working with their agendas. In the past professionals, including health visitors, were often guilty of imposing their own ideas and agendas about what families needed. This often led to conflict between families and professionals. The assessment should not only identify needs, but also family strengths and resources. Too often professionals have overlooked the many and varied ways families have of meeting their own needs, sometimes using creative and imaginative strategies.

Once needs have been identified the family and health visitor should plan how these will be met and by whom. The family may need access to other agencies, such as the local council, benefits agency and health or social services. Here the health visitor acts as a referral agency and may also act as the family's advocate, helping them to present their case. Parents who have been involved in designing family health plans have often chosen topics such as work, relationships, stress, smoking, diet and illness. In terms of issues affecting a community, work may be undertaken in the areas of housing, transport, play facilities and childcare. Parents have also wanted advice and information on bringing up children, dealing with issues such as feeding, bullying, sleeping problems, children's fears, growth and development. You can see from the list that the possible range of issues the health visitor may need to deal with is vast.

Working with Groups

Health visitors don't only deal with individuals and families. They may also be involved in running or facilitating groups dealing with issues such as parenting, baby massage, stopping smoking, etc. Health visitors are encouraged to seek out those groups who are likely to have the biggest threats to their health and also who have the poorest access to services. Such groups include asylum seekers, travelling families and young people leaving care. Health visitors may also be involved with supporting groups dealing with HIV/AIDS, alcohol and drug misuse, family planning, contraception, pregnancy, the menopause, disability, housing and homelessness, isolation and depression.

Health visitors who lead or form part of a multidisciplinary team can focus on a local neighbourhood and target particular individual and family work. Community development involves working alongside local people to enable them to find ways of identifying their health needs and ways to meet them by working in partnership with local agencies and the community in general. Health visitors are public health workers and in keeping with the principles of public health they need to work using a partnership and empowerment agenda. The traditional priority given to individual and family work is being replaced with an emphasis on a family-centred public health approach. The family-centred public health role means a change of emphasis to increase community-based and targeted public health activities that have long been advocated by the profession.

Activity

Make an appointment to see your local health visitor, or work with your tutor to organize a visit by a health visitor. Ask them what factors affect their role.

REFERENCES

Council for the Education and Training of Health Visitors (CETHV) (1977) *An Investigation Into the Principles of Health Visiting.* London: CETHV.

Department of Health (1992) *Child Protection Guidance for Senior Nurses, Midwives and Health Visitors.* London: HMSO.

Department of Health (1999a) *Saving Lives: Our Healthier Nation.* London: HMSO.

Department of Health (1999b) *Working Together to Safeguard Children.* London: HMSO.

Department of Health (2001) *The Health Visitor and School Nurse Development Programme.* London: HMSO.

FURTHER READING

Department of Health (2001) *The Health Visitor and School Nurse Development Programme.* London: HMSO. Health visitors and school nurses are already making great strides in developing their family- and child-centred public health roles and this pack draws on the numerous examples of innovation that are taking place.

Emond, A. (2001) An evaluation of the First Parent Scheme. *Archives of Diseases in Childhood,* Vol. 86 (3): 150–7. This article covers one particular method of working with new parents to help them develop confidence in childcare.

Health visitor website: http://www.healthvisiting.org/. An NHS website that provides information on what health visitors do, as well as a wide range of advice for parents dealing with information about childcare and services for children and families.

Law

Chapter *Twenty-six* Overview of the Legal System

ANGELA BRENNAN

The law affects every one of us in many aspects of our day-to-day lives. It determines what is acceptable behaviour for individuals (criminal law), the fairness of transactions between individuals (civil law) and the way our society is run (administrative law). Although you may be familiar with what is 'legal', you may be less familiar with how society decides the content and scope of the laws that govern us. By examining how and why the law changes we can see how society's views have developed, and also get some understanding of what the priorities for the future might be.

The term 'common law' is probably familiar to you – you may have heard it in relation to 'common law spouse' – but where does the term come from? To answer this we need to go back in history to before the Norman Conquest in 1066. At this time, people in Britain lived in isolated settlements and communities. The location of your home and periodically the influence of invaders would determine which laws governed you. Following the Norman Conquest, the king decided that he wanted to organize a set of laws that were common to all his subjects, regardless of where in the country they lived. Hence the term 'common law'. The king determined these laws and they were enforced by judges, who travelled around the country hearing cases and disputes and applying the same rules or laws to all similar cases. The decisions in these cases came to be written down and so a body of common law was developed which could be used by all.

The main principle of common law was the Doctrine of Binding Precedent, which basically meant that once a decision had been reached on a certain set of facts, then that decision must be followed in all subsequent cases where the same or very similar facts existed. This brought certainty to the application of the law and the principle continues to this day. 'New' law could be made when a set of previously untried circumstances prevailed, but these were made by the king or queen of the day. The monarch had sole law-making powers and could exercise these powers almost without restraint. Common law continued to develop over time and became a comprehensive set of 'rules' by which people lived. We still have common law rules in operation today; for example, murder is a common law offence and so all the rules relating to the definition, proof or evidence requirements are based on the common law rather than a statute. The judiciary and the courts still have an important role to play in developing law and determining the operation of legislation. However, no *new* common law has been made for a long time.

The Development of Statute Law

The English Civil War resulted in the monarch being stripped of the power to make laws; parliament became the supreme law-making body. The courts, in return for their support of parliament at this time, were granted some independence, which they retain to this day. This independence is important because it helps to separate the power of the executive (government) from the judiciary. Since the seventeenth century, parliament has been the only body that can make new laws and amend or repeal old ones. The procedures by which this is done are at the heart of the democratic process and this is summarized below.

The government of the day generates most of the legislation that goes through parliament (individual MPs may propose legislation in the form of Private Members Bills, though these do not stand much chance of getting through the procedures involved). The government usually precedes its decision to put Bills before parliament by issuing a Green Paper (a consultation document) and a White Paper (which sets out firm proposals).

When a Bill is introduced into the House of Commons it goes through a five-stage process:

- First Reading: title is read and a date set for the second reading.
- Second Reading: general principles are subject to debate by the House; this is a critical point for the Bill, as after the debate a vote is taken on whether to proceed.
- Committee Stage: the Bill is passed to a standing committee whose job it is to revise the bill, clause by clause, ensuring it conforms to the general approval given by the house.
- Report Stage: the standing committee reports the Bill back to the house for consideration of any amendments made.
- Third Reading: further debate can take place here, but only on the details of the bill, not on its general principles.

After all these stages the Bill is passed to the House of Lords and the process is repeated. It is then passed back to the House of Commons, where any amendments can be discussed. Under the Parliament Acts of 1911 and 1949 the power of the Lords to 'block' legislation has been restricted, though they can delay the passage of a Bill for up to a year. Sometimes the threat of this delay can be enough to force changes in the Bill if the government wants to push through a major piece of legislation.

A Bill may change considerably throughout this process or it may pass virtually unchallenged. The ease of passage of a Bill will depend to a large extent on how controversial it is, whether it is seen as a party political issue or one that is in the national interest. A government with a small majority in the House of Commons may have little success with controversial legislation; a government with a large majority will be able to impose its will quite strongly with fewer obstacles to its plans for new legislation.

Finally, a Bill requires Royal Assent, though this is now a formality. An Act comes into effect on the day of Royal Assent unless there is provision to the contrary; it is usual for an Act to contain a commencement date for some time in the future. For example, the Children Act went through the parliamentary process in 1989 but did not come into force until 1991.

How the Law Operates

We have seen how law is made and we know that law can be derived from either common law rules that still exist or more likely from statutes that have been enacted by parliament. These are the *sources* of law, but in order to see how the law actually operates we need to look at the court system. The court system varies according to the broad areas of law that the courts are serving. With regard to law affecting children, you need to understand the difference between private and public law and between civil and criminal law.

Areas of law

The main distinction between public and private law is that the former is seen to concern the whole of society; therefore it should be the state that protects public law interests, brings prosecutions and 'punishes' offenders. Private law, on the other hand, is concerned with the resolution of disputes between individuals, which may be of no interest or have no direct effect on society as a whole. The state does not therefore get involved in private law issues, but it does provide the mechanisms by which individuals can use the legal system to resolve their disputes.

In the field of child law, if we look at the Children Act 1989, we can see that this contains private and public law provision. The Act contains provision for what happens to children following divorce or separation (which is seen as a private law issue) and also deals with protecting children from abuse (which is seen as a public law issue).

Table 26.1 Differences between criminal and civil law

Criminal law (part of public law)	*Civil law (part of private law)*
A person is *prosecuted*	A person is *sued*
A person is found *guilty/not guilty*	A person is found *liable/not liable*
Proof required: *beyond reasonable doubt*	Proof required: *on balance of probabilities*
Purpose of action: *to punish offender and protect society*	Purpose of action: *to remedy the wrong, usually with compensation*
The state brings the action in the name of the Queen (R = Regina): *R vs. Jones*	One individual brings the action against the other: *Smith vs. Jones*
Cases are dealt with in *criminal courts*	Cases are dealt with in *civil courts*

The distinctions between criminal and civil law can be found in the terminology used, the standard of proof required, the purpose of the action, who brings the action and where the action is taken. Table 26.1 summarizes the differences between criminal law and civil law.

The Court System

The court system in the UK operates on a hierarchical basis, which maintains the concept of binding precedent that we explained above. Greater and greater expertise is called upon to rule on cases where an appeal is allowed. Usually, a case will start in a lower court and may proceed to higher courts on appeal. However, there are some instances where a matter may be heard first in a higher court. The distinctions that we made between civil and criminal law are also reflected in the court system.

Magistrates' courts

These are staffed by Justices of the Peace (JPs), who are not necessarily qualified lawyers but who are assisted in their work by lawyers. There are also stipendiary magistrates who are qualified lawyers and who are paid a salary. Magistrates' courts have the power to try 'summary' offences. These are defined by statute and include such things as traffic offences and common assault. The maximum penalty that can be imposed by a magistrates' court is also defined in statute and is limited to six months' imprisonment and/or a fine of up to £5,000.

There are also a number of offences that are termed 'triable-either-way', which means that they could be tried in the magistrates' court or they could be tried in a Crown Court in front of a jury. In these cases the magistrates must decide which court the case will be tried in and gain the consent of the accused before proceeding. It should be noted that in either-way offences, although a magistrates' court may try the case, they may refer it to the Crown Court for sentencing if it is deemed that the sentence should be greater than that possible for the magistrates to pass.

Magistrates also sit in Youth Courts to try children and young people. These are private tribunals, which are held separately from the ordinary magistrates' courts. This is to protect the privacy of children and young people and also to protect them from the harsher environment of the adult courts. There must be three magistrates hearing such a case and the public is not allowed access to the proceedings.

Magistrates' courts also have a civil jurisdiction in that they hear family proceedings. Justices who sit in this court must be a member of the Family Panel: people who are specially appointed to deal with family matters. Family proceedings include adoption, application for **Residence Orders** and **Contact Orders** under the Children Act, and maintenance for spouses and children after divorce.

County courts

These provide local accessible courts for small claims and minor civil matters. Again, there is a financial limit on what these courts can deal with, at present £5,000 or £1,000 for personal injury claims. These are very busy courts as they can provide a quick and relatively easy method for individuals to claim their rights. However, once a court has awarded damages or compensation to the winning side, it is up to the individual to actually get this money from the opposing side and this can sometimes prove difficult.

Crown Courts

The Crown Court hears all criminal cases tried on indictment (more serious cases) and also hears cases on appeal from the magistrates' courts. In the Crown Court the case is heard by a judge before a jury.

High Court

The High Court has three divisions: Queen's Bench, Chancery and Family. The main work of the Queen's Bench division is in the areas of contract and tort cases. The Chancery division deals mainly with land, property, bankruptcy, probate and company law. The Family division deals mainly with matrimonial matters, matters relating to minors, legitimacy and adoption and also proceedings under the Human Fertilization & Embryology Act 1990.

The Court of Appeal (Criminal Division)

This court hears appeals from the Crown Court on conviction and sentencing issues.

The Court of Appeal (Civil Division)

This court hears appeals from all three divisions of the High Court and also from some tribunals, e.g. the Employment Appeal Tribunal.

The House of Lords

We should distinguish the House of Lords when it is acting in its legislative capacity (see above) from when it is acting in its judicial capacity. As a court, the House of Lords hears appeals from both the criminal and civil appeal courts. This is the highest court in this country and decisions made here must be followed in all lower courts. Law Lords, usually five but sometimes seven, hear cases and a majority decision decides a case.

An understanding of the law helps us to think about and discuss the position of children and young people in relation to their rights under the law, how they are treated in different circumstances and whether or not the approach we take is fair and consistent.

Activity

Having read the section on the development of statute law, think about the sorts of things that may influence the type of legislation the government may want to pass.

FURTHER READING

Slapper, G. and Kelly, D. (1999) *The English Legal System*, 4th edn. London: Cavendish Publications. A basic introductory text that includes a historical perspective, sources of law, the court system and civil and criminal procedures.

http://www.parliament.uk. A comprehensive website that covers the origins of parliament through to its day-to-day working. It has a lot of information and can sometimes be a bit cumbersome to navigate, but the information is clear and comprehensive.

Chapter Twenty-seven
Legal Personnel

ANGELA BRENNAN

There is a range of people involved in supporting and representing children in the legal system. These include solicitors and barristers, the official solicitor, family court welfare officers and guardians ad litem. In this chapter we describe these roles, looking at the training required, how the people operate within the system and how they work with children and families. We also discuss whether children and young people are fairly and adequately represented in legal proceedings.

A solicitor will often be the first point of contact for people involved in the legal system. Solicitors deal directly with clients and can advise them on issues such as whether they have a viable action and what will be involved in pursuing the action. Solicitors are sometimes called the GPs of legal practice in that you go to see them first and they can refer you to a 'specialist' if required. However, this is a bit misleading as many solicitors are now specialists in their own right in different areas of law, e.g. child abuse and family law. If a case looks likely to go to court then the solicitor can engage the services of a barrister on behalf of their client (see below).

In order to become a solicitor a person is required to possess a degree in law and have undertaken a one-year Legal Practice Course (LPC), which will deal with many of the more practical aspects of becoming a solicitor. Following on from this they are required to undertake a term as a trainee solicitor, which is essentially an apprenticeship with a firm of solicitors. On successful completion of this a trainee solicitor may apply to the Law Society to be admitted to the profession and will then become an officer of the Supreme Court. A solicitor also requires a practising certificate, which is issued by the Law Society and will have to undergo ongoing professional development throughout their career.

The governing body for solicitors is the Law Society, which is responsible for complaints and disciplinary matters involving solicitors. It is also solicitors' main professional association and as such must promote the interests of its members.

There has been some concern that a dual role such as this may represent a conflict of interest. However, solicitors are not the only professional group to have such a body in both a representative and regulatory role.

Solicitors can appear in court on behalf of their clients in certain types of cases (Access to Justice Act 1999) and they can, as most other professions, be sued for negligence should their work fall below the standard required of the reasonable practitioner.

The Barrister

The barrister is thought of mainly as the court advocate, although a lot of their work also involves drafting expert opinions for solicitors or drafting **pleadings**. Barristers do not have direct access to the public; they can only be employed through a solicitor to act on behalf of a client. Barristers can act for the prosecution or the defence in a case, depending on which side employs them.

In order to become a barrister a person must undergo not only academic and professional training but must also take part in rituals and practices that date from historical times and which have little meaning in today's society. A would-be barrister must have a law degree and must register with one of the four 'inns of court' in London. They must undertake professional training for one year leading to the 'bar' examinations and during this time they must attend their inn of court to 'become familiar with the customs of the bar' (Slapper and Kelly 1999). A barrister in training is required to attend a prescribed number of dining events at their inn of court before they are allowed to take the bar examinations and must have completed a further number of dinners before being 'called' to the bar. The trainee barrister must then undertake a pupillage, which is similar to the solicitor's apprenticeship.

The governing body for barristers is the General Council of the Bar and the Inns of Court and this body serves much the same purpose as the Law Society, in that it deals with complaints and discipline but also acts as a representative of the interest of the members of the bar.

The Official Solicitor

The origins of the office of official solicitor can be traced to medieval times and the role has been abolished and reinstated many times between then and the present day. It has always been recognized that there will be people who are unable to represent themselves adequately in the legal system and who have no close friend or relative who can take on this role for them. The official solicitor is the **guardian ad litem** or **next friend** of last resort. A guardian ad litem will represent a person in public law proceedings and a next friend will represent them in private law proceedings. The fact that the official solicitor is deemed to be 'of last resort' highlights the fact that his office will only act for people who have no other means of representation.

There have been some recent changes to the types of cases that will fall under the remit of the official solicitor and this has been due to the development of the Children and Family Court Advisory and Support Service (CAFCASS), which is outlined in more detail below. In order to obtain an overview of the type of service offered by this office, it is useful to examine its strategic objectives:

- To protect the best interests and human rights of children and the mentally disabled who are unable to represent themselves in legal processes.
- To enable others to pursue legal processes where without our representation of a party they would be unable to do so.
- To contribute to a fair, swift and effective system of justice.
- To provide an effective executor and trustee service of last resort on a non-profit making basis.

(*Office of the Official Solicitor and Public Trustee 2001*)

Cases involving such issues as wardship, adoption or cases brought under the Children Act used to come under the remit of the official solicitor, but now all such cases come under the remit of CAFCASS (Criminal Justice and Court Services Act 2000). The official solicitor will now only act for children in the following ways:

- The official solicitor will act as a guardian ad litem or a next friend for a child party whose own welfare is not the subject of family proceedings.
- The official solicitor will also act for under-age or mentally disordered parents who have become involved in litigation in the High Court or county court.
- Much of the work of the official solicitor arises in general litigation when it become clear to the court that one of the parties is incapable of conducting the litigation properly, due to mental disorder or the fact that they are under age.
- In work not related specifically to children, the official solicitor represents mentally disordered adults and can act as an adviser to the court on such issues as withdrawal of medical treatment in PVS (persistent vegetative state) cases.

The Guardian ad Litem

Children who are the subject of any proceedings involving social services, such as care proceedings or child protection proceedings, usually have a guardian ad litem (GAL) appointed to protect their interests. The child will not be able to choose their GAL, who is chosen from a panel of suitably qualified persons. The role of the GAL is to ensure that the voice of the child is heard in proceedings where the child's welfare is at issue and to represent the child in their best interests.

The GAL should be independent of any local authority that is involved in the proceedings and as part of their role they may have to conduct interviews with anyone who knows the child and their family well and critically appraise any work that has been undertaken with the child. Once appointed, a GAL becomes an officer of the court for the duration of the case and is under a duty to safeguard and promote the interest of the child by providing independent 'expert' advice to the court.

The Court Welfare Officer

Family court welfare officers (FCWOs) are key workers in cases where parents are separating or divorcing. Their main role is to work with families to try to help decide the future arrangements for any children involved. There has been some criticism in the past that court welfare officers lacked the necessary formal qualifications to enable them effectively to carry out this very important role of advising the court. All new FCWOs undertake modular training as part of their induction to the role. This is in addition to a national induction programme and ongoing training in the form of resource packs. However, despite these measures, this concern still remains.

The FCWO may visit the family concerned on a number of occasions and talk to both partners and the children. Among the issues they will discuss is that of whom the children will live with following a divorce or separation. This is understandably a very sensitive area and there are many things to be taken into consideration, such as: Has there been any domestic violence? Is either of the parents opposed to the other having contact? Does the child feel torn between the two parents? The role of the FCWO is to write a report for the court about what will be in the best interests of the child in all the possible circumstances.

FCWOs have reported that certain conflicts sometimes prevent them from carrying out this role effectively (for example, where parents have agreed upon certain issues there is sometimes a reluctance to 'upset' things by disagreeing with parents). Also, where domestic violence has been present in a relationship but the children have not been physically or sexually abused, the FCWO may be reluctant to put this before the court because they have no 'evidence' of harm to the child.

The basic role of the FCWO is to be an impartial and professional observer of all the circumstances surrounding a disputed case and to help the judge reach the right decision by providing this information to the court: whether or not they achieve this goal is sometimes disputed.

Children and Family Court Advisory and Support Service (CAFCASS)

This body came into existence in April 2001. CAFCASS brought together the Family Court Welfare Service, the Guardian ad Litem and Reporting Officer Service and the children's branch of the official solicitor. It was established by the Criminal Justice and Court Services Act 2000 and is a non-departmental public body answering to the Lord Chancellor. The thinking behind this amalgamation was about improving the national service to the courts, reducing wasteful overlaps and so increasing efficiency.

The development of CAFCASS has been broadly welcomed by the agencies concerned, although there were some initial problems in relation to changes in the way that GALs were to be paid. Another major challenge is the bringing together of three distinct groups and ensuring that they work harmoniously together.

Although a lot of the literature about CAFCASS states that this body is about improving services, making them quicker and more efficient, there is little being said about how it will actually improve the services offered to children themselves. The distinct roles that operated before will continue, so this may be more about a change in management and organization than a direct improvement for children and young people. Anthony Hewson, the Chairman of CAFCASS, has said that 'our number one aim is to provide a first-class service for every child in the family courts' (Hewson 2001), but he does not say exactly how this will be achieved other than by reorganizing the management structure.

Lawyers Associations

Lawyers associations are groups created by lawyers with a view to sharing good practice and increasing the level of knowledge of the legal system. They include the Association of Lawyers for Children and the Association of Child Abuse Lawyers. These do not have any 'legal' status but are useful in that they bring together like-minded people working with children within the legal system and hopefully help to improve the service that children receive.

Association of Lawyers for Children

This is an association not just for solicitors and barristers but also for legal executives, social workers and GALs. Its stated purpose is to be an organization that promotes justice for children and young people, provides relevant training for lawyers working with children, and also acts as a pressure group to lobby for the establishment of properly funded legal mechanisms to enable all children to have access to justice. This group is useful because its members share the common purpose of improving the system for children and young people. Children do not have much of a voice themselves within the system, so such support and awareness-raising can only assist their cause.

Association of Child Abuse Lawyers

As the name suggests, this association is concerned with lawyers who represent children who are the subject of legal proceedings in relation to abuse. The code of practice for this association includes reference to the fact that solicitors and barristers involved in child abuse cases should ensure that they are fully aware of the impact of legal proceedings on the client and that they should seek to minimize any negative consequences. The code also ensures that members have the requisite expertise to take on a case and that they only instruct experts with appropriate experience. This association is therefore more about improving issues for children by ensuring good practice in the conduct of the case.

It has often been said that any system is only as good as the people working within it. We have seen, in relation to child protection for example, that although the system may appear to be foolproof on paper and offer a high level of protection, in practice it often fails. The same may be said of the legal system as it relates to children and young people. Lawyers will be specialists in areas of law, but need not be specialists in relation to their client group, and little if anything in basic legal training prepares them for working with young children in stressful situations. This is partly alleviated by the use of specialist children's representatives, whose primary role is to provide advice to the court on what is in the best interest of the child. However, problems still arise in relation to how these representatives determine what is in the child's best interests and how much the child him/herself has a voice in this. For example, recent research has shown that many children and young people do not feel empowered or supported by their experience in care proceedings and that guardians and solicitors feel that improvements could be made (Masson and Oakley 2002). Similarly, research on the relationship between solicitors and social workers involved in child protection cases found that there was sometimes a lack of understanding of roles and that there was a concern that perhaps the overlap of responsibilities could lead to tensions and disagreements. Some people argue that the problems require a much more radical solution. The president of the Association of Child Abuse Lawyers has said: 'children [will] continue to be traumatized unless the adversarial legal process [is] replaced with an inquisitorial approach throughout the UK'.

Activity

What do you think are the main issues to be considered in relation to how and by whom children are represented in court proceedings?

REFERENCES

Blatty, D. (2001) Scottish moves to protect young witnesses gather pace. *Guardian*, 1 August 2001.

Hewson, A. (2001) Centrally managed Children's Guardian Service will ensure that the voice of the child in family court proceedings is properly heard. CAFCASS Press Release, 9 July 2001.

Masson, J. and Oakley, M. W. (2002) *Out of Hearing: Representing Children in Care Proceedings.* London: Wiley.

Office of the Official Solicitor and Public Trustee (2001) *Aims and Objectives of the Official Solicitor and Public Trustee.* London: HMSO.

Slapper, G. and Kelly, D. (1999) *The English Legal System*, 4th edn. London: Cavendish Publishing.

FURTHER READING

Brayne, H., Martin, G. and Carr, H. (2001) *Law for Social Workers*, 7th edn. Oxford: Oxford University Press. A useful overview of practice and procedures in representing children in public law hearings.

Family Court Advisory and Support Service (CAFCASS) website: http://www.cafcass.gov.uk. This website for CAFCASS includes background as well as new developments and publications.

Representing Children (1999) Vol. 12 (4). A quarterly journal for all those concerned with the rights and welfare of young people and children. Articles are from practitioners and academics involved with representing children in court hearings.

Chapter *Twenty-eight*

The Children Act 1989

ANGELA BRENNAN

The recent history of the Children Act 1989 is described. Key definitions are explained along with some of the underlying philosophies. The chapter concludes by reminding you that more recent legislation continues to affect children.

The Children Act 1989 was hailed as 'the most comprehensive and far reaching reform of child law which has come before parliament in living memory' (Lord Mackay of Clashfern LC 1989). The Act simplifies many aspects of law relating to children and for the first time brings together public and private law in one piece of legislation. The Act repealed eight previous statutes relating to children and child welfare and significantly reduced the Children and Young Persons Act 1969.

Over the twenty or so years before the Children Act came into effect (October 1991) there had been a number of highly publicized incidents involving deaths of children who were in the care of social services. Deaths of children who are in the care of social services are rare, but they are taken very seriously because it is felt that society has failed these children. Public inquiries are the result of such tragic events, with the aim to avoid the same things happening in the future. The transcripts of these inquiries are available in libraries and they make for harrowing reading, conducted as they are with the benefit of hindsight. An overview of the reports reveals some key problems:

- A lack of communication between various agencies involved with the child (social services, education authorities, health authorities, housing authorities). In some cases it was as if various agencies had a piece of a jigsaw puzzle which by itself did not mean much, but if put together with the others would have presented a picture of concern.
- A lack of power by personnel (health visitors, social workers) to gain access to children about whom there was a concern. These staff had no right of entry into homes and could only be invited in by the householder. This meant that sometimes

children could not be seen for days or weeks, or they were seen in situations that were 'managed' by parents/carers.

- A failure to balance the rights and needs of the parents and the children involved. On the one hand, we saw instances where the needs and rights of the child were almost completely subsumed to those of the mother (for example, in the Jasmine Beckford case). On the other hand, in another highly publicized incident we saw the rights of the parents almost completely ignored in the rush to protect the child (Report of the Inquiry into Child Abuse in Cleveland 1987).

Ways in Which the Children Act 1989 Addresses Problems

The first way in which the Children Act 1989 attempts to address problems identified by Committee of Inquiry Reports is what is known as the paramouncy principle, found in section 1 of the Act. It states:

> 1 (1) When a court determines any question with respect to –
> (a) the upbringing of a child; or
> (b) the administration of a child's property or the application of any income arising from it
> the child's welfare shall be the court's paramount consideration.

These statements seem to suggest that the interests of the child will always come before those of other parties in a case. However, it should be noted that the paramouncy principle does not apply in all circumstances, but only those outlined in section 1. This means that it does not apply in other areas of child-related law; for example, when deciding on ancillary relief (financial arrangements) following divorce, in adoption cases, or occupation of the matrimonial home following divorce. In these cases the welfare of the child will be *one* of the issues taken into account, but it will not take precedence over any other issue.

Local authorities also now have a duty to investigate concerns about a child when they are brought to their attention. Anyone may contact a local authority to raise c[illegible]s about a child: it could be a neighbour, a relative, a friend or a professional [illegible] with the child in another capacity (e.g. teacher). In the case of professionals [illegible] with children there is a duty placed upon them to contact the local authority th[illegible] the relevant channels when there is concern about a child. When the local authority receives the report it must decide whether it fits the 'criteria' laid down by the Act:

> S47
> (1) Where a local authority –
> (a) are informed that a child who lives, or is found, in their area –
> (i) is the subject of an emergency protection order or
> (ii) is in police protection or

(b) have reasonable cause to suspect that a child who lives or is found in their area is suffering or is likely to suffer, significant harm, the authority shall make, or cause to be made, such enquiries as they consider necessary to enable them to decide whether they should take any action to safeguard or promote the child's welfare.

In the past a lack of power to enter children's homes resulted in a failure to protect the child even when concerns were held by local authority staff. The Children Act has attempted to address this issue by making the failure of a parent or carer to allow reasonable access to a child a ground for the granting of an Emergency Protection Order (EPO).

S47 states that when conducting the investigation outlined above the local authority should ensure that it gets access to the child. It also states that if the authority is denied access it shall apply for an EPO unless it is satisfied that the welfare of the child can be safeguarded without the order. It is highly unlikely that the welfare of the child can be ascertained without a visit to the home, therefore S47 is almost giving statutory right of access to a child by the local authority. This is a reasonable 'middle way', as it will only come into effect when access to a child is being unreasonably denied by parents.

Another way in which the Act attempts to address issues raised by Committee of Inquiry Reports can also be found in S47. This relates to the duty placed on various agencies involved with the child to communicate with one another. When a local authority conducts enquiries it is the duty of people who are part of the local authority, the local education authority, the local housing authority, the health authority or any person authorized by the secretary of state for the purposes of this section, to assist them with those enquiries by providing relevant information and advice. This should ensure that there is no breakdown of communication, as highlighted in pre-Children Act cases.

It should be noted that at the time of writing this chapter yet another young child had died as a result of neglect and abuse by parents, despite being under the care of the local authority. There are now calls for a major review of child protection procedures. Whether this results in a change of legislation or procedures (or both) remains to be seen.

The ways in which the Children Act attempts to balance the needs and wishes of children and parents can also be seen in the private law provisions, which deal with what happens to children when their parents divorce or separate.

Parental Responsibility

Parental responsibility is defined in the Act as 'all the rights, duties, powers, responsibility and authority which by law a parent of a child has in relation to the child and his property'. Historically, the emphasis in definitions of parenthood concerned the rights of the parents in respect of the child and his property. Originally, society did not think in terms of both parents, but of the father as having the ultimate say over what happened to their child. The notion was very much that of 'ownership' of the child. The mother's legal status in relation to her children was very much secondary to that of the father, so much so that in the early nineteenth century, if the father died, the mother may have had to leave the upbringing of her child to a guardian appointed by the father before his death. It was only with the Guardianship of Infants Act 1886 that this changed and we have seen subsequent improvements in the legal status of the mother over the years. The Children Act 1989 gives parental responsibility to the mother and the father equally if they are married. Unmarried fathers therefore have no legal parental status unless they apply to the court for a Parental Responsibility Order (S4) or they 'legitimize' the child by marrying the mother.

Other people may also be granted parental responsibility by the court through the granting of other orders such as a Residence Order or a Care Order. It is interesting to note that the granting of parental responsibility to one person does not diminish the responsibility held by others. When parents divorce, regardless of whom the child may live with, both parents retain their parental responsibility. This is in keeping with the philosophy of the Act, which regards parenthood as a responsibility that is permanent. When more than one person has parental responsibility each can act independently of the other in making decisions about a child's care and upbringing. Where there is a dispute between those with parental responsibility which cannot be resolved by the parties (e.g. giving consent for a medical procedure) then the court can be called upon to decide the issue. Parental responsibility cannot be wholly delegated, but can in part be delegated to someone having temporary care of a child (e.g. nanny, childminder). S3 of the Children Act states that a person who

> (a) does not have parental responsibility for a particular child
> but
> (b) has care of the child may . . . do what is reasonable in all the circumstances of the case for the purposes of safeguarding and promoting the child's welfare.

This would be for the purposes of getting medical treatment for the child in an emergency, for example.

Common law

The notion that parental responsibility exists for the benefit of the child rather than the parent was highlighted in the landmark case of Gillick vs. West Norfolk Area Health Authority, 1985, in which it was stated that parental rights 'are justified only in so far as they enable the parent to perform his duties towards the child, and towards other children in the family' (Lord Fraser: London Borough of Brent 1985). In the Gillick case, a mother sought a declaration from the court that a Department of Health and Social Security circular was unlawful because it advised doctors that they could prescribe contraceptives to girls under the age of 16 years without parental consent. The House of Lords held that it was not unlawful and stated that parental rights yielded to the child's rights to make decisions based upon proof that the child had sufficient understanding and intelligence to be capable of making up their own mind – the notion here being that parental rights and responsibility diminishes as the child's independence develops and the child is deemed to be what is called Gillick Competent. (Some people now refer to the young person as being Fraser Competent following a case where Mrs Gillick tried, unsuccessfully, to sue the Brook Advisory Centres for young people for misuse of her name.)

It would seem at first glance that this gives the child's wishes precedence over those of their parents; however, this is not necessarily the case. The court may rule that a child's wishes can be overruled despite the fact that they have been found to be Gillick Competent. The court will look at all the facts and a review of cases will show that there are some decisions that a court will not allow a child to take. Such decisions may include those *not* to have treatment where the child's life is at risk.

Private Law Orders

Much of the above describes the procedures and rights involved in child protection cases. However, the courts are also called upon to make decisions about a child's welfare and upbringing in cases where the child is not in danger of significant harm but, rather, where the parents are divorcing or separating and decisions need to be made about such important issues as whom the child will live with and have contact with. In many instances these issues are decided amicably and without the intervention of the court in the actual decision making. The court will want to look at provisions that have been made for children in a divorce, but if these are reasonable and uncontested then the court will not interfere.

However, there will be instances where parents cannot agree upon these important issues and in the past children have sometimes been used as bargaining tools or means of 'punishing' one parent by the other. The Children Act 1989 aims to overcome these problems by making decisions about the child based on what is best for the child rather than what parents necessarily want. The types of orders which a court may be called upon to make in these circumstances include Residence Orders, Contact Orders, **Specific Issue Orders** and **Prohibited Steps Orders**.

In making or considering any of these orders under S8 of the Act, the court must consider the paramouncy principle in S1 of the Act and also the statutory welfare checklist in S3. The checklist details the points which the court must take into consideration. It contains the following:

- The ascertainable wishes and feelings of the child concerned (in light of the child's age and understanding).
- The child's physical, emotional and educational needs.
- The likely effect on the child of any change in circumstances.
- The child's age, sex, background, and any of the child's characteristics that the court considers relevant.

- Any harm which the child has suffered or is at risk of suffering.
- The capability of each of the child's parents, and any other person in relation to whom the court considers the question to be relevant, of meeting the child's needs.
- The range of powers available to the court under the Children Act 1989 in the proceedings in question.

None of these points is given any more importance than the others and they should all be considered and mentioned in the decision of the court.

The underlying philosophy of the Children Act 1989 is undoubtedly meant to be more 'child-centred' than was previously the case, as it attempts to balance the rights of parents against the responsibility of parenthood and tries to acknowledge that as children get older they should have more of a say in their own lives.

Although the Children Act is the most significant piece of legislation, there are other Acts that impinge on children's rights; for example, the Child Support Act 1991, the Education Act 1997 and the Crime and Disorder Act 1998. These and other pieces of legislation at times undermine some of the principles of the Children Act.

One final point remains to be made about the Children Act and all child-related law and that is that people, especially children, must know about it. Those working with children should ensure that they are aware of the relevant law and how to operate within it; children should be educated about their rights and status within this area of law, which should be *for* them, rather than merely *about* them.

Activity

Think about the problems that the Children Act 1989 was trying to address. How successful was it?

REFERENCES

London Borough of Brent (1985) *A Child in Trust: The Report of the Panel of Enquiry into the Death of Jasmine Beckford.* London: London Borough of Brent.

FURTHER READING

Bloy, D. J. (1996) *Child Law.* London: Cavendish Publishing. An overview of public and private child law, with chapters on parental responsibility and court orders.

http://www.compactlaw.co.uk/child.html. A website aimed at lay people who wish to know more about the Children Act 1989 and the orders found within it.

Chapter *Twenty-nine* The Legal Status of the Child

ANGELA BRENNAN

This chapter examines the legal status of children and young people in relation to their legal rights, both as parties seeking to bring an action and also as defendants. We look at how the law views children's capability to make decisions about lifestyles and life choices and examine some of the thinking behind these views.

Having 'legal status' means that the law recognizes that you are an individual who can independently take legal responsibility for your actions and/or use the legal system to seek redress when someone else has infringed your rights.

An unborn child has a right to life as determined by the provisions of the Abortion Act 1967. This Act states that an abortion will only be lawful if the situation meets the criteria defined by the Act: that continuation of the pregnancy will have a detrimental effect on the physical and/or mental health of the mother. Two doctors must confirm that this is the case before the termination can be carried out. It is often said that in some parts of the UK we have 'abortion on demand' because most women seeking an abortion can meet the criteria, especially in relation to mental health. A termination can be carried out up to the 24th week of a pregnancy, or even later if there are medical grounds. There have been occasions in the past where the father of an unborn baby has tried to use the legal system to prevent the woman having a termination, but these have not succeeded where the woman has met the criteria laid down in the Act.

An unborn child has no legal rights as against anyone who may cause them harm through negligence, etc. Once a child is born they may sue retrospectively for damage caused while *in utero* through the deliberate or negligent actions of a third party (e.g. a midwife or doctor, or the driver of a car who negligently injures the unborn child). This course of action is open to the child as against any third party who has caused them injury or damage while they were in the womb, with one exception. A child may not sue their mother for any damage she may have caused to her unborn child through her actions. So, for example, the child cannot sue a mother who abuses alcohol or drugs and causes abnormalities in the child as a result of that abuse. This is because it is thought to be impossible to separate the mother from her unborn child when thinking about rights. If the unborn child's rights had precedence over the mother's then we might see circumstances in which a pregnant woman could have her freedom and rights severely restricted for the duration of the pregnancy so as to ensure that the child's rights were protected. In the USA, some states operate a policy whereby pregnant women who are drug or alcohol abusers are incarcerated for the duration of their pregnancy in order to prevent them from damaging their unborn child. This has given rise to protests from women's rights groups, who say that this is an abuse of the woman's fundamental rights.

In the UK, if a woman has caused damage or injury to her unborn child through her own deliberate actions, then it is possible that the child could be made the subject of a Care Order even before it is born. This would mean that as soon as the child was born they would be removed from the care of the mother unless or until the mother could prove that she was capable of adequately looking after the child. This would be done under the child protection legislation, but one could argue that in those circumstances it is a little late to protect the child once the damage has been done. Whichever way you look at this issue it is difficult to make an argument for one side or the other which does not substantially interfere with the rights of the other party. It is indicative perhaps of the status of young children generally that the law will give preference to the mother's rights.

There is one further thing to mention in relation to the rights of the unborn child and that is an exception to the rule that a child cannot sue their mother for damage caused *in utero*. By virtue of the Congenital Disabilities (Civil Liabilities) Act 1976 a child, once born, can retrospectively sue their mother for damage caused through careless driving. This may seem to be an anomaly, but as we all have to be insured before we drive a car then it is actually the insurance company that is being sued.

At birth a child acquires what is called a 'legal personality', which means that the law now recognizes them as a separate human being who can take part in legal proceedings in their own right. Of course, as a baby or very young child it would be physically and cognitively impossible to take part in legal proceedings, so a child will always be represented by a 'next friend' in private law actions or a guardian ad litem (CHAPTER 27) in public law actions.

It is a bit misleading to say that from birth a child can take part in legal proceedings because there are many proceedings that a child would be excluded from purely on the basis of their age. It is probably more accurate to say that once a child is born the law recognizes them as a separate individual who is entitled to the protection of the law in terms of anyone who has harmed them or may harm them. As the child grows up they will still be entitled to the protection of the law, but they will also be more and more accountable to the law for their actions. There is sometimes a problem when we look at the way the law seeks to protect children and the way in which it holds them accountable: some of the approaches seem to contradict each other.

UNIVERSITY OF WINCHESTER
LIBRARY

The Law Protecting Children

Each of us as individuals is entitled to be protected from harm to ourselves or our property. The way the law does this is through policing and through punishment of those who infringe the rights of others. The child, like anyone else, is entitled to be protected from physical harm, sexual abuse or exploitation, theft or damage to their property. They are not entitled to protection of other rights, such as rights under a contract, social welfare rights, some employment rights, etc., because the law does not deem that they are able to enter into a contract, claim state benefit or work full-time below a certain age. Legal commentators may say that this in itself is a form of protection: the law decides for you at what age you are capable of doing certain things, it protects you from making mistakes that could hurt you, it keeps you safe from exploitative adults who may take your money, or worse, and it gradually introduces you into the fully accountable world of the adult.

It is sometimes hard to see the reasoning behind the decisions made in relation to the age at which children are deemed capable of doing certain things. Look at the following summary list and see if you can identify what the child is being protected from.

Under 5 years you can:
- Have your own passport.
- Have your ears or nose or other body part pierced (with parents' consent).
- Drink alcohol at home.
- Own a pet.

At 10 years you can:
- Be fully accountable for your actions in terms of committing a crime.
- Be prosecuted in a juvenile court.
- Be cautioned by the police.

At 12 years you can:
- Buy a pet.
- See a 12 Certificate film.

At 14 years you can:
- Go into a pub but you cannot buy or drink alcohol there.
- Be employed part-time (with some restrictions).

At 16 years you can:
- Leave school.
- Give consent for sexual intercourse.
- Leave home.
- Buy cigarettes.
- Drink alcohol with a meal in a pub.
- Obtain a National Insurance Number.
- Work full-time if you have left school.

At 17 years you can:
- Drive a car.
- Give blood.

At 18 years you can:
- Serve on a jury.
- Vote.
- Buy alcohol.
- Buy fireworks.

At 21 years you can:
- Be a candidate in local, national or European elections.

Let's have a look at some of these protective measures: at 12 you could drink alcohol every night at home, but you may not buy any. At 10 you could be held fully accountable for your actions in terms of committing a crime, but you are not deemed old enough to buy your own pet. At 16 you can buy tobacco, but you can't buy alcohol. At 12 you could be prosecuted in a juvenile court, but you cannot consent to sexual intercourse. You may be able to find other anomalies in this list, which is not exhaustive. It can be quite complicated to think about how the law is aiming to protect children by these measures. What is the thinking behind such seemingly  arbitrary decisions on access to rights that are couched in terms of **legal capacity**?

Parental Responsibility

A lot of the measures discussed above rely on parents to exercise some influence and 'control' over their children. For example, the fact that it is not illegal for a child of any age to drink alcohol means that there must be a belief that parents will act in a responsible manner and not allow children to abuse alcohol in the home. This may be the difference between a relatively young child having a glass of wine with a meal or celebration at home and that same child drinking spirits every night before bed. Of course, the latter may well fall into the category of child abuse and so would be dealt with in that way.

A child of any age can own a pet, but they must be 12 years of age before they can buy one for themselves. This presumes that a child under 12 has had their pet bought for them by adults and that the adult will ensure that the child behaves responsibly towards the animal. This notion of parental responsibility is one which is worth exploring in a little more detail, as it links with our ideas of when a child should be able to exercise some degree of autonomy and self-determination in their lives.

Prior to the Children Act 1989 legal references to the parent–child relationship used such terminology as 'rights and duties', 'powers and duties' or 'rights and authority' to describe the position of the parent *vis-à-vis* the child. The Children Act 1989 brought in a new concept of 'parental responsibility' and much was made of this in terms of having a new philosophy underpinning the parent–child relationship. Parents would not 'own' or 'have rights over' children; rather, they would have responsibilities towards them. However, when the Children Act came out we saw parental responsibility defined in the Act as 'all the rights, duties, powers, responsibilities and authority which by law a parent of a child has in relation to the child and his property' (section 2). It would appear that the word 'responsibility' has merely been added to the long list of powers, rights, etc., and you may wonder what real changes this addition might actually make.

Some commentators have put forward the idea that adding the notion of parental responsibility to the legal definition of parenthood has a hidden agenda. By placing responsibility for children with the parents it legitimizes the withdrawal by the state of financial responsibility for children. The Child Support Act 1991 is seen as an example of where the concept of parental responsibility has been used to reduce state spending on social welfare for one-parent families (Edwards and Halpern 1992).

Other ways in which the notion of parental responsibility has been criticized include the fact that placing the responsibility for children with parents means that when things go wrong (juvenile crime, truancy, etc.) the state can lay the blame firmly at the door of the parent and can conveniently ignore socio-economic factors which may have contributed to such family breakdown. It also means that if parents 'fail' in their responsibility the state can be justified in stepping in and overriding or removing the rights of the parents.

So we can see that this idea of parental responsibility does little if anything to promote the rights of the child to self-determination. Everything depends on having parents who will respect the rights of the child and will allow the child to make decisions, learn from mistakes, etc. The law lays down rules of what children may and may not do at certain ages and relies on parents to act in accordance with the spirit of the law. When children step outside the boundaries of what is acceptable behaviour the state does not look for the reasons why, but seeks to place blame either on the children themselves or on the parents.

Children in the Criminal Justice System

We have looked at the 'legal capacity' of children in relation to some areas of private law and their perceived ability to take part in certain activities. We will now look at the rights and capacity of children who become caught up in the criminal justice system through being a victim of a crime or through being a perpetrator of a crime.

Children as defendants

In the UK children are deemed to be criminally responsible from the age of 10 years. This is a relatively new idea, coming as it did with the Crime and Disorder Act 1998. Before this act there was a presumption that children between the ages of 10 and 14 were incapable of committing a crime, but the prosecution could bring evidence to show that the child did know what they were doing and if the evidence was proved then the child could be found guilty of a crime. In many ways this previous approach fixed the age of criminal responsibility at age 14 and allowed a sort of buffer zone between the ages of 10 and 14, where the presumption of inability to commit a crime would favour the child.

But what do we mean by 'inability to commit a crime'? If a 7-year-old child walks out of a supermarket without paying for their food then surely they have committed the crime of theft? If a 9-year-old child hits another child with an iron bar and that child is severely injured then this presumably is grievous bodily harm. What the law looks at when deciding whether a child is 'capable' of committing a crime is not so much the physical act that might take place but the state of mind at the time. A crime is defined as having two elements, the physical element (the act or conduct) and the mental element (intention to do the act or recklessness as to the result of your act). Both elements must be proved before a crime can be said to have been committed. In relation to children under the age of 10 years, the law presumes that the child does not have the intellectual or cognitive ability to perpetrate the mental element of a crime and so they are 'incapable' of committing a crime. Once a child has reached the age of 10 years then the law presumes that they then have the cognitive ability to form intention and therefore they are capable of committing a crime. This has been a fairly simplistic explanation of what is quite a complex area; however, what is important to note here is that the law decides that once a child reaches 10 years they have all the decision-making and self-determination processes in place to allow them to plan and carry out a crime.

The young defendant will not be tried in an adult court and often their identities can be kept secret from the press and public. The physical organization of the court and the way the proceedings are conducted is intended to be less intimidating for the young offender. For example, parents may be present, the legal team does not wear wigs and gowns, the press are excluded. A young person, if found guilty of an offence, would be sent to a Young Offenders Institution rather than an adult prison.

However, in many ways this approach is a contradiction because if young people need this kind of protection from the legal process itself then surely this is making a comment about their 'maturity' in dealing with normal court proceedings, and yet they are deemed to be capable of the mental processes required to commit the crime in the first place.

Children as victims or witnesses to crime

The protection that young offenders can rely on is not always present for the young person who is the victim of a crime or is a witness to a crime. Firstly, the child or young person who is a victim of a crime, especially a crime against their person such as physical or sexual assault, must know that a crime has been committed against them before they can report it to anyone. Many of the allegations of sexual assault against children originally manifest themselves in less direct ways than straight accusation. The child may demonstrate behaviour changes, depression or even self-harm, the investigation of which may show that the child has been the victim of assault. This lack of knowledge that a crime has been committed against them is something that perpetrators of such crimes often rely on. This ignorance is something that we as a society may even perpetuate by our unwillingness to talk about such things as child sexual abuse openly with children and young people.

Having established that a crime may have been committed, the child must then convince the court that they are competent to give their evidence. This is not a right as it is with adults. The child must be questioned by the court to establish if they are competent and the court has quite wide discretion in deciding this issue, always of course in the best interest of the child but sometimes with the result that the child is denied access to justice. In 1989 the Pigot Committee put forward some recommendations which would allow child witnesses and child victims to give their evidence in court with the minimum of trauma. These recommendations include the following:

- The offence is reported.
- Police and social services interview the child on video and a tape is made (tape 1).
- Police show tape 1 to the suspect.
- Judge views tape 1 and rules on admissibility.
- There is a preliminary hearing in the judge's chambers. The defence puts questions to the child on video and a second tape is made (tape 2).
- If necessary there could be a supplementary interview of the child before the judge in chambers and a third tape made (tape 3).
- At the trial of the defendant, tapes 1, 2 and 3 replace the live evidence of the child.

The main objections to these proposals were that the defence would have to disclose its defence before the trial and also lawyers felt that the opportunity to discredit a witness in live cross-examination in open court would be lost. The recommendations of the Pigot Committee were reduced somewhat to allowing children to give their evidence via video provided the child attends the court for live cross-examination. The Criminal Justice Act 1991 allows for the child victim to give their evidence via video and be cross-examined via live television link while the child is in another room. However, there are restrictions on the use of such live links. Firstly, this technology is not available in every courtroom in the country. If the technology is not there then the child may not use it. They may be allowed to use screens that would act as a barrier between themselves and the defendant in the courtroom, but this is a poor substitute. The second restriction, which applies to live video link or screen, is that it is at the discretion of the court – it is not a right that the child can claim. The defence will always argue that the use of such methods disadvantages their client as it puts their client in a negative light with the jury before the trial even starts. The prosecution must bring evidence that giving evidence in the normal way will harm the child and there must be a balance of risk to the child as against prejudice to the defendant.

It has been suggested that 'decriminalizing' the offence of child abuse would actually lead to more protection for the child victim, as the threat of prison and all that that entails for sex offenders means that defendants will always be advised to plead not guilty even if they want to address the thing they have done. This forces a trial with the child victim, as often they are the only witness. Decriminalizing these offences would mean that people accused of them could be cautioned and made to undergo therapy/treatment if they admit to the offence, thereby avoiding the trauma of a trial for the child and also ensuring that treatment/therapy is offered to offenders, making them less likely to re-offend. This is a contentious area, because such an approach may be interpreted as society diminishing the offence of child abuse after so many years of fighting to have it recognized as an offence in the first place.

It is interesting to consider the different ways in which the law and the state treat children of the same age when they are offenders as opposed to when they are victims. A 10-year-old child who is alleged to have committed an assault will be tried, will have to give evidence, and if found guilty will be punished. A 10-year-old victim of assault may not be able to give evidence if deemed not competent, may be able to give evidence in a protected manner or may not (at the discretion of the court), and has no redress if the evidence against the defendant is discredited by aggressive cross-examination.

It is a confusing approach that we take towards children in the criminal justice system. It is difficult to pin down any unambiguous rationale for the way that children are given legal rights or given access to legal rights in this country. The legal status of the unborn child, however viable the foetus may be, is subsumed in the rights of the mother. The legal capacity of the child once born is almost entirely dependent on adult intervention and advocacy. The child's right to justice is largely based on beliefs and values about children and childhood which may or may not be true for that individual child. The way the child is treated by the system will vary according to whether the child is a victim or an offender.

There is no doubt that there have been improvements in the way the legal system recognizes and upholds the rights of the child. We have seen in previous chapters that many people in the legal and social welfare system are concerned with child advocacy and allowing the voice of the child to be heard. However, there is also no doubt that we have a considerable way to go before we can say that children and adults have equal rights and equal access to justice.

Activity

Now that you have read what children are 'allowed' to do at certain ages in England, think about and list the main anomalies that occur to you.

REFERENCES

Edwards, S. and Halpern, A. (1992) Parental responsibility: An instrument of social policy. *Family Law*, Vol. 113.

FURTHER READING

Children's Rights Alliance England website: http://www.crights.org.uk. This is a useful site because it includes some full texts of debates in parliaments on child rights issues and shows possible and potential developments in this area.

Flekkoy, M. G. and Kaufman, N. H. (1997) *The Participation Rights of the Child: Rights and Responsibilities in Family and Society.* London: Jessica Kingsley Publishers. Looks at the rationale for children's rights generally and with a particular emphasis on participation rights, including during legal proceedings.

Franklin, B. (ed.) (1995) *The Handbook of Children's Rights: Comparative Policy and Practice.* London: Routledge. An overview of child rights in the UK, including those in education and the criminal justice system. It has a useful section on international comparisons.

Part *Three*

Children and Society

Chapter Thirty

Interdisciplinary Perspective: The Demonization of Childhood

DOMINIC WYSE

One of the main changes in people's attitudes to children over recent years has been the emergence of a strongly held view that children have the capacity for evil and that more and more children are demonstrating this capacity. In this chapter we reveal some of the ways that the media has contributed unhelpfully to this distorted view. The important case of James Bulger's killing is reviewed in order to expose the media's inappropriate reporting and clarify some of the facts of the case, of which many people are unaware.

Three chapters in this book focus on interdisciplinary issues. Chapter 1, 'Histories of Childhood', dealt with the historical basis to our changing understanding of childhood. It concluded that smaller families and the influence of liberal thinking had resulted in a new construct of childhood. However, at the same time, the move to compulsory schooling created an ambiguous state for children. It is not only in education that this ambiguity is reflected. Chapter 15, 'Children's Rights', illustrated how there is still much work to be done to ensure that children are able to claim the rights that are enshrined in the UN Convention on the Rights of the Child. This final interdisciplinary chapter looks at the way childhood has become demonized by a powerful element in our society.

Many people work with children. The wide range of these occupations has resulted in ever more specialized knowledge required to cater for children's needs and interests. However, there are some aspects of working with children that are shared across all occupations. One of these concerns *beliefs* about children and childhood. In chapter 8 you saw how people have different beliefs about the extent to which child development is a result of nature and/or nurture. Another important theory relates to the way that we view childhood in general. Many people talk about childhood as a time of innocence, that all children are born intrinsically good, or that children are born as a 'blank slate' and the experiences that they have in life fashion their characters. These issues have exercised people's minds for a very long time.

The ideas of the French philosopher Jean-Jacques Rousseau have been influential for many people who work with children. Rousseau believed that when children are born they are pure and unaffected by some of the negative influences of their society. For this reason Rousseau felt that adults should not be in a hurry to press their versions of the world on children. Rather, children should be encouraged to discover the world for themselves and their innate positive characteristics will guide them in the early stages. The following quotes are taken from Rousseau's classic text *Emile*, a novel that expresses his views about learning and teaching:

> Respect childhood, and do not hurry to judge it, either for good or for ill. Let the exceptional children show themselves, be proved, and be confirmed for a long time before adopting special methods for them. Leave nature to act for a long time before you get involved with acting in its place, lest you impede its operations.

This quote emphasizes the point that children should be respected and that we should not judge them too early, either positively or negatively. Rousseau also suggests that we need to wait to see the positive and even exceptional aspects of children's characters before we rush to educate them. He explains that inappropriate intervention too early might stop nature taking its natural course.

> As for my pupil, or rather nature's, trained early to be as self-sufficient as possible, he is not accustomed to turning constantly to others; still less is he accustomed to displaying his great learning for them. On the other hand, he judges, he foresees, he reasons in everything immediately related to him. He does not chatter; he acts. He does not know a word of what is going on in society, but he knows very well how to do what suits him.

Rousseau's book about childhood uses the fictional character Emil as a means to explain his theories about childhood. Early independence is stressed as an important way to encourage children to learn at their own pace. He refused to accept the idea that children are lazy and suggested that they actively think about their lives. However, like the later ideas of Jean Piaget, Rousseau seems to suggest that children are egocentric: in other words, they tend to think more about their own concerns than those of others. This last idea perhaps needs some careful thought, as many children are capable of thinking about other people (for example, those children who act as carers for poorly relatives). However, it is certainly true to say that children's ability to think about others is different from that of adults. The difficulties that children find in first learning why we sometimes need to say sorry are an interesting example of this.

Literature and films for children have often emphasized the idea of childhood as a period of innocence. Stories of long summer holidays where children become absorbed in their own fantasy adventures are common. Harry Potter's miserable experiences at the hands of the Dursleys confirm his vulnerability and innocence. Rather than focus on the impact this might have on his schooling and life in general, J. K. Rowling transports Harry to a world of magic in which he learns to triumph over his adversity. Other authors, such as Jacqueline Wilson, have dealt seriously with the difficult issues that many children have to confront.

Although the idea of childhood as a period of innocence has a long history, periodically this view is challenged by events in society. One of the most serious of these is when children kill other people, in particular if they kill other children. Adults find this very difficult to deal with. On a straightforward level we are all shocked by any kind of killing. We are shocked if children are killed by adults. In recent years the murders of children carried out by Fred and Rosemary West and the earlier murders by Ian Brady and Myra Hindley were widely reported. These reports reflected society's revulsion. Reaction to these kinds of killings is partly reinforced by the belief in the innocence of childhood: the killing of vulnerable innocent children is seen as much worse than the killing of supposedly less vulnerable adults. In part this is because adults are assumed to have greater responsibility for their actions. This kind of generalization – that all adults are capable of being responsible for their actions and all children are not – is contentious. Many adults repeatedly show an inability to think before they act and often regret the consequences – something to which some children are also prone.

The kinds of emotions generated by adults killing children are magnified when children kill children. In these cases a child who is supposed to be innocent carries out murder, which is the most serious kind of crime. The murdering child has lost their innocence through the act. The victim has also had their innocence irrevocably taken away from them. This clashes very strongly with our perceptions of how children should behave and how childhood should be characterized. Thus, it is a much greater shock for adults. This is in stark contrast to our desensitized response to the regular killing of thousands of adults across the world, in wars for example.

Child killings and children who kill are very rare. Statistics on child deaths show that the rate has remained fairly constant over several decades. However, society's attitudes to crime do seem to be changing. There is greater unease in the population about the risk of violent crime to both adults and children. Fearful parents are much more cautious about their children's independence. The problem here is that restrictions on appropriate opportunities for independence can damage children's life chances by stopping them from developing their own strategies for coping with life. This is a high price to pay if attitudes to crime have been fuelled by inaccurate media coverage rather than proper attention to objective evidence.

Although child killings are rare, unfortunately they do happen. Society's concern for children means that whenever there is a child death there is often much soul searching. Huge inquiries are usually set up if a child dies due to abuse, and people try to work more effectively to minimize the risk of such tragedies happening again.

In recent years, one case in particular of children killing another child has been the subject of much debate. The case is interesting because it reveals a lot about the ways we view children and childhood.

The James Bulger Case

In 1993 the two-year-old James Bulger was killed by Robert Thompson and Jon Venables. One of the most powerful images of the case was an extract of CCTV footage, which was repeatedly featured in television news bulletins following the trial. In the extract two ten-year-old boys are seen holding the hand of a two-year-old boy and leading him away from the shopping centre where he had been with his mother.

Visual images are often at the heart of society's understanding of an issue (CHAPTERS 1, 33). Holding a young child's hand is normally a protective and loving action. The image of two older boys with a toddler would normally still be seen in this way. The shocking reality that the toddler was being led to his death conflicts strongly with our expectations. It is not difficult to imagine the awful consequences for the family that such an event must have created, even if it is impossible for us to fully understand the extreme emotions that will have been generated.

The case provoked a furore in the media, particularly once the guilty verdict was reached:

> How do you feel now you little bastards? (*Daily Star*)
>
> Born to murder. (*Today*)
>
> Freaks of nature: The faces of normal boys but they had hearts of unparalleled evil. Killing James gave them a buzz. (*Daily Mirror*)

The first thing to say about these newspaper headlines (the *Daily Star* headline in particular) is how inappropriate the vindictive tone is. Criticisms continue to grow about the standard of some sections of the British press compared to other European countries. Editors of such papers have an ethical responsibility to think carefully about the impact of the language in their newspapers. The extreme language of these headlines almost incites violent reactions to the killers without due regard for the possible circumstances that may have contributed to their act. One outcome of this reporting was that even when the killers had finished their sentences they had to be given new identities because it was feared they might be killed.

Bob Franklin has written at length about the implications of the Bulger case and its reporting. He makes the point that specific reporting about the two killers (distasteful as it was) quickly became generalized into suggestions that all children had the dangerous potential to be 'evil'. Right-wing leaning papers such as the *Daily Mail* and *The Times* often blame the alleged freedom of the 1960s as the cause of a whole range of problems in society. The idea of Rousseau and others that children are inherently innocent was challenged in particular by an editorial in *The Times*:

> Popular reaction to the behaviour of James' youthful killers has been conditioned by the belief, prevalent since the Victorian era, that childhood is a time of innocence . . . But childhood has a darker side which past societies perhaps understood better than our own . . . children should not be presumed to be innately good. In the lexicon of crime there is metaphysical evil, the imperfection of all mankind; there is physical evil, the suffering that humans cause each other; and there is moral evil, the choice of vice over virtue. Children are separated by necessity of age from none of these. (*Franklin and Petley 1996: 139*)

This raises some complex issues. In this book we have advocated that positive views of children are an important belief for people who work most effectively with them. This is not to say that children are incapable of doing bad things; rather, we presume that they normally do not. In a way this is similar to the adult right to be presumed innocent until proven guilty. Therefore, we disagree with the notion that the 'darker side' of children should be emphasized. It has been argued that children are routinely denied the right to contribute equitably to society despite strong legal measures which protect their rights (CHAPTER 15). If children are given these rights then they also have to accept responsibilities. Those responsibilities are not just individually based; they include more general recognition about children's place in society. They include the recognition that just as some adults are capable of crime, so too are some children. We should never forget, however, that adults are of course responsible for the vast majority of crime, including that which is perpetrated against children themselves.

If we return to the specifics of the Bulger case, one of the things that contributed to the demonization of the two killers was a lack of attention to the possible causes of the crime or any explanation of why they did what they did. While they do not in any way amount to a *reason* for the killing, a number of factors should be taken into consideration:

- Jon Venables had been referred to a psychologist by a primary teacher because he harmed himself. This self-harm included banging his head against a wall, cutting himself and hanging himself upside down on a coat peg.
- Jon Venables was bullied at school.
- Robert Thompson's family lived in poverty.
- Robert Thompson's mother and father had separated and his mother drank heavily.
- Robert Thompson's house was destroyed by fire.
- Robert Thompson's brother was taken into care after he was threatened with a knife by another brother. When he returned the brother took an overdose to pressure social services to take him back (Franklin and Petley 1996: 142).

In addition to these specific circumstances, there are a number of general characteristics of children who kill, as Wolff and McCall Smith (2001) point out. Most children who kill have serious **neuropsychological abnormalities**; they find it difficult to control their impulses; they are failures at school, which leads to truancy. All have experienced severe problems in their families, such as domestic violence, abuse, drug misuse, mothers who are depressed, and absent fathers. These things show that we must be very careful before we start labelling all children as evil, particularly as many of these mitigating circumstances can be attributed to the failings of adults. It is perhaps *this* which is at the root of our unease about children who kill, because we all feel a deep sense of responsibility and failure.

It is easy to assume that the way that problems are dealt with in the country you live in is the only way. Of course, this is not the case and the more experience and understanding that you gain of other countries, the more you see that there are many ways of addressing problems. Franklin and Petley (1996) compare the Bulger case with a child murder in Norway.

In 1994 a five-year-old girl was found dead in the snow near her home. The police asked parents in the area to discuss this with their children. Two days later they determined that the girl had died of hypothermia after she was kicked unconscious by three six-year-old boys. One of the boys told the police that they kicked the girl until she stopped crying. One of the boys was upset by the event and took his mother to the place where the girl was lying, but she was already dead. The age of the boys meant that further investigation was carried out by health and welfare authorities rather than the police. The sensational and vengeful tone of the British press was not a feature of the Norwegian press, which took care not to prejudice the views of witnesses. It also reported an extraordinarily compassionate attitude by the parents concerned. The mother of the dead girl was reported as saying:

> I FORGIVE THEM. I forgive those who killed my daughter. It is not possible to hate small children. They do not understand the consequences of what they have done . . . I can sympathize with the boys' parents. They must be going through a lot now. I do not know all of them yet, but they are welcome to contact me if they so wish.

Norway has a strong reputation for its human rights and children's rights approaches. It is probable that this commitment results in a much more compassionate and thoughtful response to such dreadful events. Of course, it should be stressed that these two killings are not identical. In particular, the ages of the children could be regarded as significant. The law in the UK places importance on the child's ability to understand that what they did was wrong. The quote from the Norwegian mother indicates that the children who killed the girl may not have properly understood their actions. It is certainly true that in general younger children have less understanding about the implications of their actions than older children.

The consequences of British society's response to the Bulger trial as portrayed in the media were serious. The home secretary of the day intervened in the case and ensured that Venables and Thompson were given much harsher sentences than would normally be the case. Because of this, lawyers representing the boys appealed to the European Court of Human Rights. The judgement found that the context of an adult court – complete with hostile crowds and press – meant that the boys had been intimidated, with the result that they did not understand the implications of the court process as well as they might have. It was also found that the home secretary had breached human rights law because he had intervened in a way that was unfair: sentencing decisions should be made by judges who are independent and who are not subject to political pressures to the same extent as politicians. Wolff and McCall Smith (2001) argue that children should be treated differently from adults in the courts. They provide evidence which shows that adolescents who have committed murder have a better chance of rehabilitation than adults partly because they are still developing. They also argue that the age of criminal responsibility should be raised from 10 to 12 or 14, as recommended in the judgement by the European Court.

Looking to the Future

Fortunately, child killings are rare, but it is important that lessons are learned from every death. Will McMahon and Lisa Payne (2001) suggest a number of areas that need improvement. One issue featured in the media was that instead of going to an adult prison Venables and Thompson received therapy and other support from the state. It appears that this support proved to be the right decision, as recent reports have indicated that the boys have shown remorse for what happened and are rehabilitated, even though the pressure of being given new identities will be considerable. In contrast, the victim's family has received very little support, something that needs to be addressed.

As we described earlier, there were clear signs at school that one of the boys in particular was in need of help. Primary teachers have been under considerable pressure over the last decade in relation to the school curriculum. This has had the effect of reducing the attention paid to the pastoral care of children. Teacher-training curricular prescribed by government also pay very little attention to issues such as children's rights and child protection, so we should not be surprised if schools are unable to offer the kind of support that such children might need.

Some people argue that the notion that childhood is a period of innocence helpfully cocoons children and enhances their lives. James, Jenks and Prout (1998) have suggested that the consequences of regarding children almost as a tribe apart can have both positive and negative consequences. One of the positive consequences is the greater level of control over their lives that some children might achieve by keeping themselves to themselves. Other people suggest that adults continually categorize children in particular ways in order to control them, which acts as a barrier to children achieving their full rights. The categorization of all children as demons – a feature of society's reaction to the Bulger case – was extremely inappropriate. The way that we view children in general is directly linked to the way we deal with them practically and specifically. If we regard children mainly in a positive light it can help us maintain high expectations of their progress and contribution to society. Children have a right to be treated with respect and dignity. It is the responsibility of us all to seek, understand and reward their many positive features before we begin to blame.

Activity

Collect as many examples as possible of media reporting of a serious crime that affects children. Analyse the way that children are portrayed and think about the categories of childhood that emerge.

REFERENCES

Franklin, B. and Petley, J. (1996) Killing the age of innocence: Newspaper reporting of the death of James Bulger. In J. Pilcher and S. Wagg (eds) *Thatcher's Children? Politics, Childhood and Society in the 1980s and 1990s*. London: Falmer Press.

James, A., Jenks, C. and Prout, A. (1998) *Theorizing Childhood*. Cambridge: Polity Press.

McMahon, W. and Payne, L. (2001) Lessons from the Bulger case. *Children and Society*, Vol. 15: 272–4.

Wolff, S. and McCall Smith, A. (2001) Children who kill: They can and should be reclaimed. *British Medical Journal*, Vol. 322: 61–2.

FURTHER READING

Franklin, B. and Howarth, J. (1996) The media abuse of children: Jake's progress from demonic icon to restored childhood innocent. *Child Abuse Review*, Vol. 5 (5): 310–18.

Guardian newspaper website: http://www.guardian.co.uk/. Includes an archive of articles since 1998 for which you could use 'children' and 'childhood' as keyword searches.

Pilcher, J. and Wagg, S. (eds) *Thatcher's Children? Politics, Childhood and Society in the 1980s and 1990s*. London: Falmer Press. A very important text which explores the issues to do with the demonization of childhood in addition to the important influence of politics.

Culture

Chapter Thirty-one

Toys and Games

NELL NAPIER

The value of toys is discussed. We explore how the choice of toys can influence the nature of children's play. The difference between pre-structured and open-ended toys is explained. The idea that particular toys suggest hidden messages about children's role in society is introduced. It is concluded that the choice and monitoring of the use of toys are key tasks for people who work with young children.

Imagine a very young child opening some presents. You expect them to play with the toy inside, but instead they seem to enjoy the wrapping paper. This situation is obviously quite amusing to adults because of the conventions of how we should react when given a present. There is also a possible link with children's learning. Most children spend considerable time playing with everyday materials and objects and putting them to their own imaginative uses. This is all part of their natural curiosity and desire to understand and control their own world. Roland Barthes, a French philosopher writing in the 1950s, believed that children should be encouraged to do this. He maintained that modern plastic toys were often just small copies of the objects used by adults and that such toys encouraged children to be *users* rather than *creators*.

Writers such as Tina Bruce (Bruce and Meggitt 1999) talk of pre-structured and open-ended materials. Pre-structured toys are those which have a fixed use (e.g. shape sorters, tea sets, etc.). The way in which children play with these toys is predetermined. Open-ended materials include sand, water, dough and other natural materials, and toys with a variety of potential purposes, such as bricks. When children are playing with open-ended toys there is more opportunity for them to create their own play. For example, bricks might be used to build a high tower or a fairground. Professionals who work with children often favour open-ended toys because they offer the children the opportunity to initiate their own play. Furthermore, with the help of the adult they can develop play in ways which enable them to gain skills and abilities ranging from the physical to the intellectual and creative.

Eleanor Goldschmeid (1991) rejects commercially produced toys because they limit sensory experience rather than encourage it. She pioneered heuristic play, which actively encourages exploration and discovery. This kind of play capitalizes on the fact that babies are essentially sensory beings. She advocates the use of treasure baskets (described in DfES 2003), which contain natural materials for children to explore. These should be used as soon as babies can sit comfortably and can grasp and handle objects. The objects should be a range of everyday items, but not plastic or bought toys. The basket itself should have a flat bottom and be strong enough for the baby to lean on without it tipping. It should be filled to the brim with objects so that there is plenty of scope for the baby to sort and explore. The objects provide the baby with a wealth of sensory experiences and promote curiosity and high levels of concentration. There are various categories of objects that should be included in the basket:

- *Natural:* fir cones, large pebbles, dried gourds, large chestnuts, tooth brush, shaving brush, big feathers, pumice stone, piece of loufah.
- *Wooden:* small boxes, napkin ring, pegs, cubes, bobbin, bamboo whistle.
- *Textiles, including leather and fake fur:* puppy bone, leather purse, ball, small teddy, bath plug, golf ball.
- *Metal:* spoons, egg whisk, lemon squeezer, garlic crush.
- *Paper and cardboard:* greaseproof paper, small cardboard boxes, spiral bound notebook.

Hidden Messages

Toys play a large part in helping children to develop socially influenced roles such as gender. Gender 'refers to the behaviours, attitudes, values, beliefs and so on which a particular society expects from or considers appropriate to males and females on the bases of their biological sex' (Gross 2000: 576). As societal expectations for men and women change, so too should the kinds of toys that are available, but this change appears to be painfully slow. Barthes (1993: 53) found that dolls were meant to 'prepare little girls for the causality of motherhood, to "condition" her to her future role'. It is interesting to reflect on whether Barthes's findings from the 1950s in France are true of the UK in the twenty-first century.

Toys and images of toys can also encourage negative stereotypes in relation to the world of work. For example, the packaging of doctors and nurses sets might feature boys as doctors and girls as nurses. While this may reflect the majority of cases the constant repetition of such images can help to perpetuate stereotypes. Ethnic minority children of either gender are rarely used on packaging, yet they are a large and growing section of UK society.

Bob Dixon (1990) carried out a study of children's toys, games and puzzles (Sindy, Action Man, He-Man, My Little Pony, Dungeons and Dragons, Monopoly, Death Race Bob and many more). He found that gender divisions were reinforced and male aggression emphasized. He also noted an ethnocentric emphasis: the toys encouraged children to see the world from the perspective of a Western capitalist society. Games like Monopoly are based on the idea that companies and people should operate in a competitive financial environment. While this may be the dominant world model, it is repeated endlessly in hundreds of money games and denies children access to alternative ideas. For example, in recent times there has been a growing feeling that investments should be ethical. This means that companies that look after our pension funds or our savings accounts, for example, have to ensure that the stocks and shares that they buy are from companies that do not exploit their workforce or the environment. More and more we require companies to ensure that the poorest people of the world are not being disadvantaged by capitalist activities. The Fairtrade brand, which ensures that workers in developing countries receive a fair wage, is another example of this. It is important that children grow up understanding that countries organize their societies in different ways, all of which are equally valuable. You can see that the selection of toys is not the simple task that at first it may seem.

As well as choosing toys, adults should also play a mediating role during their use. There are many things that children learn through play without an adult present. It is important that they have frequent opportunities to do this. However, this should be complemented by adult-supported play. Adults can extend children's vocabulary when they are playing, they can answer children's questions, they can scaffold their learning by posing problems or giving guidance, they can also help children to solve disputes. Adults can also help children to deal with difficult social and emotional problems; an approach that has been called play therapy.

Adults also have a role to play in encouraging children to use materials which they may not have experienced in the past. There has been concern that boys and girls are disadvantaged in various ways because they do not have the full range of experiences in the early years. For example, it has been suggested that girls are not usually as experienced as boys when they demonstrate spatial ability. In later years this might have a negative impact on their ability to understand map reading or geometry. In order to improve spatial ability children should experience play with constructional materials such as wooden bricks and Lego. In the past these activities were considered to be boys' toys. Even today there are early years workers who fail to challenge the idea that it is natural that boys prefer construction activities and there is nothing that can be done to change that.

Because of the concern about girls' lack of spatial ability a report from the office of Her Majesty's Chief Inspector of Schools and the Equal Opportunities Commission (1996: 18) recommended that 'schools can introduce specific initiatives in nursery and key stage 1 classes targeting girls who lack experience in constructional activity'. This was a welcome recommendation. However, teachers need to monitor what is happening when girls use construction materials. Epstein (1995) showed that when girls play with constructional apparatus they often do traditionally female things, such as build a home and play domesticated games in that home. Epstein accepts that in physically building the home they also carry out a traditionally male task, but cautions that we should not assume that simply giving girls the opportunity will be enough.

When choosing toys and games you should be aware that they are powerful tools for the development of skills and understanding. They are also vital in developing children's values, views of society and self-perception. In all cases careful consideration needs to be given to their use and potential.

Activity

Make a list of about thirty different toys that you know. Use a large sheet of paper to categorize the toys as pre-structured, open-ended or a mixture of both. Discuss the pros and cons of the different toys and list your main conclusions about a selection of the toys.

REFERENCES

Barthes, R. (1993) [1957] *Mythologies.* London: Vintage.

Department for Education and Science (DfES) (2003) *Birth to Three Matters – A Framework to Support Children in their Earliest Years.* London: Department for Education and Science.

Dixon, B. (1990) *Playing Them False: A Study of Children's Toys, Games and Puzzles.* Stoke-on-Trent: Trentham Books.

Epstein, D. (1995) Girls don't do bricks: Gender and sexuality in the primary classroom. In J. Siraj-Blatchford and I. Siraj-Blatchford (eds) *Educating the Whole Child: Cross-Curricular Skills, Themes and Dimensions.* Buckingham: Open University Press.

Goldschmeid, E. (1991) *Babies and Toddlers: Carers and Educators Quality for the Under Threes.* London: National Children's Bureau.

Gross, R. (2000) *Psychology: The Science of Mind and Behaviour.* London: Hodder and Stoughton.

Her Majesty's Chief Inspector of Schools and the Equal Opportunities Commission (1996) *The Gender Divide: Performance Differences between Boys and Girls at School.* London: HMSO.

FURTHER READING

British Association of Early Childhood Educators. *Equal from the Start* (booklet): 111 City View House, 463 Bethnal Green Road, London E4 9QY. Further information regarding equal opportunities in early years settings.

Bruce, T. and Meggitt, C. (1999) *Child Care and Education.* London: Hodder and Stoughton. Resources for toys and games, videos, puppets.

National Children's Bureau website: http://ncb.org.uk. Explore the work of the Children's Play Council here.

Chapter *Thirty-two*
Children's Literature

RUSSELL JONES

Children's literature is a powerful influence on childhood that helps young people explore their identity in relation to the texts they read. A brief look at the history of children's literature helps you to understand the significance of some of the modern texts for children that we refer to.

> *Storytelling weaves a spell that binds us all into one world community. We enter that world where anything is possible, to think, to feel and to grow together. Our stories help sustain and create our society. They help to shape and fashion who we are, and help us to know and feel what is right and what is wrong. Stories should cherish the human spirit and as such should be a central part of every child's upbringing.* (Corbett 1993: 5)

We are living through a renaissance in children's literature; there has never been a time when texts were so accessible, so plentiful, so rich and diverse. When we talk about children's literature we tend to mean conventional printed texts. But if you think about 'text' in a much broader way then the developments in technology have created new and equally powerful narratives for children. The development of film, television and radio started this process, but in recent times we must also include forms such as computer games and other electronic texts. One of the key features of these new texts is the way that they can have non-linear structures such as hyperlinks.

Stories existed well before the technological advances that made it possible to capture, reproduce and distribute them. Storytelling began as an oral experience, not a printed one. An example of the powerful oral tradition of storytelling is reflected in the range of Celtic mythologies, and we know that children took a full and active part in passing on these tales over time. Tales of courage, spirituality and community were all part of the child's developing sense of belonging, and these narratives served a clear social purpose.

In historical terms, literature for children is a relatively new phenomenon. Even by the end of the nineteenth century there were very few texts that were written specifically *for* children and almost no examples of published texts written *by* children. Children's literature was entirely dominated by adults. Typically, the literature in question was written to serve a particular purpose. There are several examples of English grammar manuals being adapted for the use of children in the eighteenth century, and many other examples of texts from this period which were securely rooted in religious practices and moral instruction. Stories from the Bible or the Book of Common Prayer were often used as starting points in the production of texts for children, and these were clearly aimed not only at encouraging literacy development, but also at providing examples to aid moral development. For many children, Sunday schools gave them their introduction to literacy.

The eighteenth century saw the production of many cheaply produced tales aimed at teaching children moral lessons through their literature. Short stories, poems or social observations would be followed by written moral instruction and guidance. At the same time one of the first texts that could be called literature for children was written. The *Tales of Mother Goose* and collected nursery rhymes were designed to appeal to children with much less of an emphasis on instruction. These short tellings were often funny and sometimes grotesque.

Although fairy tales are regarded as aimed at children, originally there was much less distinction between the interests of children and adults. The themes of abandonment and abuse were common and children were often taken into the woods to be killed (Snow White, Hansel and Gretel), child characters were forever in danger of being eaten (Red Riding Hood, Hansel and Gretel, Goldilocks), and adults (particularly women) were often portrayed as predatory creatures only too willing to place children in dangerous and life-threatening situations (Snow White, Hansel and Gretel, etc.). While fairy tales were never conceived as being child-specific, many were used to fulfil the socialization role already undertaken by religious and moral texts: children were 'encouraged to sort out their lives through fairy tales' (Zipes 1997: 10). Today, this sorting out process means they can negotiate between the 'traditional' printed versions, film versions such as Disney, and the more recent versions of tales such as those by Jon Scieszka (1991) (where we get the wolf's side of the story as opposed to the three little pigs'), or Babette Cole's (1996, 1997) reversal of gender stereotypes.

It wasn't until the later part of the nineteenth century that wider forms of children's literature began to appear. It is important to remember that up until this time the vast majority of children were still functionally illiterate. The children of wealthy families were educated, and there were church schools that attempted to provide basic forms of education for poorer children, but huge numbers of children had little or no education at all and were expected to become wage earners as soon as possible in order to contribute to the family's economy. The notion of these children having their own literature was deemed to be irrelevant for both economic and educational reasons.

Many texts from this period still retained clear notions of Christianity and moral instruction – *The Selfish Giant* and *The Happy Prince* by Oscar Wilde (1995) are two clear examples – and this progression can be traced through to twentieth-century stories such as *The Lion, the Witch and the Wardrobe* by C. S. Lewis (1991). By contrast, however, in 1864, *Alice's Adventures in Wonderland* (Carroll 1998) stood out as a novel that portrayed childhood in a very different way. Alice speaks with authority, experience and clarity, in a world populated by adults who demonstrate unfathomable rules, anarchic behaviour and nonsensical logic. While the novel might be seen as a simple dream-state role-reversal for adults and children, children themselves saw in the novel reflections of their own experiences of the adult-dominated world. Children who read the novel recognized the apparent arbitrariness and inconsistency of rule-making in the adult world and saw that Alice found ways to negotiate her way through this world, displaying frustration, bemusement and incredulity at adult behaviour.

Although Alice was a turning point in children's literature there were precious few examples of strong engaging texts by authors who had picked up the challenge of creating a vigorous and lively body of literature for children. Many novels aimed at children during this time were still rooted in the politics of behaviour. As the First World War dawned typical novels for children were about military academies, public school regimes and tales of heroism. The vast majority of these publications were aimed at boys, as not only were they seen to need further moral instruction but also because they would be the wage earners for their families when they got married.

However, a crucially important development in children's literature was about to take place. For the first time, children began to have literature written for them and about them, and this took the form of comics. Characters from comics began to appear in newspapers for children and their popularity spread among children and adults alike. It is interesting to note the many examples of comics being used as propaganda during the First World War, where typically chaotic and humorous characters would begin to demonstrate heroic (and often **xenophobic**) acts for their readership. Clearly, this form of children's literature was being recognized as a powerful tool in the shaping of people's minds.

Theorists such as Jerome Bruner and Margaret Meek have explained at length their beliefs about the significance of narrative in the construction of the social world for the child. Many others have discussed the ways in which concepts of fiction and reality become blurred as children grapple with story narrative. These narratives can be fictitious or based in actuality, but in either case it is the need to structure, to sequence and to communicate that is the driving force. A fundamental aspect of the relationship between child and text is that of meaning. Some might argue that meaning is (in a novel, for example) predetermined, and that the child's relationship with this narrative is passive, whereby the meaning is merely passed on as a narrative experience. The child adds little or nothing because the text itself carries the author's meanings. Others, however, have a very different version of this relationship, where the act of reading actually *creates* meaning. Margaret Meek referred to narrative as a 'primary act of mind' and emphasized the ways in which children *construct* the narrative through their interpretation.

So where does this leave us when considering children and their literature? What is clear is that there seems to be a need for story and narrative – this need transcends historical period and geographical location. All societies at all periods of recorded history up to and including the present demonstrate the need to shape and understand their social world through the medium of narrative, and our children in the twenty-first century are no different. The forms may have altered to meet the advances in technology, but the need is unchanged.

Activity

Look through a collection of picture books from different periods of time. Choose one book that you particularly like and identify the key childhood themes. Think about the way that books have changed over time.

REFERENCES

Carroll, L. (1998) [1865] *Alice's Adventures in Wonderland.* Harmondsworth: Penguin Books.
Cole, B. (1996) *Princess Smartypant.* Harmondsworth: Penguin Books.
Cole, B. (1997) *Prince Cinders.* Harmondsworth: Penguin Books.
Corbett, P. (1993) *Tales, Myths and Legends.* Leamington Spa: Scholastic.
Lewis, C. S. (1991) [1950] *The Lion, the Witch and the Wardrobe.* London: Collins.
Scieszka, J. (1991) *The True Story of the Three Little Pigs.* Harmondsworth: Penguin Books.
Wilde, O. (1995) [1888] *The Happy Prince and Other Tales.* London: Everyman.
Zipes, J. (1997) *Happily Ever After.* London: Routledge.

FURTHER READING

Bearne, E. (ed.) (1995) *Greater Expectations: Children Reading Writing.* London: Cassell. A collection of powerful insights into the ways children construct meaning through their reading and their writing.
Marshall, J. (2002) In my book. *Literacy and Learning,* Jan./Feb. 2002: 8–12. Children's enthusiasm for (and relationship with) literature; ways of using narrative as a device to promote understanding.
Website: http://falcon.jmu.edu/~ramseyil/childlit.htm. Extensive essays and illustrated guides to children's literature.

Chapter *Thirty-three* Visual Art

NICHOLAS MEDFORTH

Visual images tell us many things about the way that society views its children. In chapter 1 you read about the work of Philippe Ariès and the debates this caused. We take the notion of analysing artwork further by examining some paintings from the nineteenth century. Many of the concepts that this uncovers are ones that are still a feature of modern images.

The notion that childhood was a special time of growth and development, a time to be treasured and nurtured, emerged following Rousseau's ideas about how we should support children. These ideas were transformed by the adult culture of the time and childhood became sentimentalized in ways which bore little resemblance to the lives of most children. You will remember from chapter 1 that Philippe Ariès used paintings to gain clues about what childhood was like in medieval Europe. In a similar way more recent paintings can provide us with insight into ideas that the adult world had about childhood. Postle (1998) describes the genre of the 'fancy picture' in eighteenth-century British art. In an exhibition catalogue called *Angels and Urchins*, Postle describes the way in which painters represented contrasting themes of innocence and experience by showing children of the time as mythical figures. Nymphs, shepherds and angels are contrasted with beggars, match girls, oyster sellers and the deserving poor (CHAPTER 39).

This idea that childhood was a special time of natural goodness and innocence which had been lost to the adult world was picked up by such poets of the Romantic movement as Blake, Wordsworth and Coleridge, who tended to provide a particularly sentimental view often associated with an idealized rural or naturalistic setting. This perspective on childhood is illustrated by William Wordworth's short poem *My Heart Leaps Up*, written in 1807:

My heart leaps up when I behold
A rainbow in the sky:

Plate 1 *Little Speedwell's Darling Blue* by John Everett Millais, 1896

So was it when my life began;
So is it now as I am a man;
So be it when I shall grow old,
Or let me die!
The Child is father of the Man;
And I could wish my days to be
Bound each to each by natural piety.

At the same time, opposite ideas about children emerged in Victorian England, with church leaders and evangelists fearing that children were born inherently evil or corrupt and needed to be controlled and subjected to the will of God, so that they did not become too great a threat to adult society (Hendrick 1997).

In a 1992 art exhibition in Manchester called *Innocence and Experience*, Holdsworth, Crossley and Hardyment (1992) demonstrated that numerous themes have been used in the portrayal of children in British art from 1600. These include family, identity and the transience of childhood, and the comradeship of children, as well as darker  themes such as fear, cruelty, **sexual exploitation** and death. Overall, though, the emphasis appears to be on the more idealized and romantic perspective, which provides little insight into the challenges, hardships, distress, fears and exploitation faced by children of the time.

Diana Gittens (1998) suggests that images are a particularly powerful way of communicating an idea or viewpoint, as they seem solid, concrete and real yet they may not always simply resemble the reality of what they show. Visual art contains symbols, icons and references to cultural ideas that have been applied by the artist to their subject. Gittens reminds us that representation is not an easy concept because any explanation must take account of the fact that images are products of their time and the culture within which they are painted. As such they give us useful clues about the ways in which children and childhood were seen at the time, at least by the adults who painted them.

Often the paintings of the Romantic period were about a view of childhood which was passed between wealthy adults, although children who were privileged enough to see them might also have gained some ideas about how childhood was supposed to be. It is not difficult to find such paintings, which can be seen in civic galleries around Britain. For the purpose of this chapter we have chosen just three of the many paintings in a local gallery, the Lady Lever Gallery in Port Sunlight, Merseyside.

In *Little Speedwell's Darling Blue* John Millais represented the Romantic view of childhood by placing the child in a natural setting (symbolizing a childhood shaped by a natural goodness) and wearing white clothes to represent innocence. The child is clearly regarded with great affection: a *little darling*, as is suggested in the title. As a result the child becomes an icon of an angelic childhood. This is reinforced by the rather passive posture of the child. Such paintings reflect the oppressive and almost claustrophobic expectation that good children are clean, quiet, able to entertain themselves and who do not challenge adult authority. The gender of the child may represent the painter's view that girls fitted this particular childhood ideal

Plate 2 *Street Arabs at Play* (also titled *Head Over Tails*) by Dorothy Tennant, 1890

better than boys. The yellow cornfield in the background may suggest a golden time of childhood.

The painting was bought by Lord Lever and later bequeathed to the gallery because he was attracted to the 'pretty light-hearted painting', which was far removed from the sombre poem (Tennyson's *In Memoriam*) on which it was based. It is possible that Lever's interest in a particularly romantic view of childhood was part of the manipulation of images that is a feature of advertising media. He will have been aware that the majority of children's lives were nothing like those portrayed in the images that he held in his gallery. But as a successful businessman he recognized how attractive such images of children might be to a public who would buy his soap powder. Similar images were later used in posters advertising soap powder, along with unsophisticated captions and superimposition of soap products.

On first glance, another painting from the same period provides a rather different view of childhood.

Dorothy Tennant and the French painter Jules Bastien Lepage were interested in painting 'unwashed' street children. London flower girls and shoe-blacks became the subjects of an illustrated book, *London Street Arabs of 1890*, from which this painting was originally taken. The setting of Tennant's painting is a typical British industrial scene of the time, with the townscape indicated by the chimneys and factories in the background. The painting is clearly about children from a different class and background to the child portrayed in *Little Speedwell's Darling Blue*. The clothes worn by the children are ragged and made of rougher cloth (without the bows and decorations of Millais's little darling) and the children are barefoot. The children are likely to have been workers, but may have been school children, as during the 1870s and 1880s educational reforms made schooling compulsory. Authors such as Hendrick (1997) suggest that the reforms came about due to a religiously based idea that children were born bad or evil and needed to be corrected and controlled by adult society. Concerns were also expressed that street and factory children were becoming delinquent and a threat to future society. Reformers of the time attempted to solve this perceived problem by attempting to reclaim childhood for all children and provide a form of schooling which would prepare all children for the future needs of society.

Tennant's painting is interesting because it contains several ideas about childhood which do not always sit comfortably together. For example, the painting includes notions of play and freedom and a rather sentimental view of working-class childhood. Tennant has chosen to challenge the negative perceptions of the day by portraying the children from a more romantic viewpoint, hence the innocence of their play. Although this is a more positive portrayal of working-class children, it is an image that is too sanitized and one which tells little of the problems or hardships faced by such children.

The way in which the gender of the children is reflected in the painting is also of interest. The left- and right-hand sides of the painting are almost mirror images of each other. The boys are central, active and boisterous, demonstrating their athletic skills, while the girls towards the outer margin are in a more passive, admiring and

Plate 3 *This is the Way We Wash Our Clothes* by George Dunlop Leslie, 1897

reflective role. It is also interesting to note that the original title of the painting was *Street Arabs at Play*, suggesting a slightly patronizing and subtly racist treatment of the subject as well as positioning the children as mischievous. The title was later altered by Lord Lever to describe the activity of the children, hence the slightly sentimental and nostalgic *Head Over Tails*.

George Dunlop Leslie's painting *This is the Way We Wash Our Clothes* has similar themes to the others we have explored: the relationship between work and play, innocence, class, gender and a sentimentalized idea of childhood experience from an adult perspective. Like *Head Over Tails* the painting was one of the first used as a poster in an advertising campaign for soap powder. At first glance the child appears to be happily playing in her own family kitchen, rehearsing a role she might later take on in her adult life. Alternatively, she may also have been a worker, as working-class girls of a similar age were sent out to supplement the family income by working for minimal pay as skivvies in the homes of the wealthy. The context and use of the painting show how an image can be used to exploit children and childhood for financial gain by appealing to adult sentimentality.

According to Ann Higgonet (1998) this is not the only way in which childhood might be exploited by adults through commercialism. She describes the ways in which subtle themes of power, coyness, sexuality and availability may also be woven into paintings to satisfy an adult painter and audience, and their preferred ways of viewing children.

Gittens (1998) reminds us that the twentieth century onwards has resulted in a proliferation of images which are accessible to both adults and children in ways which have not been experienced by previous generations. These are communicated through still and animated media, paintings, billboard posters, picture book illustrations, catalogues, magazines and newspapers, comics, film, television, logos and advertising campaigns, charity flyers, video and the Internet. These images and representations of childhood are diverse and contain a range of cultural ideas and represent a variety of lived experiences, but they are, in most cases, communicating an idea about childhood from an adult viewpoint.

Childhood continues to be depicted predominantly from a white, middle-class, romanticized, idealized and *cosy* perspective. Themes such as innocence, natural childhood, the deserving poor, schooling, play and development are contrasted with images which fuel adult fears: delinquency, challenges to authority and control. As we have seen, these are all a product of earlier generations. It is too easy for these to shape the ways in which we think about children and childhood, unless we consciously seek to challenge and critically evaluate such themes.

One of the striking new ways that images have been used is represented by a recent series of Barnardo's advertisements. These deliberately subvert conventional images of childhood in order to shock the adult viewer. The adverts deal with issues of child abuse, social exclusion and prostitution, and use graphic and disturbing images of children in threatening situations to communicate the idea of a stolen childhood. These portrayals of childhood are necessary to highlight the significant problems that children face and as a corrective to the other kinds of images which predominate. However, it is still the case that all images are owned and shaped by those who have the power to create and disseminate. When adults have this power the images rarely reflect the reality of the lived experiences of the majority of children.

Activity

Visit your local art gallery. Look at any images of children or childhood you can find. What kind of themes can you identify? Relate your ideas to more contemporary images, such as those on television, film, posters, newspapers and magazines.

REFERENCES

Gittens, D. (1998) What do children represent? In D. Gittens (ed.) *The Child in Question*. London: Macmillan.

Hendrick, H. (1997) Constructions and reconstructions in British childhood: An interpretative survey, 1800 to the present. In A. James and A. Prout (eds) *Constructing and Reconstructing Childhood: Contemporary Issues in the Sociological Study of Childhood*. London: Falmer Press.

Higgonet, A. (1998) *Pictures of Innocence: The History and Crisis of Ideal Childhood*. London: Thames and Hudson.

Holdsworth, S., Crossley, J. and Hardyment, C. (1992) *Innocence and Experience: Images of Children in British Art from 1600 to the Present* (exhibition catalogue). Manchester: Manchester City Art Galleries.

Postle, M. (1998) *Angels and Urchins: The Fancy Picture in Eighteenth Century British Art*. Lund Humphries/Djanolgy Art Gallery, University of Nottingham.

FURTHER READING

Cunningham, H. (1995) *Children and Childhood in Western Society Since 1500*. London: Longman. This very readable book provides a detailed and comprehensive overview of the history of Western childhood, focusing on issues such as the social construction of childhood, family, school, work and the state.

Walther, N. (1998) A picture of innocence, or something more sinister? Children, art and exploitation. *Guardian*, 9 June. This article critically explores the notion of innocent childhood portrayed by adults through art and visual imagery.

Chapter Thirty-four Multimedia

DOMINIC WYSE

We live in a society where visual images are becoming more and more important. This chapter explores some of the issues to do with children's exposure to television and the influence of film. It concludes with some thoughts on the links between learning and multimedia.

Visual images are a powerful medium through which we all view society. Children engage with visual images first because the ability to read and write develops much later. For example, the television is probably one of the first things that children see and hear, and is something which can later occupy large parts of their time. Adults, on the other hand, engage much more with print, although television, film, the Internet and visual images in the environment remain strong influences on adults' lives.

Ever since the invention of television many people have suggested that children watch too much and that it is bad for them. Of course, there are undesirable aspects to excessive television watching. For example, it is not a physically active experience, so if it is done to excess it can contribute to poor physical health. There are also some subjects to which children should not be exposed, such as excessive violence and/or programmes that deal with themes in an adult way. The obvious example is sex. Some people might argue that children should never watch programmes about sex. However, if we think about that in more depth it does not make sense. The important thing is that children are exposed to programmes that are appropriate for their level of development and understanding. It may surprise you to know that there is a book suitable for children of all ages about having babies and which includes some humorous images of sexual positions! (*Mummy Laid an Egg* by Babette Cole).

Another potential problem with excessive television watching is a lack of discrimination. It is all too easy to 'channel hop' in a mindless way. Children are likely to benefit more if they are taught to identify favourite programmes and choose to watch them at the appropriate time. This requires adults and older siblings who are prepared to mediate or help younger children understand television listings in order to remember when particular programmes are showing.

Among early favourites with children are cartoons. Drawings – both children's own and those in picture books – are precursors to the animated images in cartoons. Although animated cartoons are a relatively recent development there are already some classic cartoons which have amused several generations: *Tom and Jerry* is a good example. Regular squabbling and its consequences (a feature of most children's development) are graphically illustrated by the antics of Tom and Jerry. Interestingly, we only ever see the lower body of the main adult in the cartoon.

Violence is one of the issues that relates to *Tom and Jerry* and other cartoons. Recurrent images such as the iron torpedoed down Tom's throat that leaves its imprint in his neck, or Tom being squashed by an enormous weight that leaves his tiny legs popping out of an otherwise flat body, have amused millions of people. Why is it that these images are so less worrying than, say, horror movies such as *Friday the 13th*? It is perhaps children's own opinions on this that give the clue. Often, children will say 'it isn't real'. Realism is an important facet of the extent to which violence on television might be damaging to children. Films and programmes which depict extreme violence with great realism are much more likely to disturb than the typical children's cartoon images. We might think of a scale which at one end has nursery rhyme violence like Humpty Dumpty falling off a wall and at the other end has real-life murder. All programmes will fit somewhere along the scale, with those closest to real-life violence being potentially the most damaging.

The extent to which the combined output of all programmes features violence is something that also needs careful thought. If a child's diet of programmes is predominantly violent, or if over time the output of television programmes markedly increases in violence, this might not be a good thing. It might mean that society is becoming more violent, or it could be that television is 'dumbing down'. These things are very difficult to prove, but we would argue that an environment in which children have access to excessive violence is a damaging one.

Some more modern cartoons produced in the USA are fascinating. *Rugrats* features interaction between siblings and their friends. We see the stereotype of the bossy sister, although she is also shown to be creative and resourceful. The cartoon is *multi-layered*, which means that it has messages for both children and adults alike. Another important feature is that the Rugrats know far more than the adults give them credit for. As with *Tom and Jerry*, the adults tend to be seen as tall and distant, viewed from the children's visual perspective. However, the adults often engage in conversations which explore issues that are common to many parents – sometimes with comical consequences, as when the children misinterpret what they are saying.

Since the 1980s, comics for adults have gained in popularity. Japanese culture has a long tradition of graphic stories, with *Manga* being particularly notable. In the West the author Art Spiegelman has written a Pulitzer prize-winning graphical novel called *Maus*, which features cats and mice portrayed as Nazis and Jews.

Film

The cinema has grown in popularity over the last ten years, with multiplex cinemas catering for this expansion. The Walt Disney Corporation is now a globally influential brand of films for children. One common concern expressed about Disney films is the extent to which they are stereotypical. For example, in *The Little Mermaid* many of the original stories feature a grandmother along with the little mermaid herself, who is the central character. In the Disney version the opening scene focuses heavily on the male lead character and his crew aboard a ship. Shortly afterwards we are introduced to the little mermaid's father; grandmother does not even feature. Sebastian the crab also appears to be a well-worn stereotype of a West Indian comic character.

In order to appeal to as many people in the world as possible such stories are tidied up and any sharp details smoothed off, giving something which at times is rather bland but which sells well. However, other films have been successful without doing this: *Shrek* is a good example. In this film the sugary sweetness of Disney is replaced by an irreverent bitter-sweet portrayal with a disgusting but at times touching main character. *Shrek* is a deliberate antidote to Disney and its many imitators. In one scene, which pokes fun at Disney's *Snow White,* the princess sings a duet with a bird as a reward for beating up a French Robin Hood and his not so merry men. As the duet rises in pitch the bird begins to swell up until eventually it explodes!

A film which perhaps has had the biggest influence of all in recent years is *Star Wars*. In the 1970s, when George Lucas began the *Star Wars* saga, he said that these were 'stories for a generation who had grown up without fairy tales'. Jack Zipes (1997: 1) observes: 'We never abandon fairy tales.' We seem to have a deep-seated need for stories, and it is only the format that changes through history. *The Lion King*, *Beauty and the Beast* and *The Never Ending Story* are all examples of our continued passion for fairy tales in the twenty-first century. Of course, the other driving force behind film making is profit. *Star Wars* was one of the first films to link merchandise with a film in order to enhance profit. This very successful strategy is employed with most children's films these days. An interesting example of this was the publication of books by the company Dorling Kindersley. Initial media reports suggested that the company had vastly over-produced *Star Wars*-related products (including the books), so they tended to receive a negative media image. A closer look reveals a fascinating account of the *Star Wars* myth:

> In the last days of the Republic, Senator Palpatine used deception to become elected President of the Galactic Senate. Once in office he appointed himself Emperor. He declared martial law throughout the galaxy and began to rule through the military forces of the newly created Imperial Navy. Palpatine affected the simple clothing of a simple man, but drew his powers of persuasion and control from the blackest depths of the dark side of the Force. While the Force has twisted his face, it has also sustained him beyond his years, and even in his old age the Emperor remains a figure of terrible power. (*Dorling Kindersley 1988: 33*)

UNIVERSITY OF WINCHESTER
LIBRARY

An intriguing aspect of these books is the way they mix the genres of fiction and non-fiction. Dorling Kindersley produced a visually attractive series of books called *Eyewitness Guides*, which covered a range of factual topics of interest to children. The *Star Wars* books used this same factual format but with subject matter that was entirely fictional:

> Herein you will find the tangible elements of the 'Star Wars' saga explained in detail and presented with clarity as never before. Here you may come very close to touching all this imaginary reality for yourself. You hold in your hands a guidebook and a passport to a place where the blaster bolts smell of ozone and the rock canyons of Tatooine hide mysterious eyes in the dark. Join us. (*Dorling Kindersley 1988: introduction*)

Perhaps most telling of all is the use throughout the book of the initial capital letter in 'Force', suggesting the religious idea of God and bizarrely coincidental with the email that exhorted people to enter 'Jedi' as their religion in the national census. Global marketing could hardly have a stronger weapon than fiction made reality.

Multimedia and Learning

One of the things to think about when using different media with children is the extent to which their experience is passive or active. Passive work involves *analysis* of still and moving images, which at its best is a stimulating experience for children, but at its worst can simply involve the adult transmitting their own views about particular images. For example, photographs can be positively used in a variety of ways to stimulate discussion and even the simple sharing of personal experiences can be valuable. It should be remembered that encouraging children to *create* using multimedia is also a very important learning opportunity. Parker (1999) describes an example of such learning. His research featured a project that involved year 3 children adapting Roald Dahl's story *Fantastic Mr Fox* into an animated film. One part of this involved some children working towards a simplified version of the book for younger children, while others were getting ready to use an animation package on the computer. Parker felt that some of the children's writing to support the script had particularly strong visual characteristics:

> 1 'I saw some metal in the moonlight night.'
> 2 'All I can see is the 4 walls. Brown, dim and muddy like a pison' [prison].
> 3 'I can see the opening to our den. Its daytime the light light is coming in.'
> (*Parker 1999: 31*)

Buckingham's (1999) research has focused on two areas: computer games and creative use of multimedia. In contrast to public concerns, he found that games-playing was very much a social activity. Although games were played alone, they were also played collaboratively. The games provided a topic for much discussion that included swapping games, sharing cheats and hints, and discussion about the wider world of games playing, such as television programmes about the subject, games shops, games arcades, and magazines. Buckingham also added the cautionary note that much of the discussion was influenced by consumerism. This is perhaps further justification for helping children to become *critical* consumers of media messages, so that they are not unfairly influenced by advertising.

In another piece of research Buckingham tried to find out 'to what extent, and how, were children using computers for digital animation, design work, sound or video editing, or for what is sometimes called "multimedia authoring?"' Some of this survey's results mirrored the previous piece of research. For example, overall he found that 'boys were generally more interested and involved' in this area than girls. He also found that although many of the children claimed to be involved in multimedia authoring it was rarely a creative process. For instance, some of the children thought that they had made animations, but they confused their own input with examples that were already available on the computer. The low levels of creativity were due to parents' own lack of skill and ability to help their children, the children's view that computers were mainly to be used for 'messing about' when they were bored, and the absence of meaningful audiences for their work.

The pace of developments in information technology is dramatic. It is for this reason that children are often far more knowledgeable about such things than their parents or even their teachers. Children's lives are very heavily influenced by images of all kinds. It is important that all who work with children celebrate this rather than see it as a threat. If adults talk to children about their multimedia interests and skills and try to learn new skills themselves then they are connecting with an important part of children's lives.

Activity

Use a digital video camera and a computer editing package to make a film with a group of children, either based on a favourite story or one that is improvised.

REFERENCES

Buckingham, D. (1999) Superhighway or road to nowhere? Children's relationships with digital technology. *English in Education*, Vol. 33 (1): 3–12.

Cole, B. (1993) *Mummy Laid an Egg!* London: Random House.

Dorling Kindersley (1988) *Star Wars: The Visual Dictionary*. London: Dorling Kindersley.

Parker, D. (1999) You've read the book, now make the film: Moving image media, print literacy and narrative. *English in Education*, Vol. 33 (1): 24–35.

Zipes, J. (1997) *Happily Ever After: Fairy Tales, Children and the Culture Industry*. London: Routledge.

FURTHER READING

British Film Institute website: http://www.bfi.org.uk/. A useful site for extending your knowledge of film. Includes publications which suggest ideas for working with children: *Story Shorts* is a recent example.

Buckingham, D. (2000) Children's media rights: Protection, empowerment and the role of education. *Childright*, 164: 7–9. Buckingham addresses some of the debates about sex, violence and consumerism, but suggests that children can and are defending their rights.

Warner, A., Williams, J. H. and Katzenberg, J. (producers) (2001) *Shrek*. DreamWorks. This film is very funny and takes a wry look at the culture of fairy tales.

Equality

Chapter *Thirty-five*

Ethnicity and Race

RUSSELL JONES

Children experience childhood differently in relation to the key areas of language, race and culture. A relationship between identity and the experience of contemporary education is outlined. Recent research is used to demonstrate that many children from minority ethnic backgrounds feel marginalized and isolated by the education process.

Children's experiences vary dramatically according to their ethnic background. The institutions of the education system (educare settings, schools, colleges, universities) have the best opportunity to make these experiences positive. Unfortunately, the government's own recent research has concluded that a black Caribbean pupil is almost 50 times as likely to be permanently excluded from school as Chinese children (Howson 2002). This is of particular concern because there is also a worrying relationship between suspensions, expulsions and subsequent criminal behaviour (Blair 2000). Furthermore, there is evidence that even when black pupils achieve more highly on tests than their white counterparts they still find themselves in lower sets, and that even when African-Caribbean children entering the school system at five years old have the highest test scores they can still leave at 16 producing the worst examination results (Berliner 2002).

Numerous studies have shown that young children are aware of racial differences. The work of Milner (1983), Wright (1992) and Gaine (1987, 1995) clearly shows how young children can use racist language (such as 'Paki') and express discriminatory views. Such research has repeatedly called for practice where children's views on issues to do with race, multilingualism and culture are discussed in order to counter learned prejudice. Too often, adults working with children deliberately avoid dealing with any of these issues because they either consider this to be a 'fair' approach or because they don't want to deal with contentious issues. Who is losing out when this sort of practice is the norm?

In day-to-day work with children, people come across children from a wide range of racial and cultural backgrounds. At other times they work with a large majority of children who represent a distinct racial or cultural group. In either case, an important starting point is whether issues such as the child's race, culture or language actually matter in the settings where you work with them. There are two conflicting schools of thought informing this debate and it is worth spending some time considering each of them.

Firstly, there are those who believe that characteristics such as race and culture are largely irrelevant in the classroom. They argue that teaching can only be delivered effectively when all children receive the same curriculum regardless of their race or culture. The teaching is better organized and the learning is stronger because everyone receives the same input. Often, this approach is described as a 'colourblind' one, whereby the teacher deliberately tries not to accept race or skin colour as issues for the classroom. This view is an important one to take on board because it remains commonly held.

Secondly, an alternative position is that characteristics such as race and culture are centrally important in the classroom. Proponents of this view suggest that a colourblind or monocultural approach to teaching actually distances and even alienates some children. It also denies the majority of children access to a wider range of perspectives on society. To ignore characteristics such as language, race and culture means that you are ignoring crucial aspects of the child's identity, which is central to the teaching and learning process.

Let's take an example of the colourblind approach. If the teacher assumes that the English language, traditional English food, traditional English clothing, etc. are the norms which form the basis of the approach, then minority ethnic children are unlikely to find links with many of the important things in their lives. Imagine a British Indian Sikh child in this situation: they are likely to see many aspects of their lives as different and possibly of less value. This is likely to have a negative effect on their self-esteem. It is incorrect to argue that this child is being treated the same as everyone else, because their experience of the colourblind approach is in fact so *different* to that of their white peers.

The colourblind approach has been a feature of the English education system for many years. The radical changes that have been made to education in the past twenty years or so have done little to change this and have even made the situation worse. There are fewer opportunities for teachers and learners to bring personal aspects of their lives (including cultural ones) into the curriculum because the levels of prescription are so extensive. In addition, there are problems with the notion that religious education should be 'broadly Christian in nature'. For the white child this kind of education may consolidate and link with their experiences out of school, but for minority ethnic children those same broadly Christian school experiences are usually radically different from their lives at home. Some schools have recognized that multi-faith worship is a sensible alternative where leaders from the different religions organize different assemblies. Unfortunately, rather than celebrating this diversity, some educators can regard it as a problem.

The Importance of Language

The primary function of language is to enable us to communicate, but it is also a very important means to support growth of knowledge and concept formation. These can be acquired through many forms of language use, including the tentative, exploratory and hypothetical. We constantly use our language in order to speculate about the social and physical world and this language use crosses the boundaries of traditional subjects. For example, many early years settings will have leaf prints on the wall during autumn. A good early years practitioner will be aware that the point of this process is not only for artistic reasons. The talk that takes place alongside this activity supports a range of knowledge and understanding. For instance, the close observation required for further artwork might lead to a mathematical discussion about the irregular symmetry of the leaf veins and a scientific discussion about their purpose.

The acquisition of concepts and knowledge is common to all children, but there are special considerations for multilingual children. Their learning is best supported when all the languages that the child knows are valued and where possible used in the setting. Specifying that children only use English is not only damaging to the development of the home language, but it also slows the learning of English. Because language is central to learning generally, restrictions on its use can also damage cognitive and social development.

The links between language and identity are strong. A positive self-image is in part helped by other people's positive responses to your social and cultural characteristics. Judgements are made about intelligence, commitment and attitude solely on language features and often just the surface features of language. For example, bilingualism featuring languages such as English, French and German is given greater status in the education system than bilingualism with Urdu or Arabic. The following quote provides an example of the way in which it is far too easy to make mistaken assumptions:

> Student teachers judged recordings of a middle-class white boy, a working-class white girl, a recently arrived Jamaican girl and a British born girl from a Barbadian background who spoke twice – once using a working-class English accent and once a Barbadian dialect. The middle-class boy was consistently evaluated most favourably: he was felt to be more intelligent, better behaved and so on. Next came the two working-class recordings, one white, the other black, followed by the two Caribbean children. The crucial point is that the same child was judged more positively in her English than in her Caribbean 'guise'. The student teachers were also prepared to make judgements about the children's educational outcomes, predicting high academic successes for the middle-class boy and very low levels of achievement for the black children. (*Brown 1998: 70*)

There are clear lessons to be learned here about the ways in which we work with our young people and the ways in which we recognize and deal with our own prejudices and stereotypes. Jones (1999) outlines the ways in which teacher training in predominantly white areas of the country has systematically ignored the linguistic and cultural needs of minority ethnic children. Sewell (1997) worked with disaffected young black males in the north of England and found that many of their negative experiences of the education system stemmed from teachers who were unable to offer them respect as individuals. One recent article by a young black school leaver describes how he spent his school life feeling isolated by those whose job it was to educate him.

> I became disruptive in school – talking in class, mouthing back at the teachers when they chastised me and playing tricks all the time . . . I was so bored in school. My mum had taught me a lot of stuff [she] used to give me books to read about black history – but there was nothing like that at school . . . all my schools felt like white places where there happened to be black kids who had to fit in. (*Neustatter 2000*)

Policies have been implemented at national and local levels to deal with the monitoring of minority ethnic pupil progress, but policy makers are yet to address the central issues of identity and marginalization.

For all people who work with children there is a need for high levels of knowledge about the experiences of ethnic minority families and the courage and sensitivity to tackle racism. For some people it is easier to adopt a colourblind approach, but as we have shown this is not in the best interests of the children that we work with. If children are to develop positively then they need to feel secure from racism and know that all cultural experiences represent an equally valuable contribution to society.

Activity

Make a list of some of the issues that this chapter raises that you find controversial. Identify the reasons that make them controversial for you. Make a further list of questions that this thinking raises.

REFERENCES

Berliner, W. (2002) The race is over. *Guardian*, 12 March.

Blair, M. (2000) 'Race', school exclusions and human rights. In A. Osler (ed.) *Citizenship and Democracy in Schools: Diversity, Identity, Equality*. Stoke-on-Trent: Trentham.

Brown, B. (1998) *Understanding Discrimination in the Early Years*. Stoke-on-Trent: Trentham.

Gaine, C. (1987) *No Problem Here*. Stoke-on-Trent: Trentham.

Gaine, C (1995) *Still No Problem Here*. Stoke-on-Trent: Trentham.

Howson, G. (2002) Reach out to black boys. *Guardian*, 25 January.

Jones, R. (1999) *Teaching Racism*. Stoke-on-Trent: Trentham.

Milner, D. (1983) *Children and Race 10 Years On*. London: Ward Lock.

Neustatter, A. (2000) I felt hated. *Guardian*, 17 October.

Osler, A. (ed.) (2000) *Citizenship and Democracy in Schools: Diversity, Identity, Equality.* Stoke-on-Trent: Trentham.
Sewell, T. (1997) *Black Masculinities and Schooling.* Stoke-on-Trent: Trentham.
Wright, C. (1992) *Race Relations in the Primary School.* London: David Fulton.

FURTHER READING

Commission for Racial Equality website: http://www.cre.gov.uk. Well-maintained, regularly updated and informative official website for the CRE.
Jones, R. (2000) Out of the abyss: The current state of multicultural education in primary education. In *Education 3–13*, March. This paper outlines recent policy and practice, linking these to issues related to cultural identity.
Richardson, R. and Wood, A. (2000) *Inclusive Schools, Inclusive Society: Race and Identity on the Agenda.* Stoke-on-Trent: Trentham. A well-written book outlining the key ideas and principles relating to identity, 'race' and racism.

Chapter *Thirty-six* Disabled Children

JANE BAKER

One of the measures of a healthy society is the extent to which it supports and includes disabled people. The reasonably clear definitions of disability that are offered by legislation are clouded by the realities of life for disabled people. People's attitudes to disabled children are one of the main barriers to them leading enjoyable lives.

David is a disabled young person. When he was little, people would say to his mother things like, 'It's a shame isn't it'; 'He's good looking in spite of it'.

As David grows up people are less open in their expressions of sympathy. Looks of embarrassed awkwardness have replaced the well-meaning but ignorant comments made when he was younger. People see him as someone that does not fit within their normal expectations. Future employment, relationships, marriage and independence are likely to be harder for David than many other people. David now faces a lonely adolescence, which causes him to feel increasingly angry about having a disability. 'I want to be normal!' he shouts.

If you see a child with a disability what is it you first think? Do you feel sorry for the child's parents? Do you feel slightly embarrassed? Do you wonder what caused the disability? Do you feel the need to befriend the child? We all experience these feelings and for most people they are rooted in compassion. Our reactions to disabled children can be helped by better understanding of the realities of being disabled.

It is important to be clear what is meant by disability. Definitions are important because they provide a common reference point for people who work with children. For the child with disability the way that adults interpret the definitions will affect the nature of the services that he or she will receive.

Impairment: is any loss or abnormality of psychological, physical or anatomical structure or function.

> Handicap: is a disadvantage for a given individual, resulting from impairment or disability, that prevents the fulfilment of a role that is considered normal (depending upon age, sex and social and cultural factors) for that individual.

> Disability: is a restriction or lack (resulting from impairment) of ability to perform an activity in the manner or within the range considered normal for a human being. (*World Health Organization*)

> A child is disabled if he is blind, deaf or dumb or suffers from mental disorder of any kind or is substantially and permanently handicapped by illness, injury or congenital deformity or such, as may be prescribed. (*Children Act 1989*)

> A person has a disability for the purposes of the Act if he has a physical or mental impairment which has a substantial and long-term adverse effect on his ability to carry out normal day-to-day activities. (*Disability Discrimination Act 1995*)

It is interesting to note here the way that the British legislation regards disability as 'substantial and long term' whereas the WHO definition regards as the benchmark *any* loss of physiological function resulting in a lack of ability to perform what is considered normal. Part of the reason for this is the fact that once it has been agreed that someone is disabled there is a cost implication. Legal definitions are one thing, but this is not the only way that we understand disability.

Society's perceptions of disabled children are particularly noticeable in the media. On the one hand, the lives of disabled people rarely feature in the media. On the other hand, there is much talk about developments in genetics helping to stop disability occurring. Although this is done with the best of intentions, the implication of these messages is that disability needs to be eradicated. Clearly, if you are a disabled person, this can be viewed as a negative perspective on your worth to society. When this is coupled with the overwhelming numbers of 'perfect' children who are a feature of adverts in particular, the effects on the self-esteem of disabled children can be great.

> We live in a society that makes children very vulnerable, one that has very ambivalent feelings about disabled children. We live in a society in which disabled children are often excluded from the mainstream of life, where it is often not very safe to be disabled and where disabled children are often oppressed. (*Marchant et al. 1999: 215*)

There are of course adverts and slogans that deliberately attempt to attack the thoughtless aspects of negative media portrayals. For example, the memorable phrase that you should 'see the child not the disability' is important because it prompts us to remember that disability is only one part of the child.

The causes of disability can be inherited, environmental, trauma at birth, accident and illness. Some categories of disability include:

- physical disability;
- learning disability;

- hearing impairment;
- visual impairment;
- mental disability;
- speech and language impairment.

Each category can range in complexity and severity. Many children experience short-term or long-term disability. It is important when looking at a child with a disability to remember that each child faces different experiences and problems.

Constructs of Childhood Disability

Medforth, Fenwick and Wyse (2000) note that there are clear themes or 'constructs' that affect the way we view children. Disabled children are no exception.

> Images of children are invariably constructed by adults to convey messages and meanings to adults. The meanings that are used to convey childhood change and vary, although there are certain recurring and central themes: dependency, victimization/helplessness, loss, nostalgia, innocence, danger and nature. (*Ibid.: 3*)

Children with a disability are invariably regarded as dependent and as victims. The medical and charitable models are prevalent. The medical model approaches disability as it does disease, something that should be eradicated, treated, contained. It perceives the individual with the disability as someone that is in need of treatment. The charitable model is one which is driven by sympathy and which is exemplified by fundraising activities such as the televised Children in Need events. Its advantage is that it generates much useful financial support for children's charities. The disadvantage is that it is a one-off event which can be seen as a way for society to feel better about itself rather than tackle the issues of inclusion in a sustainable way.

The *social* model emphasizes that those with disabilities should be seen as people first and foremost. Children and adults with a disability are viewed as equal and valuable members of society. The importance of medical care for people with disabilities is recognized, but this is not a dominant issue. There is a recognition that society's response is often more of a problem than the disability itself. In the social model, prejudice and discrimination are clearly seen as major contributory factors to the more negative aspects of the lives of disabled people.

The construct of the working child has a mixture of positive and negative connotations that are reversed in the case of disabled children. In the Western world the idea of children working before they are old enough is generally seen as negative (CHAPTER 39). In British society children cannot have full-time work before they are 16. However, there are many examples of children working at a young age which are seen as positive. For example, increasing amounts of homework set by schools is seen as a good thing. Having a part-time job like a paper round is also seen as positive. Helping in the home is required and for some children this can be onerous if they are caring for other family members or if they help with the family business. All of this work is demanding. It attracts little if any wage, yet it is generally seen as positive because it is establishing the kinds of habits that will be needed once children enter full-time employment. For disabled children it is much harder to get work as a child. This is partly because there are restrictions on what disabled children can do, but it is also strongly linked to the fact that expectations of the kind of work they will do as adults are so much lower. A child born with a disability thus faces a struggle to function within a society that is driven by how useful for employment people are perceived to be. One of the main arenas where children are prepared for the world of work is in schools, yet there are still many problems to overcome.

The education system uses the term 'special needs' when talking about children with a disability. The Education Act 1993 states that a child has special educational needs if they have a learning difficulty that has an impact on their ability in comparison to a child of the same age. The legislation introduced within the past fifty years has shifted from segregation to an inclusive approach. The SEN Code of Practice, amended as recently as 2002, has moved the importance of working with the child and parents higher up the agenda. It also provides a framework that places emphasis on integration within mainstream education. However, many children still do not enter mainstream education and are therefore educated within special schools. If society is to change how children with a disability are viewed, education provides an appropriate opportunity. The biggest negative impact special education has on children with a disability is the reinforcement that they are different from their peers. One way this is highlighted is in the relationships that they can form. The simple expectation that children within mainstream education will make friends who live locally is undone by sending a child to a special school. These schools are often some distance from the local area and bring children from wide and diverse communities. Children are faced with isolation from friendships outside the school, which in turn impacts on social experiences and skills. Unfortunately, disabled children's experiences in mainstream schools have been so bad that their parents have found that the best special schools give children a much better education. This, of course, is a choice by default.

Activity

Read the following short case study. Note down some of the things that are likely to be done by the school and the local education authority to assess and support the child.

Simon is 5 years old and has just started at the local primary school. The teachers are immediately concerned about Simon's behaviour and learning. He has poor concentration and is very disruptive within the class. Simon is clearly isolated from the rest of his classmates. He finds it very difficult to make friends and is unable to follow and understand rules. The teacher speaks to the parents and with their agreement it is decided an assessment should take place.

REFERENCES

Foley, P., Roche, J. and Tucker, S. (eds) (2001) *Children in Society: Contemporary Theory, Policy and Practice.* Basingstoke: Palgrave.

Medforth, N., Fenwick, G. and Wyse, D. (2000) Images of childhood. In D. Wyse and A. Hawtin (eds) *Children: A Multi-Professional Perspective.* London: Edward Arnold.

FURTHER READING

Marchant, R., Jones, M., Julyan, A. and Giles, A. (1999) *Listening on all Channels: Consulting with Disabled Children.* Brighton: Triangle. This work underlines the importance of listening to children who have a disability. It illustrates how valuable it is to involve children in making decisions about the services they require and their life choices.

Roffey, S. (2001) *Special Needs in the Early Years: Collaboration, Communication and Coordination*, 2nd edn. London: David Fulton Publishers. A useful text for the early years practitioner which notes how important the role of the professional is.

Tassoni, P., Beith, K. and Eldridge, H. (2000) *Diploma Child Care and Education.* Oxford: Heinemann. This book simply outlines essential issues surrounding disability. It is directed toward the student practitioner and covers many areas of childcare.

Chapter Thirty-seven
Poverty

JANE BAKER

Poverty is one of the most serious problems facing children in the twenty-first century. This chapter looks at some of the features of child poverty and its effects. Reference is made to a significant government strategy called Sure Start.

> *Poverty means going short materially, socially and emotionally. It means spending less on food, on heating, and on clothing than someone on average income. Above all, poverty takes away the tools to build the blocks for the future – your 'life chances'. It steals away the opportunity to have a life unmarked by sickness, a decent education, a secure home and long retirement.*
>
> *(Oppenheim 1990: 3)*

Child: I am eight years old. I have been hungry for three days now. We might get some food tomorrow. My father is dead and so are two of my brothers and a sister. My mother is very ill and will die one day soon. I am just going to get some water, but it will take me an hour.

What country do you think this child lives in?

A radio advert used a white British child to say these words. At first, you tend to be outraged and wonder how could such a thing happen in Britain. It then becomes clear that the real child lives in a developing country. Although poverty in Western countries doesn't compare with the extremes of deprivation faced by some African countries in particular, it does seriously affect many children in Britain. The UN Convention on the Rights of the Child clearly states that children have the right to live without poverty:

> State parties recognize the right of every child to a standard of living adequate for the child's physical, mental, spiritual, moral and social development. (*Article 27*)

It is important when thinking about poverty that you understand what is meant. The terms used are *absolute* poverty and *relative* poverty. Absolute poverty means being so poor that the basic requirements for life are endangered: a lack of access to food, shelter or water. Relative poverty is based on economic calculations which examine the gross income of the country and the average income for the citizens of that country. If people fall below a particular threshold (or 'poverty line') they are defined as 'in poverty'. Poverty in relation to children is caused by a number of different factors, many of which relate to the circumstances of their family. In the UK the income level of many families falls below the level considered to be an appropriate standard of living.

In the 1970s, 1 in 10 children were below the poverty line. Towards the end of the 1990s, the figure was 1 in 3. Currently, over 4 million children are living in poverty in the UK. Although there has been overall growth in the wealth of the UK, the increase in the number of children living in poverty stems from an increase in income inequality. The UK, especially, has experienced a widening gap between people who have access to a high level of income and those who do not.

Gregg, Harkness and Machin (1999) undertook research which found that 4 million children lacked at least one thing from a list of 27 items that people consider to be important. The list includes:

- New shoes
- Waterproof coat
- Fresh fruit
- Fresh vegetables

The research concluded that the money spent on items such as fresh fruit, vegetables and clothing was no higher in 1995–6 than in the 1970s. It highlights the huge gap in the spending ability of the poorest group, and shows that the inequality of income has a direct impact on children's well-being. Although society has changed in the intervening years, repeated research has found that the impact of unemployment and low-paid work continues to be the principal cause of poverty among children in the UK (Daniel and Ivatts 1998).

The education of children living in poverty is an area of great concern. Research evidence, which has looked at the most effective schools, has consistently found that the socio-economic conditions of the pupils have a direct impact on their achievement and hence, in our test-driven system, the results of the schools. In the 1980s the Conservative government introduced the idea of parental choice of schools, similar to the idea of a 'free market'. Many people have argued that this system is a further disadvantage to families in poverty because they do not have the resources to choose schools other than those that are closest to their home. In addition, families with more money are better able to provide additional educational resources for their children.

The health of children living in poverty is also worrying. Although improvements have been made in the health service, including a substantial investment announced in 2002, children who are born into or live within a poor family still experience great inequality. Fagin (1984) noted that the impact of unemployment had an effect throughout the family, including the symptoms of mental and physical illness.

Government Strategies

The British prime minister made a pledge in March 1999 to eliminate child poverty in 20 years. To support this pledge a number of legal and policy initiatives have been introduced. These new initiatives, alongside the ones already in place, provide a comprehensive package which is part of the government's attempt to eradicate child poverty:

- Child benefit
- Working family tax credit
- Childcare credit
- New deal for lone parents
- Minimum wage
- Educational maintenance for young people
- Nursery places for 3–4 year olds

One of the most important recent initiatives is the Sure Start programme. This is a local community-centred initiative informed by a holistic approach to the child's developmental needs. The Sure Start programme has been developed to help families who are disadvantaged within society. An examination of Sure Start helps us to identify areas that should be considered and tackled when looking at child poverty. The overall aim and targets of Sure Start highlight the impact of poverty on all aspects of child development.

The aim of Sure Start is:

> To work with parents and children to promote the physical, intellectual and social development of babies and young children – particularly those who are disadvantaged – so that they can flourish at home and when they get to school, and thereby break the cycle of disadvantage for the current generation of young children. (*Sure Start, n.d.*)

Sure Start targets:

- Improving social and emotional development
- Improving health
- Improving the ability to learn
- Strengthening families and communities

The targets above show us that poverty is a factor that can invade every part of a child's development, and is not just a factor in the traditionally perceived area of material needs.

While recent initiatives might look new, Western society has not been particularly successful in tackling a problem that has been known about at least since the nineteenth century. Harry Hendrick described the children who were targeted by the Poor Laws of that period.

> Poor Law children occupied a transitional position between the state as the arbiter of rescue, reclamation and protection, and as the provider of services for children as publicly recognized citizens of the future. The welfare of Poor Law represents an era of social policy that saw the free flowing of ideas on the treatment of deprivation, as reformers and administrators looked, often unwittingly, for ways in which to conceptualize institutional child care in a changing environment. (Hendricks 1994: 74)

Hendricks's suggestion that the welfare of Poor Law represented a time of change is clearly not unique to that era or those pieces of legislation. Neither is the concept of 'free flow of ideas' by a wide network of professionals. Without a doubt, the current government recognizes the importance of investing in the future of children. The rapidly changing environment that children are brought up in today means that strategies such as Sure Start are needed to impact on social exclusion, adverse health, and employment outcomes associated with long-term poverty. However, the children of today's society face a similar problem to that faced by Poor Law children: the *quality* of policy ideas. To provide a satisfactory response to poverty, Sure Start needs to be sustainable; it has to show that it is reducing the widening gap between rich and poor. This kind of sustainable solution is very difficult to achieve. It is important to remember Hendricks's reflection on one of the major limitations of previous initiatives: 'The children of the poor, as well as those who were orphans, found themselves living experiments in the cultivation of environmentalism. It was a tradition that would linger in British childcare policy' (ibid.: 84).

Activity

Discuss with a partner how poverty will negatively affect children's physical development, intellectual development, emotional development, language development and social development.

REFERENCES

Daniel, P. and Ivatts, J. (1998) *Children and Social Policy*. London: Macmillan.

Fagin, L. (1984) *The Forsaken Families: The Effects of Unemployment on Family Life*. Harmondsworth: Penguin Books.

Gregg, P., Harkness, S. and Machin, S. (1999) *Child Development and Family Income*. York: Joseph Rowntree Foundation.

Hendrick, H. (1994) *Child Welfare: England 1872–1989*: London: Routledge.

Oppenheim, C. (1990) *Poverty: The Facts.* London: Child Poverty Action Group.
Sure Start (n.d.) *About Sure Start.* Retrieved 6 November 2002 from http://www.surestart.gov.uk/aboutWhatis.cfm?section=2.

FURTHER READING

Child Poverty Action Group website: http://www.cpag.org.uk. The Child Poverty Action Group promotes and campaigns for the rights of children to live without poverty.

Piachaud, D. (1987) *Poor Children: A Tale of Two Decades.* London: Child Poverty Action Group. This work explores child poverty and the current issues children face. It looks at the different ways children are marginalized by the poverty they experience.

Townsend, R. (1979) *Poverty in the UK.* Harmondsworth: Penguin Books. This important work draws on much research to illustrate the divides within UK society. It provides readers with an insight into the experiences of children at the end of the last century.

Society

Chapter *Thirty-eight*

Non-Government Organizations

JOHN HARRISON

We examine the development of non-government organizations (NGOs) both in this country and in the wider world: the issues that shaped them and the barriers that they have overcome. This leads to an examination of NGOs today and the problems they face. Finally, we ask if there is a future for NGOs and try to picture the part they will play in the lives of the world's children.

There are over 4,000 NGOs helping millions of people all over the world (Edwards and Hulme 1996). Their work ranges from projects to aid isolated villages, to international campaigns that try to influence whole governments (Korey 1998). But what are NGOs? What do they do and how do they affect the lives of children?

An NGO can be defined as any non-statutory organization that offers support and services to people. As their name suggests, NGOs are not part of any government. They are set up by those who wish to offer more help than is given by local and national governments (although most NGOs work with official bodies in order to help others).

Early History

Early societies' treatment of children seems very strange to us (Roy 2001): they were cruel and violent towards children, using brutal methods in childrearing and education. However, there is evidence of individual adults helping children, particularly those from disadvantaged backgrounds. Wealthy people who wanted to display their wealth and generosity to impress others often took on this role. Many were also motivated by a sense of duty.

Poor children continued to be seen as a good cause in the Middle Ages. Wealthy individuals established schools for 'poor scholars'. Often there would be a religious aspect to these schools and the wealthy expected that the pupils would pray for them. Some of the most famous schools in Britain were established to educate the children of the poor. Both Eton and Winchester began life in this way. Schools with names such as Merchant Taylor and Haberdashers were established to help children gain an education. Yet it should be remembered that when these schools were formed there was no formal education for the vast majority of children and what little there was at first was exclusively for boys.

The Development of NGOs

For many years there were no formal organizations that worked for the benefit of children. As society changed, more and more people became involved in helping those around them. Some people established orphanages and tried to provide children with the skills they would need in later life, such as dressmaking and woodwork. For the majority of children life was very hard, with starvation and brutality an everyday reality.

With the onset of the industrial revolution poor children became ever more involved in all aspects of work. Many activities were dangerous and thousands of children died or were terribly injured. Outside work many lived in poor housing and lots of children fell prey to illnesses such as typhus and cholera. Despite the immense wealth within Britain, most of its children lived and died in appalling conditions. It was in this environment that many of the NGOs we know today were created. In order to understand how NGOs were able to help children, we concentrate on two particular organizations: the National Society for the Prevention of Cruelty to Children (NSPCC) and Save the Children.

In 1884 the London Society for the Prevention of Cruelty to Children was established following the development of a similar organization in Liverpool. Like many other charities, its driving force came from the religious community, in this case the Reverend Benjamin Waugh. The charity quickly established a shelter to protect children from abusive environments. A journal, *The Child's Guardian*, was launched to highlight the plight of many children in the city. In 1889 the society changed its name to the one we know today. This was followed by the society's first real success. After lobbying parliament for five years, a Bill was passed that set down guidelines for the treatment of children: *The Children's Charter.*

As the society developed a number of inspectors were employed to help children at risk of abuse. Local committees were established to help raise awareness and collect funds. At the start of the twentieth century the society became more widely known and children and their families were approaching the NSPCC directly for help. By 1947 the society dealt with over 10,000 'advice sort' cases a year (NSPCC 2002). Throughout the century, governments were lobbied by the society, with the development of the child protection register a direct result of their efforts. Further work saw the development of the Battered Child Research Department, which strove to help understand the needs of abused children. This led to the creation of special units, which were on alert 24 hours a day to help deal with cases of abuse.

Throughout, the NSPCC carried out public campaigns to raise awareness and funds. Many of these involved celebrities who helped raise the profile of such events. You may remember one of these appeals. Think about the methods used to gain your attention.

The NSPCC altered in tandem with the society it served. As needs became more complex, so did the methods to deal with them. From local campaigns to national media events, the growth of this NGO mirrors that of many other organizations in the UK. But what of those who work outside the UK?

NGOs Working Overseas

Save the Children is one of the most influential international NGOs that support children. Like the NSPCC it was developed in response to helping children in crisis. Following the First World War large numbers of children in Europe were starving. A campaign was established to provide funds for food and clothing. This developed into Save the Children and went on to help children affected by other conflicts. In the 1920s it supplied 122 million meals to 650,000 starving people involved in the Russian Civil War. The impact of the Spanish Civil War saw large numbers of children separated from their families; Save the Children established a scheme to trace individuals. Other work involved lobbying overseas governments to reduce cases of child **slavery** and labour. By the 1970s Save the Children worked in areas as far apart as Nicaragua and Northern Ireland (Save the Children 2002).

As we can see, our two NGOs have come a long way since their inception. They were started by a small number of individuals, often in response to a particular event or dilemma. From these beginnings they developed to meet the needs of children both nationally and internationally. As the world has changed and the difficulties faced by children alter, so NGOs have adapted to these new circumstances. If we consider that for centuries children had little protection in law, the work done by these organizations in a short space of time is remarkable.

NGOs Today

Children continue to be at risk. In most societies they remain the most marginalized and the least supported of any group. As a result, the work of NGOs continues. Let's look at our two NGOs and see what they are involved in today.

Save the Children has been involved in helping deal with floods in Mozambique and earthquakes in India. It has also provided young people with the chance to empower themselves. This includes the development of school councils worldwide to allow children to take part in the decision-making process.

The NSPCC launched the FULL STOP campaign in March 1999. This is designed to raise awareness of child abuse. As in previous campaigns full use is made of the media to make this issue as well known as possible. Working alongside government agencies, it aims to 'bring about fundamental changes in attitudes and behaviour towards children in this country' (NSPCC 2002: 16).

In many cases NGOs work alongside official support agencies such as UNICEF (United Nations International Children's Emergency Fund). Many UN staff have previously worked in NGOs, so they understand the way such organizations function (Weiss and Gordenker 1996). Such cooperation has led to the merger of a number of NGOs. Despite the greater involvement of governments in the care of children, there is still a need for NGOs with no political or official affiliation to enter contested areas and act independently.

If we remember why NGOs were formed do we believe they have a future? In the UK the law now prevents practices such as child labour and institutional violence. Worldwide, there are powerful governmental initiatives that alleviate the sufferings of children. Why, then, do we need these NGOs? Do we still need to give our money to such organizations when children are supported by the state?

Simply by reading this book you will know that today's children face a whole range of problems. Issues such as child abuse and bullying continue. The threat of war is as real now as ever before: there were more wars in the twentieth century than in any other period. Children are often the first casualties in any conflict. Thus there will be a need for NGOs in the near future at least. There is a place for organizations that help children and their families in all corners of the world, regardless of political affiliation or race. Until abuse and victimization are eradicated there will be a need to protect children and educate the wider society about such problems.

Activity

In order to understand the work of NGOs in more depth why not visit some of their websites? The web addresses of the NSPCC and Save the Children are given below, but try to visit others as well. Discover how they came into being, how they developed and the work they do. By doing so, you will develop a deeper knowledge of the vital work they undertake.

REFERENCES

Edwards, M. and Hulme, D. (1996) *Making a Difference: NGOs and Development in a Changing World.* London: Earthscan.

Korey, W. (1998) *NGOs and the Universal Declaration of Human Rights.* London: Macmillan.

NSPCC (2002) *About Us.* Retrieved 31 October 2002 from http://www.nspcc.org.uk/html/Home/Aboutus/aboutus.htm.

Save the Children UK (2002) *About Us*. Retrieved 31 October 2002, from http://www.savethechildren.org.uk/functions/indx_abus.html.
Weiss, T. and Gordenker, L. (1996) *NGOs: The UN and Global Governance*. Boulder, CO: Lynne Rienner.

FURTHER READING

National Society for the Prevention of Cruelty to Children website: http://www.nspcc.org.uk.

Roy, W. (2001) *Making Societies*. Thousand Oaks, CA: Sage. Roy's text will help you to understand the differences between the societies of each country so that you can consider the impact that this has on the work of NGOs.

Save the Children website: http://www.savethechildren.org.uk.

Vittachi, A. (1989) *Stolen Childhood*: *In Search of the Rights of the Child*. Cambridge: Polity Press. In order to understand the issues that face NGOs it is important that we understand the societies in which they work. This book provides much useful information.

Chapter *Thirty-nine* Children Working

NICHOLAS MEDFORTH

Our views about children working are strongly influenced by our understanding of the history of child labour and the context of the country that we live in. Reflections on the differences between rich and poor countries' attitudes to child labour are followed by an analysis of child labour in Britain today.

In CHAPTER 33 we explored the idea that the adult world regards childhood from a rather sentimental perspective. Such a view of childhood is based upon a Romantic ideal, yet the real lives of many children are distinctly different from this. When we ask students who are embarking upon the academic study of childhood what 'childhood' means, they invariably come up with some recurring definitions. These include the notion of childhood as a time of innocence and freedom from adult responsibilities and a time for play. A consideration of the part played by work in the experience of childhood runs counter to these themes of childhood. Many people feel that play should be the only work of childhood; it is the way in which children learn about themselves and their place in the world. However, the world of work plays a large part in the lives of many children, both throughout history and in the present day.

Children's work is sometimes described as child labour, but it is difficult to reach an agreed definition for this because our ideas are shaped by the historical and cultural context. A key question that you should ask is: who counts as a child and what constitutes labour? We need to consider the fact that some types of work may have some benefits. For example, parents believe that it is part of their responsibility to teach children household chores to enable them to develop important life skills. It is also believed that by doing small paid jobs such as paper rounds children learn about the basic features of paid employment, which will be important when they become adults. In some countries children might be expected to balance education with work or household chores, such as caring for children and older relatives, or growing crops in order to satisfy basic family needs. Income from child labour in many of the poorer countries of the world may well be essential if children and their families are to avoid extremes of poverty, deprivation, starvation and malnutrition. In many parts of the world recreation time and play have less significance in relation to childhood than in countries such as Britain.

While there may arguably be some benefits for children working, child labour is also often exploitative. This means children's work is exploited for the financial and economic advantage of powerful adults rather than the benefit of the child worker. Universally agreed standards about what is appropriate childhood experience are frequently violated. Article 32 of the United Nations Convention on the Rights of the Child (CRC) recognizes the right of the child to be free from economic exploitation and from performing any work that is likely to be hazardous either to the child's health, or their physical, mental, spiritual, moral or social development. The CRC also recognizes children's rights to play and leisure time. Examples of work that violates the rights of the child include excessive hours; inadequate pay for the labour involved; work that compromises the health and safety of the child; work that restricts the child's access to education, play and recreation; work that is too taxing or physically demanding; or work that children have no choice but to endure. In the worst extremes of exploitative child labour children are forced to work through **debt bondage**, and they are caught up in child trafficking and slavery or sexual exploitation through pornography and prostitution.

Child Labour in Britain During the Age of Industry

The negative aspects of children's work in developing countries today share many of the features of exploitative child labour in Victorian Britain that we have now come to abhor. Readers of authors like Charles Kingsley and Charles Dickens will be familiar with this kind of work through following the plights of fictional children who endure harsh working conditions. Real children experienced exploitation in workhouses, factories, small businesses, domestic households and street-based services such as match selling and chimney sweeping. Stories of working children often focus on children's work in large cities like London, but children are likely to have been similarly exploited in rural Britain through work in agriculture and in the smaller mills of towns in the provinces.

Before the industrial revolution it was not unusual for children to work. However, as the childhood historian Hugh Cunningham explains, during this time there was a shift in both attitudes about children's work and the ways in which they were employed. Cunningham (1995) points out that prior to the industrial revolution children tended to work in the family home or immediate community, which tended to be rurally based. Peasant industries were small-scale and children might for example have been involved in farming or weaving to satisfy their family needs. The industrial revolution involved the shift of industry to the cities, where production was large-scale and generated a great deal of wealth for the people who owned mills, factories and businesses. The emphasis was no longer on children working to fulfil basic family needs; instead, it was on generating profit for the employer. This inevitably meant that child workers were exploited. This was often justified through the voicing of middle-class concerns about the idleness of children that bore little relationship to the reality of life for the working-class child.

Suddenly, children were catapulted from a world of casual home- and community-based work to paid work in factories, mines and mills with regular and long contractual hours. Harry Hendrick (1994: 25) traces the history of child welfare and argues that

> There was nothing new about children working in the Industrial Revolution, for it had long been established that they should contribute to the family economy. By the early decades of the nineteenth century they were widely employed in textiles, dress, mining, agriculture, domestic service, docks and navigation, metals and machinery and tools. However, it was their working in textile mills, mines and as chimney-sweeps which most dramatically captured the imagination of reformers and philanthropists who campaigned against this form of exploitation. Many contemporaries were appalled, not only by the scale and intensity of the exploitation, but also by the brutalization of the young workers, and the violence which it was felt was being done to the nature of childhood itself.

Hendrick points out that the struggle to rescue small children from long hours and cruel conditions is one of the best-known stories in the history of childhood. Reformers felt that this kind of treatment of children was inappropriate for a civilized Christian society and that it raised real concerns about the direction of progress. These concerns resulted in legal reform through a series of Factory Acts between 1802 and 1875, which led to the gradual prohibition of full-time child labour for children under 14 and the introduction of compulsory schooling. It could be argued that childhood was being *reclaimed*, but children now had to work in schools to fulfil a new set of aspirations for adult society. Although education had the potential to empower children through the acquisition of knowledge and skills, compulsory schooling also had the effect of making children dependent and unwaged.

A Global Perspective on Child Labour

Many of the changes in society seen in Britain during the industrial revolution are mirrored in changes in the developing world today. Often, poorer countries are forced to move away from working patterns that emphasize small-scale production to meet the needs of families and local communities. Instead, there is a drive towards large-scale production fuelled by the need to satisfy the desire for luxury items in wealthier nations, or the desire for profit from the shareholders of large multinational companies. The consequences of this are often the replacement of the production of staple foods by the production of cash-rich crops like coffee, and large-scale production of such things as cheap fashion items. The problem is made worse by the debt crisis faced by many poorer countries that have to pay high rates of interest to wealthier nations on money they had to borrow out of economic necessity. Production is therefore often based upon the least expensive means possible, which results in the exploitation of children for little or no pay.

It is difficult to provide exact facts and figures, as much child labour is hidden. For example, many girls work in households or in service-industry settings which are more difficult to count. Child labour appears to be most widespread in Asian and Pacific countries, as well as in Latin America, the Caribbean, the Middle East and Sub-Saharan Africa. In many of these countries child labour is a result of poverty and deprivation.

The international children's organization Unicef (2001) paints a bleak picture of children's work across the world:

> There are hundreds of millions of children and young people around the world who are imprisoned, not in physical jails, but in a state of bondage more permanent than locks or bars alone could create. These are children who labour at tasks that harm their bodies and minds, their spirits and future.

Further evidence comes from the International Labour Organization (ILO 1996), which estimates that about 280 million children from the age of five upwards work for a living in developing countries (this is almost equivalent to the entire population of the United States). About half of these children work full-time. Child labourers represent about 1 in 6 children in the world today and 73 million are under the age of ten. Children largely work in jobs that clearly contravene Article 32 of the CRC by endangering their heath and well-being. About 110 million children are involved in hazardous work, for example in mines, quarrying or the construction industry, without the protective health and safety legislation enjoyed by adult workers in wealthier countries. In this kind of work boys make up a slight majority, but girls and boys are equally involved in child labour. Children work in almost every kind of work we can imagine, including the particularly exploitative occupations of prostitution, pornography, street working, **drug trafficking** and as soldiers in armed conflicts.

The Unicef website provides some typical scenarios: a young girl who should be in school carries a large basket of merchandise for sale in Guatemala; a small Brazilian boy, his face covered in dirt, stands in the midst of a garbage dump in São Paulo where he collects rubbish for resale; an Asian girl forced into the hazardous job of breaking rocks; a Mexican girl carrying a load of tobacco leaves she has picked. Other examples include a shoeshine boy sleeping on a doorstep in Hanoi, Vietnam, his head resting on a box containing the tools of his trade, and a young orphaned boy working in an electronics factory in Rwanda (in this case his work is part of a training project aimed at helping orphaned children off the streets and into work).

Campaigning organizations like Unicef, the ILO, Save the Children and Oxfam justifiably challenge governments and the international community to take responsibility for ending child labour. However, the abolition of child labour raises some important dilemmas: would a worldwide ban in the short term lift children and families out of poverty or make the situation worse? Could it push children into more dangerous and hidden forms of labour? Would it deny the benefits of work to those children who choose to work? Might it involve the imposition of culturally inappropriate ideas about what childhood should be about? These problematic issues should be balanced against the need to protect the rights of individual children as citizens of the world.

In a report entitled *A Future Without Child Labour* the director general of the ILO highlights some of the ways in which these issues might be resolved. Key points include the need to:

1 Recognize the problem and collect valid data about how widespread different forms of child labour are.
2 Translate political rhetoric into concrete policy change; for example, reducing third world debt.
3 Develop regional, national and international partnerships to reduce poverty, promote economic growth and develop social services and education.
4 Develop strategies to allocate resources in favour of children. This might, for example, involve a guaranteed minimum income for families and compulsory free education which is flexible, accessible and tailored to children's needs.
5 Bring about enforceable legislative change in order to protect children's rights.

Children Working in Britain

Powell (2001) explains that in Britain the employment of children is regulated by law. The legal position is that children may not be employed if

1 They are under 13 years of age.
2 Work starts before the close of school hours.
3 It takes place before 7 a.m. or after 7 p.m.
4 It involves more than 2 hours on Sunday.
5 Employment involves tasks such as lifting and carrying which might cause injury to the child.

These restrictions include street trading and public performances.

It is easy to imagine that while exploitative child labour is widespread in the developing world, it is merely a historical phenomenon in the West. In 2001 a survey conducted by Mori on behalf of the Trade Union Council (2002) found that the law is frequently flouted and that the European Young Workers Directive introduced in June 2000 to regulate children's work has had a very limited effect. The survey discovered that nearly half a million (485,000) school children are working illegally; more than 100,000 admit to playing truant in order to do paid work: 12 per cent of boys and 5 per cent of girls. One in four children under 13 admitted doing paid work either during term time or during the summer holidays even though this is illegal, while just over a third of school children (50 per cent of 15–16 year olds) work. Some 45 per cent of children in paid work have worked outside of legally defined permissible hours and almost one third (29 per cent) of children who work said that it left them too tired to do homework or schoolwork. The most common jobs were babysitting (37 per cent) and paper rounds (35 per cent). These were followed by cleaning (19 per cent) and working in a shop (16 per cent). Girls were most likely to babysit, while boys tended to do paper rounds. Although 11 per cent of school children say they earn more than £5 an hour, most earned between £2 and £2.50 an hour.

These findings raise some interesting discussion points for us to consider. Has paid work always been an essential but often unrecognized part of childhood? Should children have a right to spend at least some of their time working and earning? Should children receive equivalent wages to those earned by adults? Should we reward children's unpaid work in school financially? When considering these points it is important to remember that while children's paid work in Britain may be exploitative and sometimes dangerous, the scale is not comparable to that of many child labourers in the developing world. Thinking about the difference reveals a disturbing irony. Children in the West may be engaged in low-paid work in order to buy desirable luxury items such as fashionable clothes. Unfortunately, these items are likely to have been made by child workers in a developing country who will have earned a tiny proportion of the money spent by the British teenager.

Activity

Think about some things that you could do to help bring an end to exploitative child labour.

REFERENCES

Cunningham, H. (1995) *Children and Childhood in Western Society Since 1500*. New York: Longman.

Hendrick, H. (1994) *Child Welfare: England 1872–1989*. London: Routledge.

International Labour Organization (ILO) (1996) International Programme on the Elimination of Child Labour. Retrieved 23 October 2002 from http://www.ilo.org/public/english/standards/ipec/index.htm.

Powell, R. (2001) *Child Law: A Guide for Courts and Practitioners*. Winchester: Waterside Press.

Trade Union Council (2002) Mori survey. Retrieved 23 October 2002 from http://www.fbu.org.uk/ffgtr/pdfarch/apn01/0401-16.pdf.

Unicef (2001) *Beyond Child Labour, Affirming Rights*. Retrieved 23 October 2002 from http://www.unicef.org/pubsgen/beyond-child-labour/.

FURTHER READING

Childhood: A Global Journal of Child Research (1999) Understanding child labour. Special issue, Vol. 6 (1). This special issue of a key contemporary journal explores issues relating to child labour from the perspectives of a number of researchers. These include children's rights approaches, cultural perspectives, the role of trade unions, and national and international partnerships for working towards solutions.

UNICEF website: http://www.unicef.org. This excellent website provides a wealth of information. Illustrative case studies and updates on local and international strategies help us to respond to the complex issues raised by child labour.

Vittachi, A. (1989) *Stolen Childhood: In Search of the Rights of the Child.* Oxford: Blackwell. This book explores the ways in which child labour across the world constitutes a betrayal of universally agreed definitions of childhood.

Chapter Forty

Research with Children

DOMINIC WYSE

Many programmes of study require students to carry out research. Over the last ten years it has been recognized that research with children involves particular knowledge and skills. This chapter discusses some key issues in this area, including planning research, interviewing children and ethical considerations.

High-quality research with children shares many of the features of research with adults, but there are a growing number of specific considerations that need to be taken into account. Given that all research should be well planned, there are various elements that need to be thought about. Research is stimulated by questions and/or a perception that something needs to be explored. The plans for research projects often include a series of research questions. Projects also often include a set of aims and objectives. For the kind of small-scale projects that you are likely to undertake it is helpful to restrict the numbers of such aims and objectives. As a rule of thumb, restricting your plan to one aim and three objectives can help you focus on the specific detail and not be too ambitious. In the following example you will notice the way that the aim and the objectives are very closely linked:

Question: How does the UN Convention on the Rights of the Child impact on children in schools?
Aim: To explore the nature and extent of children's participation in their school.

Objectives
Find out what groups of Year 5 and Year 6 children think about participation in their school.
Find out what school council members think about the effectiveness of the school council.
Compare lesson observations with the accounts of the children in order to explore the issues raised by the children in more depth.

It is not always necessary to have both research questions and aims. Sometimes an introductory section which puts forward a rationale for the research based on a reading of the literature is sufficient to replace the research questions, provided there are clear aims and objectives.

In addition to questions, aims and objectives there are several other basic considerations that need thought. The sample or number of participants is something that can sometimes be forgotten, but it is a very important consideration for all research. The first aspect of this is the number of participants. It is technically possible to have only one participant, something which has been done using **ethnographic** approaches. Parents' accounts of the development of a child are a good example of this kind of work. Other research can require thousands of participants if it involves statistical surveys. In addition to basic numbers you will also need to think about gender, race and other socio-economic considerations. The important thing to remember is that the sample depends on the kind of research you are doing and in particular your objectives.

Another useful thing to include in early planning is a timetable. The detail of a timetable forces you to think about a range of decisions that will need to be made. For example, if you are going to do some interviews when and where will they take place? What do you need to do to gain access to the site? How long will you spend at the site? Are you allowing enough time for ongoing analysis between your visits? Although timetables may well change once you start the research, it is helpful to give yourself an overview of how you will complete the work. The timetable should include time for the writing-up of the research and a final completion date.

You will also need to plan the kinds of data collection tools and methods that you are going to use. Once again, it is important to think about your objectives, as the methods chosen should be the ones best suited to helping you achieve your objectives. There are many good introductory texts on research methods. As space precludes a full account in this book, we have chosen to focus on some of the issues to do with interviews because this is a particularly important skill when working with children.

Interviews

Many small-scale research projects involve interviews/discussions with children. Scott (2000) offers a fascinating and rigorous account of her work on a very large-scale research project which included children. As an introduction to this work she explores some important issues with regard to interviews with children, including the significant observation that in the past children have been excluded from large-scale social surveys.

From about age 11 onwards the data collection tools that are appropriate for adults can be used with children. For younger children a range of techniques can help you achieve your research objectives. Pictures are sometimes used to enhance data collection because they can offer a more concrete representation. Simple faces have been used to represent moods or emotions in response to particular ideas. Memory aids can also sometimes help. Many surveys use the standard *Likert* type responses: 'agree strongly; agree; neither agree nor disagree; disagree; disagree strongly'. Scott suggests that these can be made simpler for children by starting with 'agree' or 'disagree' and then probing for strength of feeling afterwards.

There is no evidence that children are any less or more reliable than adult respondents, but there are some differences.

> There is little reason to discredit children as respondents; however, in highly traumatic circumstances children, like adults, have been known to lie or display memory distortion. Moreover, modern psychological and medical evidence suggests that children are more reliable as witnesses than previously thought, and reliability can be increased by skilful interviewing. The interviewing advice is very familiar to survey researchers: give the child unambiguous and comprehensible instructions at the start of the interview; avoid leading questions; explicitly permit 'don't know' responses to avoid best guesses; and interview the child on home ground, if possible. (*Scott 2000: 106*)

It is necessary to adapt standard interview practice for adults by giving children more guidance. If adults ask for clarification it is normal to say 'whatever it means for you' rather than risk unduly influencing their answer. For children, their relative lack of experience can mean that they don't fully understand the researchers' intent. Therefore it is very important that the questions are as clear and unambiguous as possible and that guidance is offered where necessary. It is also important to pilot questions with small numbers of children before the main study. Children, like adults, are susceptible to biases which can come from wanting to agree with the questioner and wanting to appear socially acceptable. In particular, peer-group conformity can be a strong influence. One technique to avoid such bias is to use more than one data collection tool or to use both group and individual interviews.

The kind of relationship that you establish with children that you interview is important. Fine and Sanstrom (1988) suggest your role should be one of 'friend' in order to interact with the children in a way which is likely to result in them trusting you. In reality this is very difficult to achieve because of the differences in age and differences in status between adults and children.

Ethics

One of the important dimensions of research with children is ethics. Professionally funded research with children requires that research proposals be submitted to an ethics committee. This is a committee of people who have expertise in ethical matters and who will decide if the research is appropriate to be carried out with children. Some universities even require undergraduate research proposals to be vetted by an ethics committee. There is a complex set of issues to be considered when you are thinking about the ethics of your research.

Children have powerful rights of their own which are complemented by general human rights legislation. As you saw in CHAPTER 15, the UN Convention on the Rights of the Child ensures that children have a right to participate in all matters that affect

UNIVERSITY OF WINCHESTER
LIBRARY

them. This means that if you are doing research with children they must give their own consent. In order to give their consent they must understand as much as possible about the research as appropriate to their stage of development. Schools can be a particularly difficult place for children to exercise consent. Too often teachers, who under the law are in *loco parentis* (which means they can take decisions as if they were a parent), sometimes oblige children to help with research without really asking for their consent. This can put you as the researcher in a tricky position because it is your duty to make sure that you have informed consent from the children. Gaining consent is particularly challenging with young children because of their general level of understanding, but even nursery children can understand a straightforward explanation about the research that you are doing and can be asked if they would like to take part. You can also explain to them that they are not going to be in trouble if they don't want to be involved and that they can withdraw at any time during the research. Parental consent is also necessary for research with children.

Confidentiality is another important ethical issue. All names should be fictionalized in any written reports. You should be honest and clear with the children about who is going to know their views. As a student, you and your supervisor will know about the children's views. Technically, it might be possible to anonymize your data to the extent that even your supervisor won't know the names of the participants, but this is probably not necessary provided it is made clear to the participants. For undergraduate research it is usually better if all data are destroyed once the research is complete. At the very least, data should be kept safely and securely so that any promises about confidentiality are not breached. Research funding bodies sometimes require that archives be established so that other researchers can test the findings by reanalysing data. This underlines the need to fictionalize names, sites and participants, or to use some kind of coding system.

Research that looks at 'controversial' topics like abuse or discrimination, or which involves children with special needs, requires particularly careful thought. People who have carried out studies about abuse have recognized that the conversations held during interviews can lead to further trauma because of the memories that are stirred. Researchers in these situations need to be trained in counselling or should have organized professional support for those participants who might need it. It is also possible that children might disclose information about being abused which would require the researcher to contact the local social services department. In this case confidentiality cannot be maintained and written agreements with older children make this clear.

Strong arguments have been presented which suggest that research that is ethically appropriate should result in demonstrable benefits to children. One way of achieving this is to involve the children themselves in the research. The highest level of involvement comes when children carry out the research themselves, from planning to finished product. However, the supervision of such work requires a high level of skill and knowledge of the research process and how children might work within such a process. Lower levels of involvement are possible. Kirby (1999: 46) suggests that for the different stages in the research process six levels of involvement can be considered:

- None
- Be informed
- Express a view
- Influence decision
- Be a partner in a decision
- Be the main decision maker

When you are planning your research you should have reasons for your decisions about the level of involvement from the children.

There are always potential benefits and potential costs for participants in research. Apart from health and safety considerations, costs can include time, inconvenience, embarrassment, intrusion of privacy, sense of failure and coercion. Benefits can include satisfaction, increased confidence or knowledge, and time to talk to an attentive listener.

Alderson (1995: 2) presents a useful list of ethical topics – accompanied by sets of key questions – that need consideration when carrying out research with children:

1. The purpose of the research.
2. Costs and hoped-for benefits.
3. Privacy and confidentiality.
4. Selection, inclusion and exclusion of participants.
5. Funding.
6. Review and revision of the research aims and methods.
7. Information for children, parents and other carers.
8. Consent.
9. Dissemination.
10. Impact on children.

The best research takes account of all the items on this list (with the exception of number five for research which is not funded). When you undertake research ensure that it is well planned, systematically carried out and ethically appropriate. If this is done there can be tremendous benefits for children.

Activity

Plan and carry out a piece of research which involves children.

REFERENCES

Alderson, P. (1995) *Listening to Children: Children, Ethics and Social Research.* Ilford: Barnardo's.

Fine, G. and Sanstrom, K. (1988) *Knowing Children: Participant Observation with Minors.* London: Sage.

Scott, J. (2000) Children as respondents: The challenge for quantitative methods. In P. Christensen and A. James (eds) *Research with Children: Perspectives and Practices.* London: Falmer Press.

FURTHER READING

Christensen, P. and James, A. (eds) (2000) *Research with Children: Perspectives and Practices.* London: Falmer Press. This is an excellent text which covers an exciting range of important topics. It includes understandings of the concept of childhood from a range of perspectives, including the historical. The importance of participation is another significant theme and the book includes the outstanding chapter by Scott referred to in this chapter.

Kirby, P. (1999) *Involving Young Researchers: How to Enable Young People to Design and Conduct Research.* York: York Publishing Services. A practical guide to support people who want to encourage children and young people to carry out research. Includes useful case studies of participatory work.

Mahon, A., Glendinning, C., Clarke, K. and Craig, G. (1996) Researching children: Methods and ethics. *Children and Society*, Vol. 10: 145–54. In addition to reflections on research methods this paper makes reference to two studies. One involved children who were caring for family members and the other focused on the impact of the Child Support Act 1991.

Appendix

Further Reflections on the Activities

Chapter 1 Histories of Childhood

It is useful to see this resource as being about a series of *cohorts*. Cohort studies take a group of people all born at the same time and follow their experiences through their lives. The National Child Development Study, for example, has followed all the children born in the UK in March 1948 and regularly goes back to 're study' the same group at different life stages. You might have talked to people who were 12 in the 1930s, a time of economic depression and high unemployment. What did that mean for the pressure to leave school and go out to earn? Or what about childhood during the Second World War: evacuation, rationing, absent fathers, etc.? You may have contrasted these experiences with the baby boomer generation of the postwar period, who experienced the growth of youth culture and new levels of affluence (for some).

Chapter 2 Self-Concept

Your answer may include a variety of examples, and the overall feelings that you have in relation to the experience of testing are naturally bound up with the consequences and outcomes of the test. You may have developed the concept that you always do well (or badly) in a certain type of test (or certain subject) as a result of the feedback you have received over a number of tests. The responses of others before and after the test will have been influential in developing your self-concept.

Chapter 3 Attachment

Your answer may include wanting to be close (proximity seeking), pleasure at seeing and being with them, able to ask them for help when needed, concern for their well-being. These are similar to those shown by infants and parents, but may differ in intensity, the ability to control situations, and the number of people involved.

Chapter 4 Peers

You might have scored one of your parents as 8, meaning a predominantly vertical relationship, but this varies according to the kind of parenting style and your age. You might have scored one of your friends as 1, meaning a horizontal relationship. One of the interesting aspects here is the extent to which one or other of the friends is dominant in the relationship and the ways that this might change the extent to which it is vertical or horizontal.

Chapter 5 Family Structures

Generally, you will find that the image of the family is of two parents with their children, often a boy and a girl. Consider brochures for family holidays. These often have pictures of parents playing with their children. All the members of the family are smiling and happy. The images of family life often also show members of the family engaged in gender stereotypical ways: mum in the kitchen, or using household appliances, while dad is in the garden or washing the car. Frequently, media sources reinforce the traditional image of the nuclear family.

Chapter 6 Parenting

You probably found that you had to make sure that your knowledge of Gillick Competence was secure. You may also have played the characters in more than one way. For example, the child could have been portrayed as either competent or not competent. The mother could have been portrayed as authoritarian or permissive.

Chapter 7 Parental Separation

For the drama to be convincing you would have had to try to explore the tension between strong emotions, which are difficult to control, and the desire to protect the children from too much argument. Actors who play emotional scenes often find that the process stirs deep emotions in themselves, even if their own experiences were quite different from the ones that they are portraying.

Chapter 8 The Nature/Nurture Debate

In relation to your own development the ideas that you came up with will be individual, but may include hair, skin and eye colour, body shape, temperament, beliefs, personality and behavioural characteristics. Mine would include the following:

I am a similar size and shape to my mother and look like her, and I have been brought up to believe in helping others before myself.

Chapter 9 Cognitive Development

Your answer to the question might have included a memory of a time when as a child you bought a present for someone because you wanted it yourself. The phrase 'it's not fair' can also reflect egocentrism. Often the child is unable to see that real equality happens over extended periods of time. The fact that on one occasion a child gets something which the other child does not get is not necessarily unfair – it would depend on what they were both given over time.

Chapter 10 The Development of Language and Literacy

You may have found that your observations did not easily compare with the developmental milestones. One of the reasons for this can be if you have only worked with the child for a short period of time. The other possible reason is the way that children's development depends on the individual child's cognitive and environmental context. For example, my own children learned to decode print at different times. My son could decode favourite texts soon after he was three and a half, whereas my daughter was nearer five.

Chapter 11 Mental Health

You may have experienced the trauma of divorce, for instance. It is very common for separation from parents to have lasting consequences in adult life. For example, people may feel greater levels of insecurity and need the constant reassurance of family and friends. This can be made more difficult if the person is naturally extrovert, because other people can assume that they have no problems. Sometimes deep reflection about such events is only possible very much later in life.

Chapter 12 The Sociology of Childhood

You may have found examples from all of the perspectives which fit your experience. Perhaps your father was the main wage earner, which is a feature of both functionalist and Marxist perspectives. Perhaps your parents divorced and you were brought up by your mother, who developed assertive ways of organizing her life and yours. Overall, you may have found that the postmodern perspective is a very effective way of theorizing modern life, but one which leaves many difficult questions related to application of the theory.

Chapter 13 Childhood and Juvenile Delinquency

The picture presented by the figures suggests that typical criminals are male, young and live in 'less well off' areas of cities. Their typical crimes involve theft of and from cars, and housebreaking/burglary. Problems include:

- The figures do not address the underlying causes for crime.
- Non-reporting of minor crime.
- Under-reporting of some crimes, e.g. rape.
- Crimes which depend on police activity to find them (e.g. drug possession) may go up and down with the levels of police activity.
- 'Crimes without victims' (i.e. where the person committing the crime is also its victim, as in drug abuse and some sexual crime).

Chapter 14 Sexuality

You may have concluded that sex education is often unsatisfactory. Frequently children do not get the information that they need, particularly with regard to the emotional and psychological consequences of a sexual relationship, rather than just the physiological ones. Many people feel that full and honest information appropriate to the stage of development is essential. For a wonderful example of how this can be done even for the very youngest children, read Babette Cole's book *Mummy Laid an Egg!*

Chapter 15 Childrens' Rights

You probably found that most of the children that you talked to had not been informed about the CRC. This in itself is a breach of the convention, because one of the articles puts the responsibility on the nation-state to ensure that children are aware of the convention. When you shared some information with the children you probably found that their first observations were about understanding the consequences of the convention. By phrasing information and questions helpfully you may also have found that children have some instinctively productive ideas about rights and in particular how they would like to participate more in their education.

Chapter 16 Overview of Social Welfare

You may have found that in recent years in particular education and health have featured strongly in media reporting. This is because the government has pinned its success on these areas, especially education. Social services stories unfortunately tend to focus on deaths of children or other tragic cases. This lack of attention is reflected in the poor conditions of work for social workers and their support staff.

Chapter 17 The Role of the Child and Family Social Worker

You will probably have found that talking directly to someone who is doing the job gives a very different perspective from what you may have read about their role. This is because texts can quickly become dated and because professionals doing the job increasingly have to respond to changes in their work as required by central and local government. One of the challenges for all professionals is to manage the practical demands of their jobs while at the same time doing things which represent rigorous research and theory.

Chapter 18 Child Abuse

Some people think that child abuse is normally sexual or physical; they are less aware of the fact that neglect and emotional abuse are also formal definitions according to the law. Another misconception is that abuse is normally perpetrated by strangers; in fact, abuse is nearly always carried out by people known to the child. The large numbers of children who are abused daily should lead all people who work with children to ensure that children are taught to be more aware. It also requires the courage to refer suspicions of abuse whenever they arise.

Chapter 19 Overview of Children's Education and Care

You may find that parents choose their childcare because of the cost or the location. They may be influenced by the opening hours. They may also talk about the philosophy of the establishment. Perhaps the carers share a belief in the way that children should be cared for and educated. What do you think? Should young children be cared for in their own home? Why do you think this? Should their parents be the ones who care for them when they are very young? Why do you think this? Is it good for children to be cared for alongside other youngsters of their age?

Chapter 20 The Role of the Early Years Practitioner

You probably found that a large number of adults are involved in early years settings. Individual members of the team will have shared areas of responsibility and some may have additional responsibilities or duties depending on their experience, qualifications and status. If the setting was well managed you will also have noticed how members of the team support each other so that, collectively, they can offer the best possible environment and experiences for children.

Chapter 21 National Curricula

If you were talking about a nursery you might have remembered role play, such as the home corner. You might also have remembered activities such as the sand pit, story reading, building with bricks or painting. Perhaps you didn't remember much science work, which was subsequently strengthened in the national curriculum.

If you were talking about a primary school you might have remembered working your way through workbooks; or else sitting in groups, each group learning about a different subject. This was something that was heavily criticized by Robin Alexander, who argued that whole-class teaching was more beneficial. Ironically, the National Literacy Strategy prescribed the use of five ability groups with each group doing a different literacy activity.

Chapter 22 Play

You will have noticed that the equipment provided has a strong influence on the kind of play. For example, some old-fashioned climbing equipment has only one entry and one exit. Modern equipment includes a variety of entry points that range in physical challenge, and a range of exit points. Playground areas that are unpainted necessitate children devising their own games, whereas those that are painted can suggest particular games and activities. A mixture of both is advantageous.

Chapter 23 International Perspectives in Early Years Education and Care

Generally, you will find that most working parents rely on a combination of nursery, childminding and perhaps even the extended family to support their childcare. You may also find that the arrangements for part-time nursery provision for three-year-olds actually hinder unemployed parents from seeking work. Continue to think about further improvements that could be made.

Chapter 24 Overview of Health

You might have come up with characteristics similar to the following:

Julia

- Very rarely absent from school due to illness.
- Parents both in full-time work with higher than average income and professional qualifications.
- Father a smoker.

- One parent particularly knowledgeable about nutrition and cooking.
- Detached house with central heating and large garden with play areas for children.
- Suburban area with quick access to open country.
- Occasional coughs and colds and typical childhood illnesses such as chicken pox.

John
- Frequently absent from school because of illness.
- Parents quite often absent from work due to illness. Father on shift work. Mother a heavy smoker.
- Two-bedroom terrace house without central heating.
- Limited access to parks.
- Many instances of bronchial infection as a baby.

Chapter 25 The Role of the Health Visitor

The health visitor will probably have mentioned issues such as size of caseload, management priorities and amount of paper work. They may also have stressed the importance of relationships with other professionals such as social workers and general practitioners, and in particular the relationships with families and groups.

Chapter 26 Overview of the Legal System

Your key ideas might have included the following:

- The government may have 'promised' in its manifesto to bring in certain legislation if it is elected or re-elected.
- The government may want to bring in legislation that will be in line with popular opinion at the time, thereby increasing the likelihood of being re-elected. An example of this might be the Crime and Disorder Act 1998, brought in when there was widespread media concern about rising crime, especially among young people.
- The government may want to 'shape' society in a certain way and may want to bring in legislation that will 'force' people to act in a certain way. The Child Support Act 1991 may be an example of this.

Chapter 27 Legal Personnel

You may have thought of some of the following: children should be able to have their voices heard in court proceedings that affect them. Sometimes children are just too young to be able to attend court and give their views, or the courts may deem them too vulnerable to be subjected to the formal and sometimes frightening atmosphere of a court. In these circumstances the adults that represent children's views should listen to what children have to say and include this in any recommendation or presentation to the court. Adults who represent children in this way should ensure that the child and no other party is their main concern. Perhaps the ideal advocates for children and young people are those who not only know the law but also have a knowledge and understanding of such issues as child development and communicating with children, and who are supportive of the child's right to participate.

Chapter 28 The Children Act 1989

You may have thought of some of the following:

- The problem of different departments/agencies not cooperating and communicating has been addressed by the legal duty placed on all relevant agencies to cooperate with the local authority when it is carrying out an investigation under S47 of the Act. However, this is difficult to police and also relies on agencies recognizing that they have information relevant to an investigation.
- The problem of local authority staff failing to gain access to a child has been addressed to some extent by the fact that failure on the part of parents/carers to allow a child to be seen can result in an application for an Emergency Protection Order under S44 of the Act.
- The problem of the needs of the child being ignored in favour of the needs of the adults concerned has to some extent been addressed by the increase in rights of local authorities described above and also in the underlying philosophy of the Act that the child's welfare shall always be paramount. There can be problems in translating philosophy into practice and again there is no way to ensure that this is being done except in hindsight.

Chapter 29 The Legal Status of the Child

Children develop at different rates and it is difficult to generalize about all children at a certain age. If such arbitrary age limits are set and adhered to then children do not have the chance to grow and mature into the adult role. One day they are deemed to be incapable of doing something, the next they are fully capable without any guidance and support.

If the goal is to protect children from exploitation and harm, perhaps it would be better to treat each case individually. However, this is considered time-consuming and costly, so perhaps the current approach is based on what is easiest and most convenient, rather than what is best for the child.

Chapter 30 The Demonization of Childhood

A recent example was the killing of two girls in the village of Soham. The media attention to this event was on a massive scale. Because the alleged killer worked for a school the result of the media attention was a crackdown on the procedures for checking employees' criminal records. However, the suspect had previously been cleared of relevant criminal convictions. As you saw in chapter 18, children are dying every day as a result of adult abuse, but the media do not find this sensational enough. They prefer to concentrate on high-profile cases. This perpetuates many unhelpful and inaccurate ideas about the real dangers for children.

Chapter 31 Toys and Games

You may have decided that Lego is open-ended and that it has the potential to be used for a variety of purposes. For example, it can be used to build models, but it can also be used to represent things in a different way, such as food for an imaginary party. It helps children to develop fine motor control. It can be used as a solitary activity or as a cooperative activity; if used with a friend it can help develop social skills. In either case it can help develop children imaginatively, as they create their own construction. You might have commented that in recent years Lego has added to its range by moving towards more pre-structured models that come with instructions and that are based on film characters and other elements.

Chapter 32 Children's Literature

There is a wealth of children's literature currently available, so choosing one book is difficult. Anthony Browne is just one example of a very successful author of picture fiction. Children's lives are often central to his books and he manages to address difficult issues in an engaging way. His book *Voices in the Park* offers four different perspectives of a walk in the park: adults versus children, and middle class versus working class, are among the issues that characterize the different voices. Even the fonts of the text are designed to mirror the characters' voices.

Chapter 33 Visual Art

You might have discovered some of the themes identified by Holdsworth, Crossley and Hardyment (1992): the family; the maternal bond; fatherhood; a sense of identity; gender and identity; the comradeship of children; play and the adult world; cruelty and fear; play and nature; work; training and school; passing childhood and the end of innocence; death; children and sexuality.

Chapter 34 Multimedia

Children have a natural interest in making up 'shows' and performing them for adults. You may have been able to tap into this interest when you made the film. One of the interesting features of this kind of work is watching the film and hearing the children's ideas about how they could improve it.

Chapter 35 Ethnicity and Race

You might have found controversial the idea that people who work with children should, in the appropriate way, open out discussion about race issues. Sometimes, regarding such things as controversial is due to the belief that young children can't understand the issues. This belief is unhelpful. It is possible to discuss most issues provided that the language used is developmentally appropriate. It is also the case that, as members of society, children will have formed a range of views about race and culture and these need to be explored with them. One further related question might have been: doesn't talking about the issue just make things worse? If these issues are not handled sensitively then this is certainly a possibility, but from the black child's perspective the colourblind approach is one that causes them many more problems.

Chapter 36 Disabled Children

In the first instance the teacher will be expected to keep more detailed records for the child than they would normally need. As far as behaviour is concerned they may record the antecedents and the consequences of poor behaviour. Early dialogue with the parents would seek to rule out any health problems, such as those connected with hearing and vision. The progress towards a statement of special educational needs is often a long one because if it is granted then there is a duty to provide extra resources for the child.

Chapter 37 Poverty

Poverty leads to restricted growth due to poor diet, which in turn can result in poor health. Lack of opportunity for high-quality education results in poorer performance in the school system, with further damage to employment prospects. The problems as a whole that are experienced by children in poverty are likely to contribute to poor self-esteem. As far as language development is concerned, progress in reading and writing can be slower because of a lack of opportunity to experience a wide range of text-based sources.

Chapter 38 Non-Government Organizations

If you visited the NSPCC site you may have read about their early influence on some of the first international legislation to protect children's rights.

Chapter 39 Children Working

Examples could have included:

- Joining and supporting one of the campaigning organizations, such as Oxfam, Save the Children or Unicef.
- Checking that things you buy have not been produced by exploiting children; raising the issue in larger retail chains.
- Writing to your MP, urging that the issue be kept high on the national and political agenda.
- Raising the issue as a campaign point within your own student or trade union.
- Developing a sound knowledge of the issues involved and informing friends, family and local community.

Chapter 40 Research with Children

Many researchers find that when they actually carry out their research things differ from the plan. Sometimes sensible decisions to adapt the methods can help improve the research. At other times the differences can reflect poor planning in the first place. One of the best ways to avoid the negative consequences is to read, read and then read some more before, during and after the research.

Glossary

Accommodation	Changing the way we respond, react or think as a result of assimilating new knowledge or experiences.
Affectional bond	A long-enduring tie to a specific individual. It is not interchangeable and includes the desire for closeness.
Antitoxin	A specific antibody produced in response to a toxin (poison) which has the effect of neutralizing the poison.
Article	The UN Convention on the Rights of the Child is organized as a series of articles, which are paragraphs used to structure the convention.
Assimilation	Taking in new knowledge or experience; an active process.
Attachment	A specific type of bond in which a sense of security is bound up in the relationship.
Capitalism	An economic system characterized by private ownership of businesses with a main aim of producing profit.
Child labour	Paid or unpaid work carried out by children involving use of their personal physical or intellectual resources.
Contact Order	An order available under the Children Act which specifies with whom the child will have contact after a divorce.
Culture	The state of artistic, intellectual, social and moral development shared and understood by the majority of people in a particular society or civilization.
Curriculum	The subjects that are studied in a school.
Debt bondage	The exploitation of child workers as a condition of family debts.
Delinquency	A term generally used to describe a pattern of antisocial behaviour, including but not limited to actual crimes, typically committed by young people.

Deserving poor	A social welfare term of the state, but also people who were patronized by the upper and middle classes. They were felt to be good and hard working despite their poverty and therefore worthy of kindness and charity.
Deviancy amplification	The process by which deviance (e.g. delinquency) can be increased rather than decreased by society's reaction to it.
Drug trafficking	The use of persons (including children) to smuggle and/or sell drugs across regional and international boundaries.
Early childhood education and care/Early years education and care/ Early childhood services	All these terms refer to the range of services for young children and families. The emphasis here is on integrated services that bring together education and care.
Egocentrism	Seeing things from our own perspective.
Ethnographic	Approaches to research which involve direct observation of social settings over lengthy periods of time. The researcher becomes a participant in these settings.
Exploitation	The unjust use of one person's labour or personal resources by another more powerful person for their own benefit rather than that of the worker.
Factory Acts	Laws to regulate the conditions of employment of factory workers which were first enacted in 1833.
Foundling hospitals	Charitable institutions for orphaned and abandoned children. The first in London was set up by Thomas Coram in 1741.
Functionalism	A perspective in sociology which stresses the ways in which different aspects of the social structure contribute to the maintenance of the whole social order.
Genre	In the widest sense this means any spoken or written language form.
Guardian ad litem	An adult who represents a child in a public law action. Guardians ad litem are usually social workers but can be probation officers.
Huntington's chorea	A chronic progressive neuro-muscular disease.
Laissez-faire	Literally translated this means 'leave alone' but it has come to mean an approach which leaves people to determine their own actions, rather than be interfered with by other people and the state.
Legal capacity	The ability to take part in the legal system, either directly or through a next friend or guardian ad litem.
Maturation	Genetically pre-programmed sequential patterns of change.
Moral panic	A term used by Stan Cohen to refer to a situation where 'a condition, episode, person or group of persons emerges

	to become defined as a threat to societal values and interests'. He used the phrase originally to refer to the reaction to mods and rockers. Scraton uses it to refer to reactions to the supposed 'crisis of childhood'.
Motor development	The development of various abilities to move around and to use the body in skilled ways.
Neuropsychological abnormalities	Problems related to the brain and mind.
Next friend	An adult who represents a child in private law actions. This can be a parent or person known to the child, or it can be a social worker.
NNEB	Nursery nursing qualification previously administered by the National Nursery Examining Board until it merged with the Council for Early Years Awards in 1994. This qualification is now administered by the Council for Awards in Children's Care and Education (CACHE).
Philanthropy	A sense of duty to help others.
Pleadings	The documents used in court cases.
Postmodernism	A recent development within the social and human sciences which rejects the idea of 'grand narratives' or sweeping overall models of social life in favour of the identification of different discourses.
Preschool services	Generally refer to the range of services described in this glossary as Early childhood education and care/Early years education and care/Early childhood services, but the term *preschool* tends to emphasize the education side and school preparation aspect.
Prohibited Steps Order	An order available under the Children Act which prohibits either one of the parents from carrying out any steps mentioned in the order, without the consent of the court.
Psychoanalysis	A movement in psychology following the ideas of Sigmund Freud.
Public health	The health of the population. Public health is made up of a wide range of activities, including health promotion, protection and prevention, as well as healthy public policy and individual and community empowerment.
Puritanism	A religious philosophy which stressed the importance of self-denial and purity of thought.
Reciprocity	This term is used to describe behaviour that is reciprocated, felt and which results in observable action by both the child and the carer.
Representation	The particular viewpoint which an artist chooses to portray a subject to the viewer.

Residence Order	An order available under the Children Act which states, following divorce, who the child will live with and where they will have their main home.
Rhetorical tactics	Skills of speech used for particular effects, often in order to generate a particular response.
Romanticism	A movement in literature and art which emerged at the end of the eighteenth century and laid stress on the purity of nature and the importance of re-establishing contact with our natural selves.
Self-concept	A multi-faceted concept made up of awareness of self as an individual and as part of the world.
Self-esteem	An evaluative component of self-concept, shaped by goals, accomplishments and support.
Sentiments	A French word referring to the combination of ideas, philosophies, beliefs and feelings people have at a particular time about a topic. It includes the idea of emotional significance, but also refers to ordinary beliefs.
Settings	The variety of nurseries, playgroups, preschools or contexts where children aged five and under are cared for and educated.
Sexual exploitation	Exploitation of a person through pornography, prostitution or coercive sexual activity.
Slavery	The ownership and exploitation of labour of one person by another.
Socialization	The process by which people learn the culture, norms and values of a social group.
Specific Issue Order	An order available under the Children Act that asks the court to determine the answer to a specific issue in relation to a child's welfare, upon which the parents cannot agree.
Symbolic interactionism	A perspective within sociology which sees social situations as socially constructed in terms of shared negotiated meanings created in interaction between individuals.
Taboo	Powerful social rules forbidding particular behaviours.
Theory of mind	An understanding of our own and other people's minds.
Total fertility rate	A statistical measure that indicates the average number of children who would be born to a woman over her lifetime if current age-specific fertility rates continued.
Xenophobia	Actions showing hatred or fear of foreigners.

Index

References to illustrations and tables are in *italic*.

UNIVERSITY OF WINCHESTER
LIBRARY